ISBN 0-9683372-

KEYSTONE

Keystone Press Inc.
15916 Patricia Drive
Edmonton, Alberta
Canada
T5R 5N4

Editor: Ric Dolphin

Research: Pamela Klappstein
John Klappstein

Printed in Canada by:
Quality Color Press
Edmonton, Alberta

Foreword

by David Frum

Hudson Bay. The city of Vancouver. The Mackenzie River. Canada has never been bashful about honoring its great pioneers and explorers, but where oh where will we find a mountain or river big enough to merit the name of Byfield? Thirty years ago, Canadian political journalism was a wilderness every bit as bleak as anything encountered by the first settlers of the west. Today, it is a booming and thriving landscape of conservative opinion. When you see the thriving streets of Alberta's cities now, it seems incredible that this land was home to nobody but buffalo and a handful of aboriginal nomads. And when you hear the dozens of confident, thoughtful and unintimidated conservative voices on our television sets, in our parliaments, in our newspapers, it seems equally incredible that there was a day when Mr. Byfield and his reporters stood very nearly as alone as those ancient Indians.

The essays gathered in this volume are vintage Byfield: by turns funny, scorching, prophetic. Reading them again is like following the wagon ruts of the pioneers. Here is Byfield, giving voice to the anger of the west at its economic exploitation. Here is Byfield again, warning of the moral decay of our society at a time when it took almost reckless courage to criticize feminism and defend religion. Here is Byfield once more, warning of the radical instability of the Canadian federation and of the imminent separation of Quebec. Here is Byfield, the patriot, the historian, the teacher, the lover of literature. And here finally is Byfield, analyzing the potential for a western-based conservative party, and then calling just such a party into being.

Journalism is perishable stuff. But any future historian trying to understand Canada's troubles in the late twentieth century will want to look at Mr. Byfield's work. Unless you read Mr. Byfield, you won't ever properly understand the anger of the west at central Canada, the reasons for the destruction of the once-unbreakable Conservative grip on the west, and the birth of the Reform Party.

Mr. Byfield has had a good many rough things to say about the modern world. He is a conservative Christian, horrified by abortion, worried by the breakdown of the family, infuriated by the moral laxness of our society. And yet somehow, he always holds onto his wit and good humor. Mr. Byfield has been likened by his (many) critics to an Old Testament prophet. But whoever heard of a prophet who made his listeners laugh?

For a quarter of a century, Mr. Byfield has put one of the most artful typewriters on the continent at the service of the conservative cause. Thanks very much to him, that cause is thriving. That seems to me to demand some token of gratitude. It may be impractical to rename one of the Rockies, Mount Byfield, although I suspect he'd like it, for Mr. Byfield ain't the bashful type. But if we can't get him a mountain, we ought at least to read, reread, and keep learning from his work. And, whatever our point on the political compass, to salute it as some of the finest journalism ever published in this country.

- December 1997, Washington, DC

(David Frum, 37, has written for *The Wall Street Journal, The Times Literary Supplement, Forbes*, and *The Washington Post*. He is the author of *Dead Right* [New Republic Books, 1994] and writes a twice-weekly column for *The Financial Post* and the *Sun* newspapers.)

Table of Contents

Table of Contents

Chapter One

The Fall of Society

*"It is time we quit bleating about our rights,
and got down to the serious and thrilling
business of our responsibilities."*

- Ted Byfield, 1982.

**If the printed word is on the way out,
our civilization won't be far behind**

The printed word, we were assured last month in *The Globe and Mail*, is on the way out. It will be replaced by computer icons, electronic voices and "motherlodes in a clean, soothing videostream." The article was written by someone identified as a "technology reporter" for the *Globe's* "Report on Business" section. Reading and puzzling over it, I've reached the conclusion that if this man is typical of tomorrow's technology, then what may be on the way out is the human mind.

To explain, I'll have to recapitulate his article in some detail. Just as velcro replaced shoelaces, CDs replaced vinyl records and touchtones replaced dial phones, he writes, the "simple icon" will replace words. "The written word is a painfully slow way to pass on information." The icon may be imprecise and unable to compress complex and detailed ideas, but "that's where technology comes in."

In the increasing multiplicity of television channels, information can be increasingly subdivided. The Internet becomes ever better at incorporating graphics, audio and video. "And if you must have a book then have a book on tape. Better yet, have it on a tiny microchip in an earpiece, so you can walk around listening to talented actors perform the book, rather than having to sit still and grind thousands of words yourself."

No longer will you need exhaustive manuals of instruction. You needn't know how to turn off the dishwasher, just tell it to do so. You needn't read the TV guide. Just tell the set what you want and it will obey. Research will disappear. Just tell the computer your subject and it will do the rest. Repair manuals will be replaced by videoscreens.

"Writing will disappear because it keeps getting in the way of the human need for information and entertainment. It's not an effective use of time, which means it's not cost-effective. Time is money. There's no piece of information or emotion conveyed in writing that can't be expressed by images or sounds." And so, concludes our technology reporter, "why bother teaching kids to read? You don't have to

be too swift to calculate the diminishing return on that investment."
Now it's obvious why this young man - I take him to be a young man; he sounds about 16 or so - is unhappy with existing methods of communication. He is certainly not very good at them.

In an article on the "printed word," for instance, present dinosaurian practice would require him to explain, somewhere, what he means by those two printed words. Is he talking about words imprinted on paper, or on a videoscreen? If the former, I would agree with him. Use of paper will almost certainly decline, though it is far from doing so at present.

But this doesn't seem to be his meaning. All this talk of icons and videocharts and the mysterious "clean, soothing videostream" (in description of which he favoured us with no printed words whatsoever) suggests that even words on videoscreens will become obsolete, replaced by grunts and icons and videocharts, doubtless right from the "motherlode," whatever that is.

But it's here that I have great trouble. For words show not the slightest inclination towards obsolescence. I remember reading somewhere (or perhaps I absorbed it from an icon; these days you never know) that the English language now has about five times as many words as it had a century ago. This does not seem evidence of impending obsolescence. But then, of course, I'm not a technology reporter, and I do not work in downtown Toronto. Perhaps they have fewer words there.

Something else bothers me. We find out west that human beings can read words between three and ten times faster than they can hear them spoken Therefore "the talented actor" will take nine hours of your "walking about" to read into your ear-borne microchip what the slowest reader would require only three hours of "grind" to read to himself, while a fast reader would have to endure the grind for only about 55 minutes. In any event, this factor makes it very hard for us dinosaurs to understand the point. Why is "the written word a painfully slow way to pass on information" if the substitutes being proposed are three to ten times slower still?

Then there's the matter of those video graphs and charts. You know - the kind that show the monthly rise in rents in urban areas, the percentage increase in manic hysteria among female office managers, etc. Do they replace words? No, as a matter of fact, they do not. What they replace is numbers. Maybe numbers are also on the way out, although somehow I doubt it.

After the invention of the telephone and the unionization of the post office, writing certainly declined. But now, of course, writing is ascending again since the invention of e-mail. This will soon store voice messages, no doubt, but they will never be as useful as written messages because it takes three to ten times longer to listen to them.

The Internet provides another case study. It is certainly redolent of icons. But for every icon, I would bet, it stores ten thousand printed words. In fact, the Internet has expanded, not contracted, the use of the printed word.

Again, iconography would seem subject to distinct limitations. Here for instance are ten English words, all in fairly general use: *earnest, eager, fervent, fervid, passionate, hearty, sincere, zealous, enthusiastic, ardent.* All generally describe a human state of mind, yet each has a quite distinct meaning. One of them may perfectly describe a certain mental state. Another would fail completely.

If we had one earnest icon to describe all ten conditions, would our communicative capacity be advancing? Or would we be headed back to the cave where - correct me if I'm wrong - iconography was indeed the chief means of graphic communication? The answer to this is not encouraging. But if we had to develop ten icons to convey the ten different meanings, why not stick with the printed words we already have? Aren't printed words, in a sense, already icons?

Which raises one final point. Running through this man's article is the unexamined assumption that society inevitably travels onward and upward. Every innovation, he implies, is an "advance." There are no retreats. If it's new, it's bound to be better.

But you wonder: where does he get this notion? Certainly not from history. Doesn't he realize that every civilization has regarded itself as irresistably advancing, and that every one of them collapsed into ruin? And one indicator of its impending ruin was proliferating ignorance and illiteracy. As someone has pointed out, there are only two centuries in history when an educated man would be able to read classical Greek, while his supposedly educated grandson could not. One was the fifth century, just as the whole civilization of the ancient world began to disintegrate. The other is the twentieth.

- August 18, 1997

Perpetrators of a holocaust, and how to manufacture them

I was invited last month by the Edmonton chapter of Hadassah to a symposium conducted by the Brotherhood of Christians and Jews on the subject of what has come to be called the Holocaust. The defacing and torching of an Edmonton synagogue and seven churches by a lunatic and the threatened development of the Ku Klux Klan in Alberta by other lunatics have made people uneasy. Hadassah wanted Albertans to be made conscious of the kind of thing that can happen when cynicism prevails in politics and recruits the lunatic element to its cause.

We heard the testimony, still piteous forty years later, of a victim of the Holocaust who lived after watching her own family being destroyed. We sat for what seemed two hours to watch a documentary record of the methodical annihilation of seven million men, women and children by the best technology that a scientifically-oriented government could devise under wartime conditions. The experience of watching even photographic glimpses of this tragedy four decades into history was, needless to say, horrible. Hadassah had made its point.

Uppermost in the mind, of course, was the question of what had caused this frightful business. Economic calamity, political dislocation social disintegration had all beset Germany at the time, but even this does not seem enough to explain the diabolism that was at work. How did it happen? How can it be prevented from happening again? What are the symptoms to which we should be always alert?

We leap, of course, to the obvious. We note the defacing of the synagogue, the Klan, crude allusions to "Pakis," and the kind of niggling racism I remember from my youth wherein certain resorts, clubs and hotels were closed to Jews, Poles, Indians and so on. Such inclinations as these must have been fanned by propagandists into a national hysteria. Yet historians do not concur that this was what took place in Germay. The German Jewish community was the most assimilated, they say, in all Europe. German Jews tended to consider themselves Germans first and Jews second.

So what did happen? What signs should we then look for? I think the root cause of the Holocaust lies much deeper, that it is not intrinsically political but psychological, and that some element of it lies in the heart of every man.

The astounding evidence of those photographs was not simply in the events themselves, but in the apparent compliance with such atrocities and their acceptance by thousands upon thousands of people, many of them no doubt very like ourselves, family men, generally honest, assigned to an unpleasant job and doing it. There seems, however, to have been one striking characteristic common to these people. The conscience, that part of them which could define the distinction between good and bad, fair and unfair, right and wrong, had apparently been rendered inoperable. It was dead. A most hideous and obvious evil was taking place before them. In fact they themselves were participating in it, but they did not seem to realize the ghastly reality of what they were doing.

To forfend another Holocaust therefore we must somehow discover how those people got that way. "No device has yet been invented," said Franklin Roosevelt, "that can permanently separate men from their own consciences." I think he was wrong. Something had certainly separated these men from theirs and that device was propaganda. A concerted government-directed assault had been made upon their ability to comprehend the elementary principles of justice and charity until that comprehension was inoperable in a whole segment of the population for a whole range of activity. The voice within them that should have been shrieking out in protest against what they were doing apparently did not speak at all. Or if it did, they had trained themselves or been trained not to listen to it. They did their grisly work because it was the "approved thing to do." And the part of them that should have questioned the "approved thing to do" simply was not there.

They had been persuaded, it seems, that right and wrong belonged to the past. There had come about what the government was pleased to call "the New Order." The Old Order might not have accepted such things, but the Old Order was obsolete. A new revelation had succeeded it, a new vision of human values, a new morality. All this they had swallowed whole and that hideous parade of photographs was the result. And so too, of course, might we swallow it or possibly something worse, the instant we begin to talk about "obsolete moralities" and new "lifestyles" or when we find ourselves saying "surely we don't believe such-and-such in this day and age," as though day and age had anything whatever to do with moral truth. When we think this way, and many people do, then what we are in the process of doing is deadening our consciences. And our enlightened consciences and reason are our only sure defence against the propagandist and the demagogue.

Each of us has within himself a voice. Sometimes it questions what we're doing. "This seems unfair, this seems wrong," it may say, or "you really should do this," or "the time has come to do that." If we fall into the habit of ignoring that voice, particularly if we ignore it on the grounds of current fashion, we may fancy ourselves as very "with it" and "modern" people. But what we are actually becoming is prime material for the propagandist and fit candidates to take part in the next Holocaust, wherever and however it may occur. - *October 10, 1980*

If Chatelaine weds Penthouse, the marriage can't last

I was given the other day the publication of one of the human rights lobby groups which cited and deplored the alarming statistical evidence of social disintegration in Alberta - suicide, juvenile crime, family breakup and so on. It struck me as odd that a civil rights group should deplore such things. If any single factor can be blamed for the contemporary social collapse, it is our ceaseless and impatient insistence upon our "human rights," and our concurrent silence on the subject of human responsibility.

While the causes of our malaise are many, most can be traced to one, notably the seeming failure of the family unit. It in turn is directly attributable to the modern instability of marriage. When the marriage fails, the home breaks up. However "civilized" the divorce (and many are not in the least civilized), the resulting trauma to both parents and children creates many of the other statistics. To solve the problem therefore we must somehow re-establish permanence in the marital partnership We need a tougher, deeper, more durable commitment that can withstand the storms that all human relationships involve, and emerge from them stronger and more resilient than ever. To achieve this, however, we are going to have to stop yapping about our rights and begin pondering most diligently our responsibilities.

The kind of yapping I'm talking about is eloquently illustrated by certain mass circulation magazines, some addressed to women, some to men. Take, for example, that bountifully profitable Maclean Hunter publication called *Chatelaine*, which is by a mile Canada's most widely read women's periodical. Much of its content has not changed for generations - advice on cooking, dieting, fashion and home improvement. But in the last ten or so years it has developed a new editorial thrust. This consists in one long, ceaseless and increasingly strident whine for assorted rights. There is the right of women to equal pay, the right of women to equal pensions, the right of women to equal job opportunities, the right of wives to minimum wages, the right of secretaries to refuse to make coffee, the right of mothers to have free daycare, the right of mistresses to claim alimony, the right of female shop workers to prohibit offensive wall calendars, the right of mothers to pass child care onto fathers, and on and on. Why is research so retarded on a male birth control pill, demands one article. Why do fifty per cent of married women in their thirties who have good jobs "cheat" on their husbands? (The answer after about five thousand words: because their husbands are no good in bed.)

The justice of most, if not all, these claims is not in dispute here. The point is that the whine is pretty well the only kind of message which the entire magazine conveys. Its whole communication is described by the single word: GET. There is not the faintest evidence of GIVE. There are no appeals to women to sacrifice their interests to that of their children, no gentle suasions for devotion to husbands, no homilies for the care of aged parents, the nursing of the sick, the bandaging of wounded shins or the healing of wounded hearts. Yet even the most superficial examination of the tough marriages, the ones that work, invariably reveals a wife and mother who does all this and a great deal more besides. And in Canada's biggest and most influential women's magazine it is almost nowhere to be found. This surely is significant.

But it pales into pedantry when contrasted with the implications of Canada's most popular men's magazine. This, as it turns out, is not a Canadian magazine at all, but an American one that outcirculates all rivals in Canada. It is called *Penthouse* and its most obvious distinction is the recurrence of four-colour, high-gloss pages full of gynaecology. Its purpose, as every male heart knows but won't admit, is to take the dignity and poise of womanhood and strip it raw, thereby fulfilling some dark desire in the further reaches of our minds that delights in the destruction of innocence. Hence the purer and younger the subject the greater the gratification, so long as it is old enough to look female. This sensation is no more related to art than it is to sex. It is an experience not of body but of mind that comes straight from hell. When women fear and banish it, they are on very certain ground, serving our ultimate interests better than their own, and in moments of lucidity we know it.

But it is not only in its pornography that *Penthouse* poisons the social order. It is in the tacit assertion of certain inalienable male rights - the right of perpetual gratification, the right to possess, exploit and abandon, the right of infidelity, the right of concubinage, the right of progeneration without commitment. And again, where is the call to responsibility? Nowhere does it declare that a man must serve, protect and nourish that which he begets, that his loyalty to his wife must be unreserved and inviolate, that her vulnerability in childbirth lies upon him as a holy obligation, and that his abandonment of that duty is not a declaration of independence but one of a despicable treachery. These things we do not read in *Penthouse*. Instead we find the ceaseless incantation of the coward who creeps away from the battle during the night. "I value my freedom," he declares, and he may therefore walk on the face of any who threaten it. That is the message of *Penthouse*.

Now it seems obvious that if many couples approach marriage, she with her mind full of *Chatelaine* and he with his mind full of *Penthouse*, the amazing fact is not that two out of three marriages fail, but that one out of three succeeds. Unfortunately, however, a two-thirds failure rate inevitably portends the impending doom of the social order. A next generation there always must be. If the conventional family cannot provide it, then the state, furnished with the new and terrible resources of biochemistry, will do so instead with all the Orwellian horror that this implies. So it is time we quit bleating about our rights, and got down to the serious and thrilling business of our responsibilities. - *November 29, 1982*

The Greek model, and why it will kill us

It is said that when the first administrators of the vigorous young Roman republic began arriving in the old and decadent Greek city states the Greeks were amazed at the simplicity of the rules with which the Romans governed themselves. The Roman authorities preserved a strict honesty, they noticed, on the strength of nothing more than the simple oath they took before assuming their duties. There were no audits, no complex accounting systems, hardly any rules at all in fact with which the Roman governor was required to conform. The Greeks, meanwhile, had been piling one set of regulations upon another to try to enforce honesty upon their officialdom, all of these ineffective. As fast as rules could be invented to control corruption, the corrupt had been finding new ways to evade them. All of which is instructive to our current situation. Day by day in almost every edition of the newspapers and in every telecast and "talk" program, we hear new demands for new laws aimed at keeping people honest and good because the laws we have already passed aren't doing it.

Hence we hear demands for laws against pornography and "hate literature" because public repugnance is no longer sufficient to prevent its circulation. We hear demands for restrictions on the powers of parents because of the increasing failure of parental responsibility. We hear demands for ever more elaborate controls of unemployment insurance because of the ever widening abuse of its purpose. We hear demands for tougher controls on "sexual harassment" because what would once be considered "intolerable" conduct is now apparently tolerable, and we raise taxes higher and higher because government must provide what was once provided by voluntary charity. Finally we hear that our health care system now faces imminent ruin because so many people are calling the doctor when they aren't really sick.

In all this we are doing exactly what the Greeks did. That is, we are attempting to produce with rules and laws standards of popular conduct that would be far more effectively accomplished by by the force of moral suasion. And as all the new laws are enacted, further and more complex legislation is required because they don't work. Pornography and hate literature continue to circulate because they cannot be legally distinguished from acceptable literature; parents continue to abuse children because the distinction between suitable punishment and outright injury cannot be drawn. Medical and unemployment insurance cheating becomes ever more rampant, and the harassers find new and more devious ways to harass. Moreover, as the law attempts to supplant old-fashioned morality, breaking the law becomes less and less reprehensible and more and more a game. "What would be the right thing to do?" a tax accountant was asked. "There is no such thing as right and wrong in tax law," he replied. "It's not a matter of doing the right thing; it's a matter of assuming a defensible position."

An incident several weeks ago illustrated the situation neatly. A man, far from retirement age, had sold a business at a handsome return and was casting about to buy another. "You know," somebody told him "you qualify for unemployment insurance." The man was astounded. "I don't need unemployment insurance," he replied. "So what?" came the rejoinder. "After all, you paid for it; the government owes it to you." He thereupon applied and soon found himself waiting in line in a government office. "Suddenly," he said, "I began to ask myself, 'What on earth am I doing here? I'm helping to destroy this whole program.' So I left the line. I just couldn't stay there. It was wrong."

The point is, whatever withdrew that man from that line is what is vanishing from our society, and our attempts to replace it by more and more laws with more and more snoops, inspectors, cops, bureaucrats and taxes seem to be getting us nowhere. Surely, we would be far better served by trying to recover what we had before, the kind of thing that pulled the man from the line. Yet the fact is you hardly ever hear this mentioned. Thousands of people are telling us what should be made illegal; hardly anyone is ever telling us what should be considered wrong.

In other words we are trying to make the law do something it cannot ever do: it cannot make us good. A law can only work when some form of conduct is so unacceptable to so many people, and the whole social order is so threatened by its commission, that society bands together to prevent by force its occurrence. But notice that this element of general disgust and repugnance must come before the law can work; the law itself can never create this attitude.

The reason we would rather talk about laws than about right and wrong is, no doubt, the fact that we live in a scientific age. Science has done marvellous things for us, making us able to move faster and farther, to escape pain, to live longer, and to better grasp the facts of our physical existence. But the problem is that science can tell us nothing whatever about right and wrong. There is no way of "proving" scientifically that I should love my neighbour as myself. That, unfortunately, is not a scientific question. Moreover, our attempts to deal with it scientifically in the school system have been nothing less than disastrous. By cataloguing moral codes and teaching them to children as "alternative lifestyles" - for such indeed was and still is, the precise purpose of nearly all social studies courses taught in North American schools - we have induced in children the notion that right conduct is entirely a matter of personal taste. Anything that feels right is right for you, says the teacher. The idea of a universal law or code that applies to us all, however inconvenient, is thereupon repudiated. Need we wonder therefore why so few people find themselves coerced by their consciences, why so few, as it were, withdraw from the lineup? We are getting exactly what we asked for.

And until we correct this situation, until we find a way of effectively teaching simple rules of right and wrong, all our efforts with legislation will be in vain. One place to start, of course, would be in the schools. But a far more important place to start is with ourselves. If it's wrong, then don't do it. - *October 15, 1984*

How come we're paying people to inflict social amnesia on us?

Derek Nelson, a columnist for the Thomson Newspapers, was dismayed this spring when he examined an Ontario high school textbook's treatment of the Second World War. It had only two themes: (a) how women working in war plants played a major role in the victory and then after the war were returned to house-bound subservience; (b) how the Canadian government deported ethnic Japanese from the west coast. The whole conflict, in which democracy had at great cost saved the world from Nazi totalitarianism, had been reduced to "a feminist and multicultural lecture."

Mr. Nelson then examined a proposed American history curriculum. Again he found a mere propaganda exercise in currently fashionable causes: women entering the work force; the treatment of the Japanese; the role played by blacks, Mexicans, natives; an exhaustive treatment of the Holocaust; the American decision to use the atomic bomb; and the allied bombing of Dresden. Of the immense sacrifices of white American males, who did nearly all the fighting and dying, there was simply nothing at all. The course, explained one of its sponsors, is intended to liberate pupils from "the prison of facts."

Last month we saw a similar "liberation" going on in Canada. A Grade 12 course in British Columbia, entitled "First Nations Studies" presents the native culture as a pristine partnership between man and his environment, which was destroyed by ruthless white settlers. One indignant teacher called the course "political indoctrination," based on the assumption that white civilization is "sort of secondary and their way is better." Natives may have been less exploitive than whites, this teacher observed, simply because they lacked the technology. After acquiring horses and guns from the white man, they slaughtered the Canadian buffalo herds within a generation. By the time the railway and the settlers arrived, the buffalo were already gone.

In advancing such an objection this teacher is citing a "fact" of history. He points to the written record and to the surviving buffalo pounds where thousands of animals were stampeded over cliffs, then butchered or left to rot. However, to academics like Robin Fisher of the University of Northern B.C., such historic "facts" mean nothing. "There's no such thing as objective history," he avers. "History is not about fact; it's about interpretation and it seems to me that all of the things [in the Grade 12 course] are valid interpretations."

Notice the line of reasoning. No one can know all the facts involved in any historic event. We cannot tell what went on in the minds of the people concerned. We cannot tell why they did whatever they did. We cannot measure its full impact upon others. Therefore all we can do is "interpret." No objective view is possible. In short, since we can't know all the facts, we can't know any facts.

Examine the following four statements about a single event in Canadian history, and the absurdity becomes clear: 1. Thomas D'Arcy McGee died at Ottawa in 1868. 2. Thomas D'Arcy McGee was killed at Ottawa in 1868. 3. Thomas D'Arcy McGee was assassinated at Ottawa in 1868. 4. Thomas D'Arcy McGee was martyred at Ottawa in 1868. Now Prof. Fisher looks at these and correctly notes that the fourth is a matter of "interpretation." Therefore, he concludes, all four must be matters of "interpretation."

But the other three are decidedly matters of fact - what historians call objective fact, meaning that the supporting evidence is strong enough to put it beyond dispute. Plainly, there are myriads of events whose factuality historians properly dispute. That's their job. But if the mind moves from there to the conclusion that there can be no historical factuality at all, one has abolished the discipline known as history. One has also abolished simple sanity. Some things unquestionably have occurred and we are quite capable of knowing it.

Some academics are fully prepared to abolish history, however, because history stands so inconveniently in their way. This is particularly true of the new polemical disciplines (you might say propaganda disciplines) like native studies and women's studies, and you can't really help sympathizing. History, as it traditionally defines itself, discriminates terribly against them. Since it is the study of the "records" of the past, it tends to restrict itself almost entirely to those human societies that left "records," meaning those that could write. Those who could not write are considered to be part of "pre-history," or prehistoric. Thus history "dawns," and the curtain goes up, when a civilization appears on earth that has developed a method of writing. This occurs about 5000 B.C., when we find three civilizations - one on the Tigris and Euphrates Rivers, one on the Nile and one on the Yangtze - already in the full flower of complex civilization.

Societies that could not write, however, tended to be left out of history altogether until they managed to acquire the ability to to make permanent records. This includes the aboriginal societies of North America prior to the white man's arrival, and it means that our earliest written records of the Indians were produced by whites. The process also tends to discriminate against women who until the Middle Ages, did very little writing; the history of ancient women is mostly told by males. Small wonder therefore that academics who specialize in native and women's studies will eagerly espouse the abolition of history. It's all "interpretation," they say, with the implication that any one interpretation is as good as any other.

However, there is a very grievous downside to what these people are doing. History serves the same purpose for a society that memory serves for an individual. I have had occasion of late to watch an individual in great age lose her memory. It was not a pleasant thing to behold her own agonized awareness of what was happening. First she could not recall, until reminded, events that had occurred the day before. When reminded, she would become horrified at her memory's failure. Then gradually even the reminders didn't work. Soon even familiar faces were scarcely recognized. Life became infantile, with only immediate sensory experiences registering on the mind and then instantly disappearing.

Now the point is, of course, that those who would abolish history are doing the same thing to society that senility does to an individual. All that is left to us is immediate sensory experience, with no frame of reference. Every event, from yesterday into the distant past, rapidly disappears into the vast quagmire of "interpretation."

How ironic that we are paying these people out of the public purse to inflict this disability upon us! You have to wonder: must everything they do go unquestioned? Are these academics accountable to no one? Is this what we mean by academic freedom? Is it the freedom to say or teach anything, however preposterous, however irrational, however poisonous? To permit such a situation doesn't seem even reasonable, let alone moral. - *June 12, 1995*

Why many generations have discouraged any tinkering with the social taboos

The Devil is a gentleman, and asks you down to stay
At his little place at What'sitsname (it isn't far away).
They say the sport is splendid; there is always something new,
And fairy scenes and fearful feats that none but he can do. *

Margaret Wente, *The Globe and Mail's* columnist, had cause to discover last week what this poem is about. She produced one of the most perceptive columns that newspaper has published in recent years. It concerned the murder trial of Paul Bernardo in the torture-death of two teenaged Ontario girls, a trial whose progressive horrors unfold hour by hour in the media.

Columnist Wente had observed the editors dealing with the story on their computer screens. "They looked sick," she said. "Some stopped reading and turned away." The trial had become "a gruesome freak show" in which "we are all spectators, but hardly any of us has the stomach to look."

"I never want to hear a word about Paul Bernardo and Karla Homolka (his involuntary accomplice) again. I never want to see another cheesecake photo of Karla in a bathing suit or of Paul and Karla on their wedding day. I wish this trial were being held on some far-off planet, with no press and no cameras to bring us our nightly Grand Guignol of grief."

She reached another conclusion. "This story makes no sense at all," she wrote. "It has no moral, no comfort, no lessons to teach, not a shred of redemption."

But there she is wrong. The Bernardo-Homolka trial has a very important lesson to teach, particularly for those raised in the generation of, and with the assumptions of Ms. Wente.

What plainly appals her is not the lurid physical details. She has doubtless read as bad or worse before. No, it's the senselessness of it. There is no comprehensible explanation - no explicable motive of love, jealousy or hatred, no rationale of unbridled greed, or overweening

* From "The Aristocrat" by G.K. Chesterton.

ambition. It seems so utterly purposeless. It is pure evil. She has never encountered such a thing before, no doubt quietly assumed it could not possibly exist. But it undeniably does exist. So put it away from me, she cries, away from my newspaper, away from my television set, away from my mind, indeed away from the very face of the earth, to "some far-off planet." But it's right here, Ms. Wente, right here in your own neighbourhood.   You know - the little place at What'sitsname.

How does such a monstrosity come about? How would a clean-cut young accountant and his equally presentable young wife descend into such a depth of diabolism that they could do such things? What happened to them? What came over them? No doubt the psychiatrists and the sociologists and the criminologists will have their explanations. But there is a very old one which even they may not refute.

It is this: he, and perhaps she too, were pursuing what the old moralists called "thrill." At first thrill came easily. It arose out of that which was almost, but not quite, normal. There always had to be a touch of "perversion." Just a touch, but it had to be there. And soon a mere touch wasn't enough. To get the thrill you had to go further, then further still. Soon thrill demanded pain, your own or someone else's. Then more pain, psychological as well as physical. Then for real thrill, you needed terror, someone else's terror, a young woman's terror, a child's terror. Down, down the soul descends until it finds itself in the grip of hell itself, more than ever craving thrill, yet with no depravity left that can produce it. That, at any rate, is the implication of the portrait the Crown paints of Paul Bernardo.

Now Margaret Wente is, like the rest of us, the child of her era. Just as mine was a generation raised to believe in wars that could be costly won and more costly lost, hers was an era that believed in freedom - freedom from taboo, from puritan restraint, from guilt, from the judgmental, from rules. Right and wrong were things each man and woman could invent for himself, and beauty was entirely in the eye of the beholder. So was ugliness. So was what some called perversion.

For who were we to say that what others did for enjoyment was anybody's business but their own? Whatever takes your fancy, whatever turns your crank. That was the principle. We were free at last from those grim certitudes of convention and religion.

Such were the orders of the day, and the day began, of course, long before Margaret Wente. Back at the turn of the century, Lytton Strachey introduced us to the hypocrisies of his "eminent Victorians." Oscar Wilde taught us to scoff at prudery, and Shaw assured us that "the Golden Rule is that there are no golden rules." All through the century, we had been systematically liberated from the "dead hand of virtue." True enough, the odious pious resisted all this emancipation, and warned that we didn't know what we were bargaining for. But by the Sixties even these had abandoned or been driven off the field, and the way was clear for Margaret Wente, and a half generation behind her for Paul Bernardo.

What do Margaret and Paul have in common? Freedom, of course. Freedom from all those restrictive things, above all freedom to dabble. And when Mr. Bernardo began his dabbling, began expressing his own idiosyncrasies, pleasing his own fancies, looking for thrill in his own way, who would have come flying resolutely to his defence at the least suggestion of criticism? Margaret Wente, that's who, along with most of her generation. She would have deplored our intolerance, lectured us on the narrowness of our views, told us that "love" must be unfettered to express itself in a thousand ways that we in our bigotry feared and rejected.

Alas, neither Margaret nor her contemporaries understood the reason that prior generations surrounded sex with rules, taboos and formulae; the reason they sought to inhibit sexual behaviour, to foster guilt and manacle our natural proclivities. They knew this instinct could go terribly, fiendishly wrong. What would begin as a playful peccadillo could end as the eucharist of hell. The rule therefore was: do not tinker with the taboos. They're there for a reason.

Well, we of the emancipated twentieth century have tinkered with them and wildly. And there will be far worse than Paul Bernardo before the consequences are over. So don't turn off the television, Margaret. Enjoy the show. You're not just a spectator. You helped produce it. - *June 5, 1995*

Crime and Punishment

"The sordid spectacle of uncontrollable crime - the daily routine of rape, murder, burglary, mugging, armed robbery and assault - evidence a simple fact: our system of benevolent criminal justice does not work. It is, in fact, a disaster."

- Ted Byfield, 1987

A new liberal challenge to the rights of the family

As an instrument of order in the public schools, the strap has all but been abolished. In some systems it is categorically illegal, in others so circumscribed as to be useless anyway. One wonders therefore how long it will be before an attempt is made to make it illegal in the home. This month we got the answer: not very long. Mrs. June Sheppard, the newspaper columnist who is as charming as she is confused, urges us all to read a book. It is "People are Not for Hitting" by the American Dr. John Valusek who, says Mrs. Sheppard, "wants to encourage the creation of a new national ethic to reduce human violence starting with the elimination of corporal punishment, not only in the schools but in the home." Would you, demands the doctor, spit upon your child? Then why do you similarly humiliate him by hitting him? Mrs. Sheppard so approves of Dr. Valusek that she confers upon him the highest praise in liberaldom. He is she says, "sensitive."

Well I might as well confess right now to Mrs. Sheppard that I am insensitive. As a parent I spanked my children. The boys in particular were paddled by both of us with assorted instruments varying from a flat board to a hair brush. There was also one celebrated occasion with a Sherwin Williams paint mixer which broke in two, much to the hilarity of the progeny. I once ventured as far as to spank a ten-year-old daughter. She had been reading a novel about Mary Queen of Scots at the time, and appeared for her spanking with the poise, dignity and consciousness of Mary before the Elizabethan executioner, which is to say, me. It was a dreadful ordeal and I never went through it again.

But as for spitting upon my children, I can honestly say that I've never done that. There are two reasons for this omission. For one, the idea never really occurred to me. For another, I have never been any good at spitting. In boyhood when the range, accuracy and substance of spitting is sometimes a matter of competitive performance, my efforts were always a disappointment. My own boys were far better at it, one of my daughters better still. She actually hit the postman once from the second floor, an achievement which rapidly led to the kind of thing which so distresses Dr. Valusek.

Which brings me to the first of two facts of which neither Mrs. Sheppard nor Dr. Valusek seem sufficiently conscious. The first is this: whether we like it or not, children do in fact misbehave. They spit on postmen, they lie, they steal, they bully, they can become quite cruel. In short, they act like human beings and therefore require the restraint of some kind of enforceable law. For if they are not effectively thwarted in this misbehaviour, some of them will expand such activity to include robbery, vandalism, assault, wounding, rape and even murder. The second is this: successful behaviour repeats itself. That is, anything a child does that seems to succeed, he will do again, probably elaborating upon it. Anything he does that leads to unpleasantness, i.e. fails, he will tend to avoid. If spitting on postmen is followed inevitably by physical unpleasantness, he will tend not to spit on any more postmen, however exhilarating the experience. In sum: we must sometimes restrain our children. We must do it making sure that the undesirable behaviour fails.

The argument therefore comes down to this: what is the most effective means of discouragement? Dr. Valusek is against spanking. There are psychological complications. The parent has an advantage because he's bigger. It is unfair to the child because he can't strike back. It leads, he concludes, to a violent community. The doctor prefers instead, no doubt, the heart-to-heart talk, a beautiful concept, gentle, loving and with most children utterly useless. Some, sad to say, become skilled at heart-to-heart talks. "Well mother gave me the Big Lecture again. So what?" There really are children who do think this way.

Taking his fears one at a time: psychological consequences follow from all kinds of restraint, whether physical or mental, and in neither case do we really know what they are. Assault upon the body may have consequences. So, too, may assault upon the conscience. The parent is not only bigger physically, he is also better at mind games, or should be. The doctor seems to regard parent and child as equals. But how could they be equals? The one has responsibility and the other doesn't. If the child is deprived, it may well be the parent's fault. Whoever has the responsibility has to have the authority. To remove authority over children is to remove responsibility for them, a development the doctor may in fact desire because it would have to be assumed instead by the state.

As to the final point, violence in the community, the doctor should read his history. Violence takes over in the community when the law fails. And the law fails when the law can no longer be effectively enforced. And the enforcement of the law is a process that begins in the home. By emasculating the power of the family the doctor is therefore helping to bring about the very condition which he abhors. So his cause is both silly and dangerous.

But what we really must prevent is the possibility of such nonsense finding its way into the statute law. It will come forward, of course, in highly respectable garb. It will be advanced as the "rights of the child" without anybody noticing that the child's rights are advanced at the expense of the rights of the parent. The horrors of child abuse will be cited, we will be shown pictures of scores of children who were punished excessively. We will not be shown pictures of the tens of thousands of other children in the juvenile courts who were also abused because they had not been punished enough. So we should be ready for this movement and we should oppose it vigorously.

- April 25, 1980

How capital punishment has been reinstituted in Calgary

It is surely more than coincidence that in the same week that parliament earnestly debates whether the state should execute criminals, a Calgary merchant is exonerated by a jury and acclaimed as a popular hero for taking it upon himself to execute one of them on his own. There is a message in this for the politicians, though it's doubtful most of them will hear it. The message is that the general populace is far ahead of its supposed leaders in (a) analysing what's wrong with our criminal justice system, and (b) knowing what to do about it.

The decision of the thrice-robbed Mr. Steven Kesler to shoot the next thug who arrived in his store is, of course, part of a current and dangerous phenomenon. Nine days before his acquittal, a jury acquitted New York subway rider Bernhard Goetz for gunning down the four black hoodlums who tried to mug him. Similar cases have appeared in Vancouver, Winnipeg and Montreal. All evidence the same principle: if the law won't protect the citizen, the citizen will protect himself, and the populace will warmly support him. The inevitable portent is, unfortunately, for civil chaos, with each man armed against his neighbour. If one wonders why things have come to this sorry impasse, he need only refer to the inanities gravely espoused in the current capital punishment debate. Here we see the liberal ideologue at his blurred, bland and balmy best. Some examples:

Contention: since capital punishment was abolished in 1976, there has been no significant increase in the murder rate. Fact: in 1976, nobody had been executed in Canada for fourteen years because juries, influenced by the same liberal lunacy as the politicians, had long refused to hang anybody. Since the time that people were routinely hanged for murder, however, the rate has doubled, or even tripled.

Contention: the state must not take away human life. Fact: then we had better remove the guns from policemen and disarm what's left of our armed forces. When the state gives these people weapons the plain purpose is surely, if need be, to take away human life.

Contention: The Bible says, "Thou shalt not kill." Fact: The

Bible does not say this. Both the Hebrew language of the Old Testament and the Hellenistic Greek of the New Testament, have one verb that means "killing" generally, and another that specifies an act of "murder." In every instance, in both Old Testament and New Testament, the word for murder is used.

Contention: capital punishment is murder by the state. Fact: a democratic state takes away a life only after the evidence against the accused has been carefully detailed and exhaustively cross-examined, only after a jury has found him guilty and only after a judge has himself decided to confirm the sentence. A murderer acts as judge, jury and executioner all on his own, and the victim is usually unconsulted. To equate the one kind of killing with the other is absurd.

(Mr. Les Bewley, the retired Vancouver judge, has logically analysed the abolitionist bumper sticker, "Why kill people who kill people to show that killing people is wrong?" Behind such thinking, he says, is the proposition: since all murder is killing, and capital punishment is killing, then capital punishment must be murder. Get the idea? Since all spaghetti is food, and corned beef is food, then corned beef must be spaghetti. Since all morons are people, and editorial writers are people, then editorial writers must be morons.)

This, as I say, is the kind of mush-mindedness that we have witnessed for years, not only in the capital punishment debate, but in the entire process by which our present criminal justice system has been constructed. The sordid spectacle of uncontrollable crime - the daily routine of rape, murder, burglary, mugging, armed robbery and assault - evidence a simple fact: our system of benevolent criminal justice does not work. It is, in fact, a disaster. But it cannot be easily changed. For the root cause of its failure lies not in ineffectual court and police departments, nor even in the phantasmagoric bureaucracy of social workers and counsellors that the system inevitably spawns. Rather it derives from the assumptions that lie, implicit and unexamined, beneath much teaching today in the fields of criminology, penology, sociology, and even, sad to say, the the law schools themselves.

Many years ago, perhaps thirty or fifty, these academic

disciplines all decided to abolish the idea of sin. Human beings, they said, do not err. They merely develop socially disruptive attitudes, or peer group alienation, always as a response to adverse environmental stimuli. Improve the environment and you will improve the individual. While this purports to be a high-minded view of society, the fact is quite the reverse. It reduces human beings to mere organisms. Prod them this way or that, and they will behave predictably, like training an animal. We are the animals and the social engineers the trainers.

And, since no man was sinful, but all were mere victims of their circumstances, how could we consider the criminal as "indebted" to society? How could we speak of a criminal sentence as "retribution?" Was it fair to use the penalty imposed upon one as a means of discouraging others? Counselling, job training, psychiatric treatment, understanding, all such improvements in the man's environment, would soon see him respond as a useful member of the social order.

What we are finding out is that it doesn't work, and that this view of human nature is therefore probably nonsense. Mr. Kesler had obviously reached this conclusion, and acted accordingly. His jury and the public generally have reached the same conclusion, and supported him. The people who refuse to reach it are social theorists and ivory-tower editorial writers. The reason for their reluctance is clear. They can see what's involved. It means far more than reinstituting capital punishment, and providing tougher judges and policemen. It means scrapping their whole concept of human nature and starting all over again. This they refuse to do. Let the streets run wild, but save the dogma. That, one suspects, is the real "crisis of conscience" in the capital punishment debate. - *July 6, 1987*

Are our new 'golf club' prisons built on a grotesque sociological error?

It becomes increasingly persuasive that most criminologists know very little about criminals. We read last week, for example, of a riot in the new women's prison at Truro, N.S., a parallel to the new one at Edmonton. The inmates - excuse me, "residents" - smashed furniture, tore out plumbing, set mattresses on fire and left one witness gasping: "I swear to God they had sledgehammers in there, or else a twister went through."

The Nova Scotia extravaganza admittedly falls short of the Edmonton jail's brief, chaotic history. Truro had no murders or recurrent wrist and throat-slashing, and one-quarter of the residents didn't escape. But together they offer a vivid picture of the government's "new concept of prison life in a home-like atmosphere."

Why so much grief and mayhem in these elaborate facilities, specifically designed to keep the residents happy? The explanation goes back thirty or forty years. In the callous, narrow, intolerant, bigoted Canada of yesteryear, a criminal sentence had four purposes: to protect the public; to serve as a deterrent to others; to exact retribution from an offender viewed as owing a debt to society; and finally to help him learn to lead a law-abiding life. These principles were not simply invented. Rooted in experience, they emerged over centuries.

At some point however, the "social scientists" reached an extraordinary conclusion. They decided there was no such thing as sin. How they learned this is unclear; seemingly it just came to them, a kind of blinding revelation. Anyhow, they began assuming that we human beings are not actually responsible for what we do. We are entirely the product of our genetic heredity and our environment. We are machines that just "respond to stimulus." Therefore we cannot be "blamed" for our conduct. The criminal is himself a victim of abuse or neglect or unfortunate genetics. That's what makes him maim, rape, rob or cheat.

The implications, of course, were vast. How would we "punish" somebody for something he couldn't help doing? Punishment became an obsolete concept. How could we speak of the criminal making "retribution?" This too implied blame. Moreover, if "unacceptable behaviour" were caused by an unfortunate childhood (you could no longer say "bad" or "evil" behaviour because these words suggested "sin"), then only by improving an offender's environment could we hope to change his behaviour.

This is what gave us the new concept of jails, well described in a *Reader's Digest* article by Celeste McGovern of the *Report* magazines. At the Ferndale Institution in B.C.'s Fraser Valley, for instance convicted killers, rapists and armed assailants live in pleasant little bungalows. They pass their time on the prison tennis or basketball courts, or on their golf course. As for work, that is optional. Even so, 52 "residents" have walked away from Ferndale; two have been charged with subsequently committing murder.

At William Head in B.C. prisoners have their own TVs and stereos, many their own computers. Guards are discouraged from "violating inmate privacy." Millhaven, Ont., residents have four tennis courts, a baseball diamond, soccer field and mini golf course. Musical instruments are supplied them. A prominent sign advises: "Know your rights." Most do. Federal prisons handle about 14,000 prisoner complaints a year.

"In Canada we have come a considerable way in transforming imprisonment away from the art of punishment," says a spokesman for the Correctional Services of Canada. "Society is best served by a system that rehabilitates rather than punishes," declares a CSC statement. As far back as 1971, Solicitor-General Jean-Pierre Goyer announced: "We have decided to stress the rehabilitation of individuals rather than the protection of society."

And if male criminals are blameless, how much more blameless must females be? Thus reasoned Jan Fox, whom the CSC describes as a "role model" for the new policy. She served on a task force known as "Creating Choices" for women prisoners, she chairs the CSC's advisory committee on women's issues, and she supervised the development of the landmark facility at Edmonton, and became its first warden.

Women are not nearly as prone to violence as men, explained Ms. Fox, and if they do become violent it's because of some violence suffered at the hands of a man.

Meanwhile a riot occurred at the ancient prison for women in Kingston Ont. The CBC's *The Fifth Estate* portrayed it as a dreadful instance of women under male persecution. The female prison staff had called in male assistance when they couldn't control the rioters. The CBC showed male guards, dressed like Darth Vader, stripping and cutting the clothes off unresisting women inmates. A lady judge reviewing the riot, saw it as an appalling example of abuse of unfortunate women. A new approach is urgent, she said. All this spurred the Edmonton project.

Some details of the Kingston riot escaped public attention. Why these women had been jailed, no one ever seemed to ask. It turned out one was serving four years for stabbing a taxi driver. Another was serving five years for tying a man's hands behind his back, beating him with a baseball bat, and threatening to cut off his penis - he didn't give her his bank card number. Another had killed a fellow inmate while serving time for armed robbery. Another was doing three years for robbing an 80-year-old man and 78-year-old woman. Another was doing fifteen years for stabbing a 63-year-old man eighteen times. The female guards had called for male help after one guard was knifed, another beaten so severely she had to be hospitalized and others attacked by prisoners swinging pillow cases stuffed with steel bed parts. Little of this made it onto the CBC program.

Such things, said Warden Fox, would not happen at the new Edmonton facility, so carefully designed to seem more like a housing development than a jail. If any of *her* residents commit a criminal offence, she told *The Edmonton Examiner*, she would resign.

The outcome is now well known. Since it opened last November one resident has been murdered, a nurse suffered a broken nose, at one point one-quarter of the "residents" had departed (several of whom were convicted killers and armed robbers), and the CSC has ordered severely tightened security, including an eight-foot fence topped with razor wire. Warden Fox remains in office.

You have to ask: could criminologists be utterly deceived in their assumptions? Could a whole prison system costing billions have been erected on one grotesque misreading of human nature? "It often happens," writes the sociologist Edward Bell of the University of Western Ontario, "that ideas gain considerable prominence in the social sciences without ever having been examined empirically." He was not writing about criminology. But he certainly could have been.

- *September 23, 1996*

Chapter Three

War & Peaceniks

*"Burying one's head in the sand
after wailing about the horrors
of war is not Christian response.
It is irresponsible role-playing."*

- Ted Byfield, 1991.

Tiananmen Square tells us why we must bring back the ogres

There are two things one might note about recent events in Beijing. One is that we do not know what happened, whether it involved the massacre of thousands or the killing of a relative few. The other is our own reaction to it. The western world was shocked, astonished, appalled, the media tell us. Now that is surely odd. Almost the whole experience of the twentieth century should have prepared us for just such an outcome. When we recoil in amazed horror at something we had been given every possible reason to expect, this must be cause for concern. It means that we have been fundamentally deceived, that we have been living in an illusion that things are not as we had supposed they were. Why, I wonder, should so many of us have looked on dumfounded and aghast when we saw on television the tanks moving into Tiananmen Square and starting to shoot at unarmed people?

"I think," said my old friend Helen Robertson,"that they should never have tried to change the fairy tales." She was for many years the children's librarian of Winnipeg and she speaks in that dreamy, far-off way in which people tell stories to children, stories whose appalling significance does not dawn on them until years later. "How," I asked, "did they try to change the fairy tales?" And I also wondered to myself what on earth this had to do with Tiananmen Square.

"Well," she said, "they tried to take the ogres out of them. There were to be no more evil people. Everybody turns out to be good in the end. Hans Christian Andersen knew better. So, Heaven knows, did the Grimm brothers. Their stories abound in simply awful creatures and people who do frightening and terrible things. But in the end they always suffer horribly themselves which is very satisfactory to the children. As Stephen Leacock said children require the villain to be 'stabb'd through and through.' But it was decided that all this was far too frightening for little ones, so in the new versions the villains always reformed, and there was no need to stab anybody."

She had as usual, put her finger on a point. A generation that is raised without ogres in childhood, that is assured from the nursery onward that real evil does not occur, and is wholly imbued with the notion that, beneath it all, everybody is prone to an inevitable benevolence, will definitely be disturbed by last week's events in Tiananmen Square. Things like that are not supposed to happen.

But surely, as they grow older, history will teach these people otherwise. The Nikka Revolt at Constantinople which left thirty thousand corpses in the Hippodrome, Napoleon's "whiff of grapeshot" for the Paris crowd, Kent State, don't all these things express essentially the same principle - that mobs, even "non-violent" ones, will sooner or later be confronted with physical force sufficient to subdue them, and often a whole lot more than sufficient?

Alas no. For most people today have been taught either no history at all, or a highly selective version of it known as "social studies," in which only the facts that fit some social thesis are extracted for public demonstration and everything else is ignored. They know nothing about the Paris commune and what happened to it, for instance, but they are very big on Mohandas Gandhi. They know that by passive resistance he successfully defied the British. What they don't know, because they were never told, is that the truly unusual was not the success of Gandhi, but the forbearance of the British. As Mr. Paul Johnson points out in his *Modern Times*, if Gandhi had tried this stuff in Stalinist Russia, he would have disappeared in the night long before anybody had heard of him. But that observation does not make its way into the modern textbooks. It doesn't accord with the thesis.

Such, then, is the world these poor people expect to encounter: a world in which there are no ogres, where all governments are sweetly liberal, where caring-and-sharing is the primal human instinct, where no one fails in school, where no one really need work and where a bounteous government eases every possible pain with funds that it borrows and never has to repay, where we need no army because no one will start wars, and no nuclear weapons because if we don't use them against others no one will use them against us, and no real jails because there are no real criminals.

It is all very wonderful until suddenly something happens. The competitor takes away our market, the treasury runs dry, or the tanks open fire. We are shocked. We are aghast. Things are not supposed to happen this way. What has gone wrong? Somebody do something. Cut off the joint-venturing with China. Hold up the grain. Send back the panda bears.

Doing something, however, means more than mere gesture. The fact is that insofar as China is concerned we can do almost nothing. China is about a quarter of the world. But we can do something about ourselves. That is, we can revert to reality, first in the fairytales, then in the schools, and then in our fiscal and economic life.

It is very important to see, says Helen Robertson, that the new fairy tales, the ones without the villains, did not work. All the books in which they appeared have gone out of print and have not been reissued. Children weren't interested in them. Children believe that evil exists. They know that it's there, and can't be ignored. It must be destroyed. It must be "stabb'd through and through."

Neither, for that matter can we really deceive them in school. Children are not fools. Educational theorists certainly, but not children. They know that the ogre of failure is really there too, and that the real job is to defeat it. Pretending that failure does not exist isn't the real job. The same is true of public policy where the ogre is the deficit and the debt. Again, pretending that it does not exist will not destroy it. One day we will find out it is altogether real, and it will destroy us. The task is to confront it. That will be fearsome, difficult, dangerous, painful, but only this way can we "stab it through and through."

Finally, the same reality must apply in Tiananmen Square where the ogre was again real. The tanks were real. Death was real. To believe that totalitarian regimes can be overthrown by peaceful student demonstrations would be to believe fairy tales without ogres, which is to believe a lie. Democracy can be neither established nor preserved without resort to arms because the brute fact is that one armoured division is more decisive than a million people, however well intended. And in the end the only thing that will persuade the ogre is to have two armoured divisions, altogether ready to "stab him through and through." Learn that, and we will have avenged Tiananmen Square.
- *June 19, 1989*

Lest we forget: the horror of war can cause one

You didn't see as many lapel poppies this year, not as many people at cenotaph services, not as much reminiscence in the newspapers and on television And this is surely understandable. People too young for any clear memory of the Second World War could now be as much as 50 years old, and anyone with a memory of the first would have to be more than 75. Remembrance Day therefore has become for nearly everyone not an occasion for remembering, but for reflecting. However, many of these reflections betray a dangerous misapprehension of what caused those two great conflicts, in particular the second one.

A University of Western Ontario student, for instance, writes in *The Globe and Mail* on what he calls "the warped message of Remembrance Day," and the headline over the article nicely summarizes it: "A ritual that commemorates the glory of dying for your country means nothing to a generation bent on individual rights, not sacrifice. Surely the day should be a time to reflect instead on the horrors of war and how to avert it." One might point out, of course, that the only reason this young man *has* any individual rights is that people were prepared to die to preserve them, but this has apparently not occurred to him.

Again, the columnist Ms. Lynn Cockburn tells us in the Vancouver *Province* that "the thing to remember" is war's horror. She spells it out, horror by horror, from Dieppe to Beirut, deploring at the same time the whole concept of the war hero. "Hero is a word we use to justify war. It is a carrot we dangle in front of young men and, increasingly, young women, to encourage them to go off to foreign countries and fight against communism and for oil." But suppose the misguided sacrifices of these contemptible "heroes" had never been made? Is it likely Ms. Cockburn could write what she pleases in a free press? Not very. Indeed, not at all. But of this, she, too, seems utterly unaware.

Both Ms. Cockburn and this student are products of the same

educational system, and Ms. Cockburn is herself a school teacher. Unsurprisingly, her message is much the same as that which is preached in most classrooms today, namely: "No violence. No physical resistance. No matter what." The thing that counts is individual rights, and rights can be preserved by teaching children pacifism, by holding peace demonstrations, and by denigrating heroism. Whether such an education will stop violence in the world, we should consider. That it certainly doesn't prevent violence in the same schools that preach it, we can see already. For many schools today are beset by violence on a scale hitherto unknown, and children, we are repeatedly told, come to school in terror and armed.

As for the world, each of the two wars taught its own lesson. The first war undoubtedly occurred in part because the leaders of both sides did not foresee the hideous catastrophe they were unleashing. The American Civil War with its awful carnage prefigured it, but it was not studied in European military academies. It is undoubtedly true that none of the leaders who brought about the First World War would have done so if they had been able to foresee the results. And one of those results was the proliferation among the western democracies of exactly the sentiments which the young student and Ms. Cockburn espouse. Their articles would have expressed the almost unanimous public view in the year 1919 - war must never happen again.

Almost unanimous is not, however, unanimous. There developed political movements which not only countenanced war, but used our very horror of it to successfully prosecute it. When Hitler took power in Germany, the French army stood, some hundred divisions strong, on his western frontier. He invaded the Rhineland, divorced from Germany by the treaty that had ended the first war, with a single brigade. Stop him, many people cried. That would mean war, replied the Lynn Cockburns of the day, and they carried the point. Thus the industries of the Rhineland fell to the Nazi war machine. Next, though his forces were still puny, he invaded Austria, overthrowing the democratically elected government. Stop him, people shouted. That would mean war, said the Lynn Cockburns again, so he acquired yet more resources. Czechoslovakia was next and with it the high-tech industries that were indispensable to Hitler's plan. Here the tragedy was most acute. The German high command had expected the French to move. They therefore stood ready to remove Hitler from power, as soon as the French attacked. But France did not attack. Why not? Because the Lynn Cockburns of the press and politics again successfully urged against war and all its horrors.

By the following year, when he attacked Poland and the allies finally did mobilize against him, his army was already invincible, and it was largely his own subsequent mistakes that cost him the victory - those, plus the unstinting heroism of may thousands of people who so strongly believed in things like "individual rights" that they paid with their lives so that a young university student 35 years later could enjoy them.

The irony, therefore, is that it was our own horror of war that led us directly into it, and the ultimate price of the kind of airheaded pacifism which we are now propagating throughout the schools was paid by six-million Jews in the gas ovens and 45 million more people on the battlefields and in the bombed-out cities of the world. None of this would have happened had the French army moved. It did not move because too many people said, with Ms. Cockburn, "Never again."

There is, we should remember, one gigantic necessity in non-violence. Whether we're applying it to individuals or to nations, it only works if you can achieve unanimity. If ten people in a room resolve never to physically fight, then as long as they observe that, there won't be a fight. If an eleventh arrives who wants the room and is altogether ready to fight for it, then either the ten must turn the room over to him, or else they must be ready to stand against him. Similarly thirty nations may want peace and disarm, but if one insists upon arming, then the others must either arm as well or submit to annihilation or enslavement. That is the lamentable lesson of history, and nothing, including atomic weapons, gives us any reason to believe it inoperative.

What we must do therefore is observe two principles. First, we

must be permanently ready for war. Second, we must be resolved to do everything possible to avert it. Neglect either one and we're in deep trouble, for the pacifist is every bit as dangerous as the jingoist.
- *November 19, 1990*

The curious racism implicit in an episcopal pronouncement

Within a week after this is published, the biggest bloodbath since the Second World War could be under way in the Middle East. Dr. Terry Morley, a political scientist at the University of Victoria, has provided the readers of his newspaper column with an altogether adequate scenario of it: Saddam Hussein, "blinded by megalomania and betrayed by pride," ignores the United Nations ultimatum and remains defiantly in Kuwait. As hostilities break out, his air force is incinerated on the ground. He looses a missile attack on Tel Aviv with heavy casualties. Israel attacks Baghdad. Saddam's response is a chemical attack against the West, whose retaliation is swift, massive, devastating and horrible. This would be no Vietnam, says Dr. Morley. The war would be as quick as its toll could be frightful.

Dr. Morley, to his great credit, deeply deplores such a consequence but in no way suggests we of the West can avert it. Unlike many on the left, he appears to know that the alternative could be much worse, namely the loss first of Kuwait, then of Saudi Arabia, then of much of the world's oil supply until an awesome economic power has been delivered into the hands of a ruthless demagogue, whose ambitions will swell with his successes.

Our situation, therefore, becomes one of "Pay Now or Pay Later," and what we wind up paying later, in terms of blood and everything else, could prove far more costly. That is, sooner or later you have to fight him, and better to do it now when he's weak than later when he's much more formidable. The technical word for such foresight as Dr. Morley exhibits is "Prudence," a Christian and classical virtue.

Moreover, the practice of facing reality rather than shrinking from it sometimes yields unforeseen dividends. Saddam, finally convinced that we mean business, just might back down. But there is a strange irony here. Only if we really mean to fight are we likely to persuade him of our resolve. So the rule is: be prepared to fight and you may not have to. Be hesitant and you will certainly have to, and if you hesitate long enough you may lose.

In great contrast with Dr. Morley's realism we behold the mindless rhetoric of the mainline churches. Anglican Archbishop Douglas Hambidge of Vancouver, for instance, joins what *The Vancouver Sun* describes as the "swelling chorus of anti-war church voices" in deploring the UN ultimatum to Saddam. The bishop declares: "Christians recognize violence has to be an absolute last resort, and I don't know if there has been a genuine effort to avoid violence." He thinks both sides should be making concessions. "When I'm in conflict the first person who has to back down is me."

His last statement is revealing. It would depend, surely, on the circumstances of the conflict. If two men were arguing over some property and each had a reasonable case, then a concession by one may set in motion a settlement. But if one has simply seized the other's property, would justice be served by the victim's "backing down?" And would the thief not simply be encouraged to rob someone else? How does the archbishop contend with this likelihood, you wonder. Nothing in the press accounts of his statements gives the least indication he has even considered it.

There is in his attitude - and it is typical of statements emanating from the leaders of many mainline churches - an implicit (if you will forgive the term) racism. If Saddam grabs Kuwait, we are to make "concessions" to avoid "violence." So next Saddam grabs Saudi Arabia and again we are called upon to make "concessions." Then he has the oil, and with the revenue from that he acquires an atomic arsenal, something he has already attempted. Again we are prevailed upon to make "concessions" considering the undoubted horrors of an atomic conflict. But then, when he is upon our own doorstep, are we finally to be given the moral sanction to fight?

If not, then plainly what the archbishop favours is slavery rather than death. In that case, he should say so now, so that we all know what values he represents. But if not, then notice the implicit discrimination. If Saddam's only victims have been a collection of Kuwaiti desert-dancers, then war is intolerable and we must avoid it all costs.

But if the possible victims are ourselves, well that's a very different matter. Western whites are worth fighting for, Arabs aren't. What an unusual position for an archbishop.

Ah yes, say some of the other church spokesmen, but notice the inconsistency. When Afghanistan was invaded we didn't go to war. When Tibet and Cambodia were invaded, we didn't go to war. Why now? Obviously because in this case, our own interests are directly involved. We didn't depend on Afghanistan, Tibet and Cambodia for oil. We do depend on the Middle East. Therefore the assertion that this is a war to halt aggression is a fraud. This is actually a war to defend American oil interests.

"American" oil interests. Ours as well surely. Canada, too must import oil, and if the Saudi supply were cut, the resulting economic calamity would affect us every bit as much as the Americans. Moreover, we would be forced to buy it from an aggressor nation that would assuredly use the revenues derived from this stolen property to further enhance his aggressive capabilities. It is true that these considerations did not exist in the case of Afghanistan, Tibet and Cambodia. It is also true that what makes us act here is a desire to protect our own interests. But what's so awful about that? Is there something sinister about protecting your interests? Doubtless these worthy churchmen believe it wrong, but on what grounds, you wonder. They never seem to say.

There are circumstances in life when the most dangerous thing you can do is nothing. And nothing is essentially what the archbishop is recommending. The response of the Bush administration and the Mulroney government has been to act, both prudently and resolutely. What may follow next week could be utterly horrible. But it is a risk that must be taken. Burying one's head in the sand after wailing about the horrors of war is not Christian response. It is irresponsible roleplaying.

"He that hath no sword let him sell his garment and buy one," a great Christian once advised. The name of the great Christian was Jesus Christ (Luke 22:36). To classify him as bellicose would, of

course, be ludicrous. But neither can he be described as a pacifist.
Perhaps he was telling us that whether to fight or not to fight would
never be a simple question. There would be times when we should and
times when we should not. We have to figure each case out as it
arises. And that requires prudence. - *January 14, 1991*

Chapter Four

The Children of the Sixties and the Sanctification of the Victim

"Lending your name to various politically correct causes and being photographed in support of them does not really make you into a Joan of Arc. Dying in a booze-caused car wreck after dining at the Ritz with an international playboy lover does not quite equate with being burned at the stake."

- Ted Byfield, 1997

Byfield as a history teacher, St. John's School, Selkirk, Man., around 1967.

Sixties people should tread carefully
in considering the euthanasia question

Twenty-five years from now I will almost certainly be dead - indeed, for all I know it could happen 25 minutes from now - so the following warning need not be considered self-interested.

If I were now forty-something, rather than sixty-something, I would be exceedingly cautious about leaping on the current bandwagon for legal euthanasia, propelled with the accustomed theatrics last week by Svend Robinson, MP, Burnaby's dubious gift to national politics.

That is, if I were a member of what is loosely termed the "Sixties generation," the generation that now runs everything, the generation with the great big numbers that has made the great big changes, I would think very hard about where this latest liberal social bonanza is likely to lead.

By the year 2019, when your generation is reaching retirement age, an enormous proportion of the population will be in their 60s and 70s, all requiring pensions and extensive, expensive medical attention. But since you have fully availed yourselves of the modern conveniences of birth control and abortion, assuring yourselves that the pursuit of personal advantage is the very essence of life, and thus you have produced relatively few children, you will discover there are far more people to support than there are to do the supporting.

Indeed, the generation that will then be running things, and to whom this weighty burden of supporting you has been bequeathed, will not only be relatively few in number. They will also be carrying an enormous tax burden to pay the debts that you, their forebears - being the caring, sensitive, concerned group that you were - ran up and heaped upon them.

Then again, these two groups of people - you, increasingly decrepit, gasping in your nursing homes, and your tax-burdened exhausted successors, straining to support you - are distinguished not only by numbers, but also by colour. You are almost uniformly white.

And everybody will know what awful people the whites are, because for years you have been at such pains to describe in exhaustive detail the sins and failings of your race. Whereas our youngers will be that vast mix of hues and colours you so often and so admiringly envisioned.

Finally, the youngers will be free. They will not be burdened by the taboos, guilts, inhibitions and moral strictures that once haunted their ancestors. You will have liberated them from all that. They will have been taught - in fact had drilled into them - that the big thing in life is ME. My aspirations, my self-fulfilment, my self-esteem, my view of life, my this and my that, are the things that matter. And when they consider you, the pensioned mass of wheezing and unproductive humanity, they may just conclude that none of it is doing a great deal for ME.

How long will it take, do you think, before the obvious solution occurs to them? Surely the sensible, practical thing, the environmentally positive thing, is to implement...what will we call it? Genocide is such an ugly word. How about Populational Planning, administered under the direction of the fore-runner of so much other social advance by then known as Planned De-Parenthood? The name is important; so is the packaging. It will be seen as the Modern Way to Go. No fuss. No cruel months or years on sickbeds. And above all, no big cost.

Some of you of course may resist. There could be ugly scenes. Unscrupulous people might try to hide their parents away. Instances will be cited where the supposedly dying weren't dying at all. In fact were in good health and went about clutching a little note: "I do not want to die." And there will be stories of the wealthy cheating the system. But with tranquilizing drugs, such evasions can surely be minimized. And, of course, there need be no legal hassles. Good old Svend Robinson and his crowd of advanced thinkers got rid of all legal obstacles back in the 1990s. That's what the euthanasia issue was all about, though few seemed to notice at the time.

Today's euthanasia advocates, of course, will scoff at such a vision. All their legal reform is intended to do, they will assure us, is to enable piteous sufferers like Sue Rodriguez to end their lives in dignity, not in agony. Moreover, this is almost assuredly all they do have in mind. But the advanced thinkers are making their customary mistake. They think always in terms of what nice people will do, and then are horrified to discover that the world is not populated entirely by nice people.

Thus over the twentieth century they have reformed the prison system so that nice people won't be mistreated behind bars, and can be quickly freed to make a positive contribution to society. They are then appalled to discover that the people in prison are not all nice, and many use their freedom as a further opportunity to rob, rape and murder. They designed a welfare system so people can be supported by the state until they are able to support themselves, and are astonished to find that not all welfare recipients turn out to be nice, so that many decide not to work again at all. They created medicare to help people in times of medical necessity, and then are amazed that so many people use the system when there is no medical necessity. They set up abortion clinics for dire cases, which might happen to a nice person once in several lifetimes, and then are shocked to learn that people not so nice were using them as a form of birth control.

This peculiar ignorance of how human waywardness seems to corrupt every social advance applies even to learned economists. John Maynard Keynes taught that nice governments could operate on deficits during economic downturns, so long as they ran on surpluses during economic booms. But governments didn't turn out to be quite that nice. They ran up deficits during hard times all right, and then ran up more deficits during good times. Doubtless Mr. Keynes was likewise shocked and appalled. He forgot or never knew the oldest lesson of all. Men sin. And any system established on the presumption that they won't is certain to fail.

Therefore, O younger generation rapidly growing older, when you are considering a euthanasia law, do not consider it in terms of what Sue Rodriguez might do with it. Think rather what an impatient heir might do with it. Think what Stalin and Hitler and Pol Pot might do with it. Imagine if it helps you, the puritanical state envisioned in Margaret Atwood's novel, and consider what they might do with it. Because they, not Sue Rodriguez, are the people for whom you are legislating. - *February 28, 1994*

How one gullible young lady wrought havoc on society

Future historians will find much to amuse them when they come
to look back on the twentieth century. It furthered technology, they will
say, more than any previous era in human history. But it is also unparalleled for sheer folly, usually occasioned because people thought that
science was advancing when it wasn't .

Take, for example, the extraordinary case of Margaret Mead.
Miss Mead is the author of a book that influenced the attitudes and values of at least two generations. It has had pivotal effects on eduction,
social institutions, the law, penology, and in fact lies behind many of
the assumptions that have dictated twentieth-century cultural change.
Now that the century is almost over, the book is discovered to be a
hoax. Those in the scientific world who have revered both it and its
author are a touch reticent about this. That's understandable. In retrospect their collective gullibility seems awesome.

Miss Mead's book, *Coming of Age in Samoa*, has gone through
several hundred printings since she wrote it in 1928. It did for the science of anthropology what Marx did for communism and Moses did for
moral theology. It became, that is, a foundational document, required
reading on first-year anthropology courses, the seminal text of whole
schools of sociological and psychological thought. Its author - a
diminutive little lady with a round face and advanced views - was cited
by *Time* magazine in 1969 as "Mother to the World." Even today, many
of the controversies between liberal and conservative innovator and
traditionalist, go back to assertions put forward in *Coming of Age*,
assertions made for so long and so irrefutably that they have come to
be accepted as self-evident truths. As the evidence mounted against
them they remained unchallenged. They simply could not be wrong. If
they were in doubt, then doubtful too must be the monumental social
changes to which they have led.

Miss Mead's book gained instant celebrity because it turned the
tide in a war that had raged for decades more or less between biology
and anthropology. Biology had given rise to what was known as

"eugenics," the endeavour to program the future of humanity by scientifically controlled breeding programs. Naziism was one of its less appealing fruitions. Eugenics rested on the theory that genetic heredity totally determined human behaviour. A person's environmental upbringing couldn't fundamentally change him. Against this, a school of anthropology, headed by one Franz Boas, mentor to Miss Mead, contended to the contrary that environmental factors, i.e. culture, shaped individuals and society entirely. It followed, therefore, that if some untrammelled human society could be found in which people of a very different culture behaved in a very different way, this "negative instance" would not only prove the eugenists wrong, it would also prove that by changing the cultural environment you could change the world.

Such a society is what Margaret declared she had discovered. Her book descended on the science of 1920s like a fireball. Among the primitive people of Samoa, she said, conflict and internecine strife are virtually unknown. They are reared without moral inhibition and rules. Their sexual behaviour is unrestricted, and young girls are actually encouraged to have many lovers. Rape is unknown, as are the emotions of hatred and revenge. Bravery is not admired. Family structures are loose and children are often raised communally. It was, indeed a paradise of free love and ease. It followed that other human societies could achieve this ecstatic condition simply by changing their own cultural environment.

It is easy to see what came of this. We changed our schools, relaxing rules and encouraging assorted freedoms in order to produce a "free" society We submerged such subjects as history in the morass of "social studies" because familiarizing children with the war-like attitudes of their ancestors would only serve to continue those attitudes. We changed our prisons because we knew that a more relaxed environment would produce much nicer people. We took away the dolls from little girls and gave them boys' playthings because we just knew that "feminine" attitudes, resulting of course in female exploitation, could be eradicated by environmental change in childhood. Female attitudes, we knew, were not biologically determined. All this went back to sociological and psychological assumptions which in the main went back to doctrines very much shaped by Mead's book.

From the start, it is true, certain doubts had been thrown upon it. For one thing, it disaccorded almost entirely with everything that had previously been written about Samoans. The accounts of Samoa dated back to the eighteenth century, were extensive, and described the people as the war-like adherents of a tough and highly moralistic pagan religion. For another, it was gradually disclosed that Margaret's intimate study of these people had been conducted over about three months, and that she had not actually lived among them but with the family of an American doctor. For another, the Samoans themselves were outraged by what she had written. But it has remained for an Australian anthropologist named Derek Freeman, who spent six years in Samoa, to produce the definitive repudiation. His *Margaret Mead and Samoa* (Harvard University Press, 1983; Penguin, 1984), which is now gaining wide circulation, details an account of Samoans that is not somewhat at odds, but in diametric opposition to Miss Mead's portrayal. They are indeed a war-like people, heavily controlled by strict moral codes, who guard the virginity of their daughters with unusual rigour. Family structure is heavily defined, and a strong Protestant puritan ethic dominates the whole culture.

So what had happened to Margaret? The Samoans, Mr. Freeman delicately explains, have a whimsical sense of humour and when embarrassed by what they consider impertinent questions will string the unsuspecting intruder a line of fabricated nonsense. Miss Mead, aged 23 at the time and asking all kinds of strange things, made a particularly attractive victim. How were they to know all this stuff was going to be put into some book? She was, in other words, duped. And so, it follows, were we all. - *May 18, 1987*

More on the Herculean task of reforming the Alberta soul

Stereotyping

Stereotyping means a fixed set of ideas, often exaggerated and distorted. It is a mental picture which regards all members of a group as being the same, allowing for little or no individuality or critical judgement. - Student's manual for use in Alberta schools, published by the Alberta Human Rights Commission.

On this brave note a 58-page booklet, apparently produced six years ago and still in use in the schools, begins its lessons on what it calls "the dark world of prejudice." The booklet was sent to me last week by a teacher. Stereotypes, it explains, "are a kind of gossip about the world, a gossip that makes us prejudge people before we lay eyes on them. Hence it is not surprising that stereotypes have something to do with the dark world of prejudice. Explore most prejudices and you will find a cruel stereotype at its core."

Now this, of course, is true. It is also true that if you "explore" nearly any novel, movie or play you will find "stereotypes" at their "core" too, often quite cruel stereotypes. The reason we are captivated by a Micawber or a Scarlett O'Hara is that they remind us of people, in other words correspond to a stereotype. What makes a Bogart or a Matthau or a Hepburn great is that they can so entertainingly depict a certain type of personality. Mr. Archie Bunker succeeded because he was an arch-stereotype. To write convincingly or teach effectively, one must master stereotype. To communicate ideas without stereotyping would seem impossible.

For everybody, that is, but the Alberta Human Rights Commission. Here we had a booklet which declared that stereotyping is an active evil, belonging indeed to the "dark world of prejudice." The intriguing question, therefore, was: how will it teach without using stereotypes itself?

The predictable answer is that it doesn't. It proceeds, in fact, not only to use stereotyped examples of bigotry to make all its points, but even to devote an entire chapter to describing, quality by quality, what it calls "the prejudiced personality," in other words the stereotypical villain, the dark monster who inhabits the dark world of prejudice. And this, of course, is exceedingly interesting because it describes the character whom the Alberta Human Rights Commission is obviously out to get. What is he like?

The booklet is effusive in its answers. It portrays in words and pictures "the prejudiced personality." Six cartoons depict the villain, as it were, in action. The most instantly notable thing about him is that he wears a hard hat, and he wears it on all occasions - when he's bossing around his wife, spying on his neighbours, beating his children, toadying to his boss, all the things that people who wear hard hats can be depended on to do.

But the stereotype in the hard hat is not the only target of the commission's educational activity. Further on we get the stereotype in the cowboy hat and the one in the baseball hat. Here we are allowed to eavesdrop on two archetypical Alberta farmers discussing in a beer parlour the problem of Hutterite absorption of Alberta farmlands. "Them danged Hutterites," the one in the cowboy hat is made to say. "How did they ever manage to sneak in here without us knowin' about it?" The other replies: "Don't ya know 'bout Hutterites? I got a cousin down Pincher Creek way. They let Hutterites in there and they say it was the biggest mistake they ever made." There follows a dialogue in hayseed English - we all know farmers invariably talk like this - intended to exhibit the bigotry and intolerance so characteristic of rural Alberta. The dialogue ends: "Who's buyin' the next round anyway?" and in the ensuing lesson the students are asked what they could do to change the objectionable qualities of such people, i.e. the Alberta farmer.

Indeed, the commission is kind enough to spell out precisely what these objectionable qualities are. The "intolerant personality," says the booklet, is that of one who (a) is "rigid in his beliefs," who (b) "possesses traditional and unchanging values," who (c) is "intolerant of weakness in himself as well as in others," who (d) "believes in punishment," who (e) is "suspicious" of people, and who (f) is "respectful of authority to an unusual degree." He is also, of course, given to that practice which the commission finds particularly abhorrent, namely stereotyping.

Now if this is the "prejudiced personality," which the commission is out to eradicate in the province, then it would follow that what it wants us all to become is people of "unprejudiced personality," possessing logically the opposite qualities to those enumerated above. We will therefore run a school system that produces a person who (a) is lax in his beliefs, (b) possesses trendy and endlessly changing values, (c) is indulgent of weakness in himself and in others, (d) opposes any form of punishment, (e) trusts everybody and everything, and (f) is contemptuous of authority to an unusual degree. He will not in the ideal of course, have a hard hat and work for an oil company, nor wear a cowboy or baseball hat and work on a farm. Rather, one suspects, he will have a degree in sociology and work for the government.

There are, however, two things to note about this booklet. One is that it further demonstrates a besetting tendency of the human rights crusader, namely the habit of himself practising the very behaviour which he denounces. But of far more importance is this: the above booklet, produced by five city high school teachers and a human rights "education officer," is plainly pursuing a social ideal. It is says a preface, "intended to be consistent with the objectives of the Alberta social studies curriculum." We need a far clearer picture of what those objectives are. We need it publicly, and we need it debated, before, not after, it is implemented in the school system. - *June 11, 1984*

The latest dogma in Canadian law: no victim will ever tell lies

The English language does not include the word "victimhood" though it sorely needs it. We have manhood, widowhood, childhood to describe the status of being a man, widow, or child. But we have nothing to describe the status of being a victim, and victimhood is one of the most privileged and respected states in which you can be placed, or more frequently, place yourself.

I counted the word "victim" about ten times on a single day last week in the headlines of Canadian newspapers. There were victims of sexual harassment, victims of rape, victims of "stalking" (a new category of victimhood), victims of racism, victims of recession, victims of war, victims of persecution and victims of indifference. There were victims of violence perpetrated by criminals who were themselves victims of abusive lay brothers, who had been victims of abusive parents, who had been victims of a coercive church.

Victimhood figured prominently in Ottawa debate. The Tory government, in its unflagging resolve to talk about cutting government spending, had introduced a law to deny unemployment insurance to people who quit their jobs. The usual ritual followed. The lobbies objected; the media agreed that this was "the wrong place to cut" (because just about everywhere is "the wrong place to cut"); the bill was emasculated. The objection centred on victimhood. What if the people who quit were victims of sexual harassment, or victims of exploitive employers, or victims of racial prejudice? In that case, agreed the government, they'll get the UI. How can you deny pogey - or anything else - to a victim of anything?

Notice that once you achieve victimhood, you also achieve innocence. Nobody will ask unpleasant questions. Why did you leave your last job? Fill in blank. What is the applicant expected to say? Because I told the boss to go to hell? Certainly not. All he need do is declare victimhood: sexual harassment. Or long hours. Or demeaning work. He gets the pogey; nobody investigates. How could they? Are all these thousands of sexual harassment charges to be turned over to human rights commissions? Hence, to be a victim is to be innocent.

Similarly, the new "stalking" law. If any woman enters a complaint that a former husband or boyfriend is "lurking about," the man will automatically be arrested. You can see the scene: "Mr. Smith, come with us." "But why?" pleads Mr. Smith. "Because your ex-wife says you were stalking her." "But I haven't been anywhere near her." "You can tell that to the judge. In the meantime for the rest of the week you'll be in custody." Who's telling the truth? The law automatically believes her and disbelieves him. Why? Because she is a victim and victims never tell lies.

Or read the recurrent stories about teenaged prostitutes. Once regarded as juvenile criminals, they have now achieved victimhood, and with it innocence. Hence I have read in *The Edmonton Journal* at least four times about "men who prey on teenaged prostitutes," meaning patronize them. One of these youngsters stands on a corner flagging cars and propositioning passersby. Who's doing the "preying?" Answer: anybody who stops and listens to her. But isn't she doing a little "preying" herself? Certainly not. How could she? She's a victim of male lust. And victims can do no wrong.

Similarly, the new "rape shield" law. It is now illegal for counsel, defending a man on a sexual assault charge, to question the sexual history of the victim. This would be too stressful to a victim, says the law. But suppose, one might argue, that this "victim" had in her past charged four other men with sexual assault on four different occasions, and in each one of them , was proved to have been blackmailing them. The law's implicit answer: no victim would do such a thing; victims never lie.

(Along with the Status of Victimhood another observable current social phenomenon should be mentioned in passing. It could be called "The Doctrine of the Most Dangerous Place." Some examples: when it is discovered that more children are abused in the home than anywhere else, we are asked to conclude: "The most dangerous place a child can be is in the home." Or when it is established that more women are beaten up by husbands or boyfriends than by anyone else, we must conclude: "The most dangerous place a woman can be is at home with her husband or boyfriend." By the same logic you can conclude that since more sick people die in hospitals than anywhere else, "the most dangerous place you can put a sick person is in hospital." Or since more people die in ambulances than in any other kind of vehicle, "the most dangerous place you can put an injured man is in an ambulance." For further specimens of this peculiar logic, consult almost any day's edition of any Southam newspaper.)

Back to victimhood. Before we confer this prized status on many more groups of people, we might bear in mind three lessons from the past:

First: victims are capable of telling lies, in fact are even more likely to do so than non-victims because they begin with a sense that they have been wronged and are owed something. To predicate any law whatever, therefore, on the presumed infallibility of the victim is to perpetrate a grotesque miscarriage of justice, and that is exactly what our federal government is consistently doing, and with the full support of the other two major parties.

Second: there are such things as victims. Real ones, with real oppressors and persecutors, who deserve the protection of the state. But by conferring the word on anyone with any complaint, however spurious, we will rapidly wear down the public sympathy that should properly accrue to such people. Like the boy who cries "wolf" too often, we are nullifying the alarm, so that when the real beast shows up, nobody listens.

Third: this whole process is teaching us to depend on government to provide protection that we might better provide for ourselves. What used to be solved by a slap on the face now requires a sexual harassment case before the human rights commission. Where each new wave of immigrants once had to earn society's respect, today respect is supposed to be conferred by the government's multicultural and anti-discrimination programs. But governments, alas, cannot make people good, and our supposedly "just society" is turning out less just and less law abiding than anything we have ever seen. Maybe we should forget about government and take care of these things ourselves. - *March 1, 1993*

Will somebody please answer Mr. Le Hir,
or will his accusers kindly back off?

Richard Le Hir is a man you'd think few western Canadians would sympathize with. The former president of the Quebec Manufacturers Association is a star candidate for the Parti Quebecois. Yet when you consider what happened to him, it's hard not to feel for him. He's raised a question which demands an answer. Instead of giving him one, the chattering classes simply heap abuse on him for asking it.

Mr. Le Hir was discovered this month to have given an interview in a documentary film two years ago. In it he raised this question: What can modern society learn from native culture? The answer, he feared, was nothing. He wouldn't say this "if it could be shown that their culture demonstrated its superiority in one form or another. But when you look at what heritage has been left by native civilizations - if you could call them civilizations - there is very little."

Such a statement must of course, be deeply offensive to any natives proud of their heritage. So you would expect to read where a native spokesman, or an anthropologist, or somebody, has refuted Mr. Le Hir and shown where modern society has a great deal to learn from native culture, citing persuasive examples.

But this did not occur. Mr. Le Hir was everywhere being accused of "racism," called an "embarrassment" and denounced, everything but answered. "My jaw dropped," said the producer of the documentary, Catherine Bainbridge. "We didn't expect him to have such ridiculously racist views." Bill Namagoose of the Grand Council of the Crees said: "Having a person like this in the cabinet won't make it easy to build any bridges between the PQ and native peoples." A Canadian Press story observed: "For Le Hir, it was only the latest in a series of gaffes that have embarrassed the party."

Notice that not one of these comments even begins to undertake a refutation of what Mr. Le Hir actually said. Maybe he was dead wrong. Maybe modern society has untold lessons to learn from the aboriginal culture. But not one of his accusers even remotely suggested what it is. Apparently that was considered unnecessary.

Precisely the same thing happened the month before to Herb Grubel, the Reform Party MP for West Vancouver. During Commons debate on the controversial Yukon land claims settlement he remarked that Canada's treatment of natives was akin to that of a "rich uncle" paying to keep his children on some South Seas island. He meant, of course, that Ottawa's native policy was a mindless and costly paternalism which helped neither the natives nor the country. Indeed I've heard more than one responsible native spokesman say almost exactly the same thing. So the assertion demanded an answer. Where exactly was his South Seas metaphor inappropriate, or in error, or unfair?

Again, he didn't get one. Instead Mr. Grubel was likewise dismissed as a "racist." One Liberal cabinet minister compared him with holocaust disputant Ernst Zundel. A native spokesman deplored his "racist, ignorant, bigoted attitude." Audrey McLaughlin discerned "clear prejudice" against natives. Southam's Vancouver *Province* (indulging in a little racism of its own) noted his German name and referred to him as "Herr Grubel." Even his own leader demanded he apologize for such an assertion which he did. But again, we got everything but a reasoned rebuttal.

Now this tactic is anything but new. In formal logic it's known as the *argumentum ad hominem*. That is, instead of refuting an argument, it launches a personal attack on the man who raised it. However, it's a dangerous expedient. It soon leads people to believe it has been applied because a reasoned case doesn't exist. They conclude that Mr. Grubel's South Sea island picture must be bang on or somebody would have said why it isn't. They assume the reason nobody told Mr. Le Hir all the wonderful things modern society can learn from Indian culture is that there aren't any wonderful things to learn, and therefore Mr. Le Hir must have been absolutely right.

But surely, you would have to think those who increasingly resort to this device must realize the ultimate consequence. People have already grown more than weary of the endlessly repeating epithets. Racism, sexism, homophobia, hate, bigotry, intolerance - all these terms have largely lost their stigma. As was noted here last week, conservatives are even adopting them as entitlements to credibility. "Redneck and proud of it!" says the bumper sticker. So if the case against such disreputable contentions as Mr. Le Hir's and Mr. Grubel's can be readily made, why isn't anybody making it? What seems to be the problem?

The answer, one increasingly suspects, is that in most instances the case against them isn't very good. It's so weak, in fact, that to state it at all is to subject it to ridicule. Take, for instace the contention sometimes advanced on behalf of aboriginal culture. What is it that modern society can learn from it? It was unswervingly conservationist, we are told. The natives did not waste, and they lived in harmony with their environment. That's why the prairies teemed with buffalo before the white man came.

But was this harmony produced by native culture or by a deficiency of native technology? If it was their culture, then when the natives gained that technology, they would have remained conservationist. The facts are the opposite. Within a hundred years of acquiring both the horse and the gun from the whites, the natives and the Metis eradicated the buffalo. In Canada, the great herds were gone before the white farmers and ranchers ever arrived. They were driven over the buffalo jumps and killed by the hundreds, most of the meat left to rot once the finer cuts were removed.

(Now watch. Having written this, I will be accused of bigotry, racism, and so on. But there will be very little, if any, historical evidence to prove the contention wrong. "Oral history" may be cited of course, but if you ask for its credentials - i.e., some kind of evidence that it existed when it was said to have existed - this is declared impossible because of its nature. Before there were tape recorders, how could you record "oral history?" But then how are we to know that somebody didn't just, well, make it up? Maybe it doesn't go back to the "elders." Maybe it only goes back to the professors. Maybe they invented it. How are we to tell?)

In any event, I think we'll soon see the public wanting real answers, real evidence when such controversial statements are made rather than streams of epithets and invective. Simply calling people names won't work any more. - *August 22, 1994*

Is it yet safe to ask the unaskable: why exactly is Diana a heroine?

Talk about luckless timing. Somewhere in the week of August 17th to 23rd, *The Globe and Mail's* columnist Margaret Wente decided to do a modest hatchet job on one Dodi Al Fayed - on his collection of yachts and helicopters, his generous gifts to young women of jewels and cash, his bad debts, and (of course) his 262 ex-girlfriends, lately capped by Princess Diana of Wales as Number 263.

Ms. Wente offered other tidbits - how despite his voluminous experience, Mr. Fayed was reputed to be "very conservative in bed," how a photographer made one million pounds from a grainy long shot of Dodi and Di lip-locking, how girlfriend No. 262 was suing Dodi for failing to marry her as promised on August 9th and how the last time she had had sex with him was only three weeks ago, how Dodi and Di secretly helicoptered to a tiny village for advice from an internationally acclaimed psychic, how a seaman named Mohammed Sead who is a Dodi lookalike had jumped ship in Toronto and was arrested for impersonating Dodi and collecting assorted freebies such as numerous tickets to Phantom of the Opera (he frankly described his occupation on the police docket as "con man"), and finally how Dodi's arms-dealing uncle was once the boyfriend of Anne-Marie Sten, who is now the wife of Matthew Barrett, chairman of the board of the Bank of Montreal.

Columnist Wente is not above a little conning of her own, of course. She was quietly playing an old media game - deploring the publication of the sordid whilst spelling out every sordid detail (which is also exactly what I'm doing here myself). But unfortunately for her it rather backfired. Her exposé of Dodi inevitably left Princess Diana of Wales looking more of a flake than ever. Precisely seven days after her column appeared, Princess Diana perished with Dodi in a Paris tunnel while Dodi's thoroughly drunken chauffeur was hurtling them through city traffic at an estimated 197 kilometres an hour, dodging crazed motorbiking photographers who were out for another million-pound shot.

The circumstances of the death, one might conclude, would tend to affirm Ms. Wente's central thesis, notably that people like this are not exactly admirable. Unhappily, however, that is not at all how the world reacted. The world in fact went ape. For fully a week, Ms. Wente has had to watch aghast as most of the English-speaking populace plunged into an orgy of deep mourning. The woman she had just depicted as a flea-brained royal courtesan was suddenly transformed into a fairy princess of unparalleled charm, grace and virtue whose loss, said a headline in Ms. Wente's own newspaper, "leaves a legacy few will ever equal."

Now Ms. Wente will no doubt have spent much of the last week pondering what exactly is this legacy. What had Princess Diana done to earn such awesome devotion? "Diana, My Idol," said the sign above the cairn of flowers erected to her in downtown Vancouver. Idol? For what?

Ms. Wente could hardly ask this out loud, of course, not wanting to be publicly flogged, hanged or fired for callous insensitivity to calamitous tragedy. She must nevertheless have wondered, though. For she is herself a hybrid, raised and educated in the outlook of a vanished society but living in a new and radically different one. Her education seemingly encumbers her with a compulsive habit of rationality which increasingly renders her a pariah among her contemporaries. (I don't know Margaret Wente, have never met her, and probably never will, but I read her very carefully because she often seems to bridge the enormous gulf that separates her generation from mine.) This compulsion, Reason, insists upon an answer to the question which perhaps it is now safe to ask: why is Diana idolized? What did she do to deserve it?

I have talked to many people about this, and have had numerous answers. She was kind to AIDS patients, came one reply, and was photographed hugging them before it was considered safe to do so. Not quite true, of course. The Pope hugged them long before she did. Thousands of medical people took far greater health risks and far sooner than either princess or Pope and they will never be internationally memorialized. She was kind to landmine victims, said another, and was photographed hugging them too. This distinguished her from her Windsor in-laws, who make a point of never being photographed hugging anybody. Hugging showed her as a loving mother, and mother-love is something the royal family know nothing about. Again, said a fourth, she refused the role of royal family breeding cow, and coura-geously defied their overbearing authoritarianism.

None of this however, is altogether satisfying. After all, lending your name to various politically correct causes and being photographed in support of them does not really make you into a Joan of Arc. Dying in a booze-caused car wreck after dining at the Ritz with an interna-tional playboy lover does not quite equate with being burned at the stake. However addicted to hugging, she nevertheless walked out on her children, not exactly a certificate of maternal devotion. And if she didn't want the role of breeding cow, the time to courageously turn it down was when it was offered to her. Rejecting a responsibility after you have taken it on does not evidence the courageous, but a quality for which there are other less flattering adjectives There must be better explanations for the idolization of Diana, such as these:

• People need heroes and the "me generation" isn't very good at producing them. So they have to settle for celebrities instead, a very different phenomenon. Diana is not another Madame Curie or Edith Cavell; she is another Elvis Presley or Marilyn Monroe, revered not for what they actually did but for what they stood for, chiefly defiance of convention and moral authority. "Wreckers," as one acid observer put it.

• Diana was eminently qualified for victimhood - victimized by divorced and negligent parents, victimized by the royal family, victim-ized by her husband's infidelities, and finally victimized to death by the media. How could anybody so richly endowed with this cherished quality be anything but an international celebrity?

• Most convincing of all, Diana legitimized our yen to escape responsibility. If the Princess of Wales can walk out on her kids, so can I. If the Princess of Wales can flaunt her adulteries, so can I. If the

Princess of Wales can tell morality to go to hell, so can I. She liberates me and is therefore my idol.

But an idol only to those on the near side of that great societal gulf, those of whom she was so thoroughly representative - spoiled, naive, childish, foolish, pitiful. She was tragic indeed, both in how she died and how she lived. - *September 15, 1997*

And then the monster she had created
rose up and swallowed June Callwood

It couldn't have happened to a nicer activist. June Callwood, who since the 1950s has been the outspoken defender of all things bright and liberal, has been pushed out of another organization for being a "racist." Now we rednecks have over the years found many unkind names to call June Callwood - mush-mind, bird brain, twithead, flake, and so forth - but "racist" isn't one of them. However, she may now bestow upon herself that status she has so lavishly bestowed upon so many others notably victimhood. Like Dr. Frankenstein, she is the victim of the monster she helped to create.

Ms. Callwood's latest acrimonious exodus is from "TWUC," pronounced, I guess "Twuck." That's The Writers Union of Canada. (Why the letter 'T' is part of the acronym I don't know, but these people, after all, are writers, and we all know what writers are like.) Anyway, TWUC apparently got into an internal fight over who should be allowed to write about oppressed minorities. Some said only "people of colour," for instance, should be allowed to write about "people of colour." That's because people without colour would be too prone to the inevitable arrogance, chauvinism, stereotyping, insensitivity, indifference and paternalism that having no colour invariably impart.

June Callwood, it seems, immediately sprang to mind - to the minds, that is, of certain members, some with colour and some without - and these dirty Twuckers really let her have it. They called her a racist. She denied it. They called her other things. She denied those too. But she rapidly became very oppressed by all this, almost as though she were a minority.

Finally some extremely prominent Twuckers thought the thing had gone far enough. Margaret Atwood, Lorna Crozier, Brian Fawcett, Timothy Findley, Graeme Gibson, Barbara Gowdy, Patrick Lane, Susan Musgrave, Daniel Richler and Rudy Wiebe (people with much recognition but not a whole lot of colour) signed a kind of open letter suggesting that the controversy should be ended and everybody should "shut the (something) up." Only they didn't say "something." At the same time June issued an open letter of her own, consisting of three words: "Enough. I resign."

Now this was really too bad because everybody agreed TWUC won't be the same without June Callwood. Just as Nellie's wasn't the same without her after she was forced out of that, a year or so ago, on the same charge. Nellie's, in case you didn't know, is a home for battered women in Toronto which Ms. Callwood founded several decades ago when she was a more active activist, serving on its board for years and raising zillions of dollars for the place.

However, it had gradually become evident that many of the women finding refuge in Nellie's were, well, people of colour, as were most of the people doing the crumb jobs around the place. Whereas the senior staff and the directors were almost entirely without colour. There was another issue too. Apparently many of the staff members who did not have colour did have something else, namely a tendency towards lesbianism and an inclination to proselytize among the others, many of whom did not have this particular inclination.

Very soon all these oppressive things and the animosities they engendered came somehow to focus upon the hapless and utterly colourless June Callwood. In the end she was forced off the board of Nellie's, just as she has been forced off the board of TWUC.

Now I can't say any more about the Nellie's case because I've never been in a women's shelter, nor put anybody in one, and I don't know anything about lesbianism including how. But on the subject of only oppressed minorities being allowed to write about oppressed minorities I know a little bit, because I've lately become enmeshed in that controversy myself.

As you may have read, we are publishing a twelve-volume history of Alberta and, not being members of an oppressed minority, we're having to do this without government grants. (Maybe it's not quite true to say we're not an oppressed minority. Anybody who does anything at a profit these days is certainly in a minority and heaven knows it's oppressive enough. But they don't count this when it comes to making grants.)

Anyhow, two years after *Volume I* came out, the *Calgary Herald* found out about it. That's standard; it took them about that long to find out about the National Energy Program. I got a call from a young lady named Wendy Something at the *Herald*. Did I know, she asked, that our book was under "serious criticism" for "racism" and "stereotyping" in its portrayal of the natives? No, I said, I hadn't heard. Who were the critics and what exactly were they criticizing? She couldn't tell me that, Wendy explained; she was a "professional journalist" and had to protect her sources. But did I have anything to say in reply?

I told her I found it difficult to reply to an unspecified criticism from an anonymous source. Well, she said, okay. The critics were a lady from a native educational council, a professor at the University of British Columbia and a retired professor at the University of Alberta. The only thing specifically mentioned was that we said the Indians once roamed the Prairies "as free as the wolf," which suggested they recognized no tribal boundaries.

I pointed out that we had gone to considerable length to define the tribal boundaries and that the whole book had been checked by Hugh Dempsey, curator emeritus of the Glenbow Institute, who so far as we knew is the province's foremost authority on native history. Since we had made every change he recommended, we assumed our account was factual.

Ah yes, she said, but did you have the book vetted by the tribal councils? No, I said, we did not. We wrote about the CPR and did not have it vetted by the CPR. We wrote about the Hudson's Bay Company, and did not have it vetted by the Hudson's Bay Company. And we wrote about the natives and did not have it vetted by the tribal councils.

I got the impression this did not altogether satisfy Wendy. But being a "professional," she didn't say anything and wrote a nice story about our being called racists. So I can at least guess what June Callwood is going through. Meanwhile, you envision a situation in which only people of colour are allowed to write about people of colour, only natives about natives, and only women about women. As for

white males, anybody can write anything they like about us - we aren't oppressed, although we certainly seem to be getting there.
- *February 28, 1994*

Chapter Five

Schools for Scandal

*"The process of teaching can never be an egalitarian exercise.
If the teacher and the pupil are equals, then plainly there is
nothing for the pupil to learn."*

- Ted Byfield, 1982

After two hundred years, the Journal is on to the John Wesley scandal

The Edmonton Journal quite abruptly last month launched a gratuitous attack on the educational philosophy of the Reverend John Wesley (1703 - 1791). It was an inexplicable thing since nothing had happened to give rise to such an outburst and two hundred years is a long time for a paper to take getting on to a story, even *The Edmonton Journal.* Yet there it was at the bottom of the editorial column on December 30th. "We have run across," says the writer, "an old quotation from John Wesley on how to bring up children," to wit:

> *Break up their wills betimes; begin this great work before they can run alone, before they can speak plain or perhaps speak at all. Let him have nothing he cries for, absolutely nothing, great or small. Make him do as he is bid if you whip him ten times running to effect it. Break his will now and his soul will live and he will probably bless you for all eternity.*

"How times change for the better," says the *Journal*... "Break his will? Man's will is his dignity. Shaping will is the challenge."

There can be no doubt that things have certainly changed. It is abundantly true that teachers today are trained in an educational philosophy that bears no resemblance whatever to John Wesley's. Neither do most of them develop such a philosophy later on because for most there is no later on. Three out of five quit the profession in failure and disgust before they complete five years in it. For myself, I completed ten years in the classroom before I drifted back into the news business. While I might not express it with the ferocity of Mr. Wesley, because I do not live in such ferocious times, I nevertheless concur with his principle. I think it accords far better with human nature than does that of the *Journal*.

The latter seems, for instance, to envision a typical class of youngsters appearing on the first day of school. Faces are eager and cherubic, hands are clasped on the desks before them, backs are straight, eyes are alert, minds wait keenly for the pearls which a smiling, competent, endlessly patient teacher will spend the next ten months dropping before them. It is an idyllic scene, and if it were even faintly true, then maybe the *Journal* would have a point. It isn't. As neither pupil nor teacher can I remember any such class. The first days of school I recall as a boy consisted of a motley collection of disconsolate trouble-makers who rued and resented the end of the holidays. We didn't like school, and we certainly had no predisposition to like teachers. If our minds were set on anything it was upon a calculated assessment of the quarry before us, with particular emphasis upon the question: how much can we get away with before he blows his top, and what's he likely to do when he blows it? We, of course, doted on the kind of teachers the *Journal* advocates, those who dast not break the will of the pupil. We were for all teachers who thought like that. We would eat them for breakfast, chew them up, spit them out, and - with any luck at all - send them off the job as babbling nervous breakdowns before Christmas. We had at least two such triumphs to our credit by Grade 9, and assorted partial victories. One teacher was overheard once in the furnace room shouting almost incoherently to the caretaker, "I wouldn't care if I couldn't teach, if they'd only leave me alone." He meant of course us little darlings whose wills the *Journal* doesn't want to see broken. They carted him off the job the following spring, as I remember it, and he never did fully recover from his ordeal in pedagogy.

Fortunately, however, there were in my youth a great many of the Wesley-type teachers, which is the only reason I got any education at all. Fine, fierce men and women they were too and I can see every one of them to this day. I can remember specific lessons they taught, examples and illustrations they used, stories they told, facts they imparted, values they implanted. All this they accomplished with whole generations of barbarians like myself, and they did it because they first broke our wills, meaning of course our wilfulness. They terrified us, they subdued us, they instructed us, they enchanted us. Only many years later were we able to see that what they gave us was themselves, wholly and unreservedly. That I should for eternity bless them seems altogether fitting.

For the process of teaching can never be an egalitarian exercise. If the teacher and the pupil are equals, then plainly there is nothing for the pupil to learn. By breaking the will of the child, Wesley meant establishing over him the ascendance of order, represented first by the parent, later by the teacher. Whether it's the parent wielding a slipper, the teacher a strap, or the professor a sharp and sarcastic tongue, all are engaged in the business of fixing and maintaining ascendancy. To do so cruelly or with unnecessary severity is a mistake. To fail to do it at all, is to abandon the whole job. And that, unhappily, is precisely what our school system did for a long time, thanks to such fatuous nonsense as that preached by the *Journal.* Of late, fortunately, sanity seems to be returning.

The weakness of the permissive approach is, of course, that it is suited only for the saintly and the virtuous. Wesley in both his faith and philosophy was concerned for the salvation of mankind which meant the self-interested, self-willed creatures that most of us, in fact, are. That's why he was a great teacher who set in motion the conversion of England in an age of moral squalor not unlike our own. We need a Wesley today, though he can expect little sympathy from such quarters as the editorial page of *The Edmonton Journal.*
- January 23, 1981

A new challenge to the ATA's vested interest in illiteracy

> *His uncle looked long after him with a countenance in which wonder was blended with curiosity, and though neither envy nor the malignant feelings which it engenders entered into his honest meditation, there was yet a sense of diminished self-importance which mingled with the pleasure excited by his nephew's favourable commencement of service.*

The above sentence is taken from an exercise in an old grammar textbook used in Canadian schools a half century ago. The student was instructed to make what was called a "detailed analysis" of this sentence. That is, he had to take each word and explain its precise function. He had to explain, for instance, that the word "which" in the second line is a relative pronoun in the objective case, the object of the preposition "in." Its antecedent (the word it referred to) is the noun "countenance" and together with its preposition it introduces the adjective clause "in which wonder was blended with curiosity" which as a whole modifies the noun "countenance." Having thus dispensed with the word "which" the student must then proceed with the next word "wonder" and so on until he had dealt with every word in the sentence. There are 27 sentences in that exercise and about 150 exercises in the year. If you could do all this satisfactorily you were considered eligible to pass Grade 10. Otherwise you failed and did it all again the following year.

The point was not simply to enable children to dissect sentences. There were two other more fundamental purposes. By thoroughly understanding how language worked, youngsters acquired an utter confidence in using it. There was no uncertainty, no guessing. They could speak and write boldly. Second, by learning to analyse the function of words, they learned the habit of logical analysis itself, and could later apply that habit to the other subjects and situations they encountered in life.

Some time during the 1930s educators began relieving students of the onerous necessity of "detailed analysis" and later of grammar itself. It wasted too much time, they said, time that could more profitably be devoted to practical subjects like sociology, psychology, accounting and hair dressing.

Small wonder that for the last five years all Alberta universities have bitterly complained that graduates being sent up from the high schools can neither comprehend what they read nor express themselves adequately on paper. The universities must now run remedial courses in English for freshmen, teaching them what they were supposed to have learned in elementary and high school. Since the students are also frequently deficient in simple mathematics, the universities teach that too, giving them the whole trilogy - reading, writing and arithmetic. A current issue of *Time* magazine, however, reports that universities in four states are now warning parents of Grade 8 children that they can no longer afford to perform the work of the lower school system. They say admissions standards are to be sharply raised in 1984.

The university faculty people talk, however, as though all these shortcomings can be corrected with a few modest changes in the current high school curriculum, as though an extra class or two of English here and there will swiftly restore the literacy we have spent about fifty years throwing away. In this they are sadly mistaken. If specific competence in language is to be once again demanded for university entrance, this would necessitate not cursory but vast changes in the schools below, and changes not only in what they teach but in their entire philosophy of education. Entrance standards can only be enforced if there are entrance examinations so that the equivalent of the much deplored "departmental exams" will thus have been restored. Worse still to the modern teacher, the emphasis would rapidly revert to what one Alberta educator calls "mere competency." The schools, instead of cherishing "social objectives," which are comfortably incapable of test and examinations, would find themselves back in the business of facing very specific standards tested by decisive and determinate examinations. These in turn would test the skill not only of the student, but also of the teacher who did or did not prepare him.

To the modern, Dewey-eyed educator all this is not merely alien, but actively wrong. The whole direction of his own education as a teacher has been opposed to it. Many, in fact, would not even know how to run classes on this basis. Most outspoken of all in its opposition to such a horror will be the Alberta Teachers Association. Consider what is implied. If the text measures the teacher as well as the pupil, there looms the awful possibility of paying teachers on the basis of measurable performance, rather than on the basis of collective bargaining and threatened strikes. Hence the ATA can be counted on to oppose the exams and favour the present blurred uncertainties. It has a vested interest in illiteracy.

The escape from this deadlock, however, is now becoming plain. It lies through the creation of independent schools outside the public system and alternative schools within it. Many of these institutions have grown up because small groups of teachers, strongly supported by parents, have become sufficiently fed up with the aimless futility they see around them. They are now in various ways redirecting education in these schools back to its historic path. For these schools, university entrance exams will come, not as an outrage but as a splendid opportunity to establish their own credibility and superiority. They can say to parents, "Send your youngster here, and we will teach him the use and function of words. We will make him a master of the English sentence, a commander of his language. That is our offer. It is tangible and testable, and we relish the chance to prove it."

But to accomplish this, they will find, as all their predecessors have found, that they must go back to the fundamentals of grammar, back to the rigours of "detailed analysis." That's why I kept that old textbook. I think of it as a relic of the future. - *February 1, 1982*

The pitfall of pretending all people were created equal

All men, avows the Christian church, are in the sight of God born equal. God, however, was not a popular concept among advanced thinkers of the eighteenth century. The concept of the equality of man, however, was their most treasured theme. So they abbreviated the formula. All men, they said, are born equal - period. It sounded so compelling a proposition, so visionary, so just, so altogether liberal, that its devotees became blinded to its one besetting disability, namely that it is plain nonsense.

In no worldly sense are we born equal. We are decidedly unequal in physical strength and co-ordination, in mental capability, in natural virtue, in mental stability and nerve, in mechanical aptitude and in a hundred other ways. Yet the lie of our supposed equality continues to deceive us with amazing tenacity. It has proved particularly alluring to the modern educator, in fact is the basis of much of the mischief he has wrought. And in this he could always count on the eloquent support of his equally befuddled devotees in the ivory towers of the media.

Consider, for instance, an editorial that appeared this spring in that citadel of comfortable complacency, the *Calgary Herald*. The Department of Education in Alberta, finally persuaded that the entire direction of public schooling since the Sixties has been a grotesque mistake, has now - to its profound credit - begun the process of restoring sanity. It has started reinstituting departmental examinations. It has announced new, tough standards for students proposing to go on to university, and it has announced a specific timetable within which these changes will be instituted. In short, it means business.

Its efforts, however, are far from applauded by the *Herald* which discovers to its dismay that "the policy erects obstacles for students not academically oriented." It will "increase the frustration and reduce the self-esteem of students who find (some) subjects difficult, and may cause some of them to drop out." Or, the *Herald* is further disquieted to note, students who are not equal to or interested in the advanced program "will not be accorded the status of a high school graduate." Public eduction, concludes the *Herald*, "should offer chances of success and satisfaction to all young people regardless of where their talents and abilities lie."

There, as I say, we see the madness of the human equality dogma in its advanced stages where all grasp of reality has begun to slip away. The mind of the writer plainly dwells in a fantasy world, where everyone succeeds, failure is unknown, and all achieve "success and satisfaction" regardless of what they do, or how well they do it. Why? Because, of course, men are born equal, and therefore all should achieve equality, live equally, die equally. Distinction of any kind is, at bottom, a failure in public policy.

Certainly if anyone wanted to absolutely guarantee the eventual collapse of a society, the pursuit of this doctrine would be one way to do it. When we argue that as much time and attention should be devoted to the education of those with little aptitude as is devoted to those with a great deal, in effect what we propose is to cheat them both. If the ungifted are deprived of education, the ungifted may suffer. (Or they may not, for education, sad to say, may be wasted on many.) But if the gifted are denied education that they require, then we all suffer, including the ungifted.

For nature is not egalitarian. The numbers of the genuinely talented born among us, will in natural occurrence be severely limited. Those able to become skilful engineers, violinists, physicists, writers, salesmen, will be statistically few. They are, as it were, rationed to us. And whether we progress, prosper or even survive as a society depends almost entirely on the performance of that few. What the rest of us do will have nothing like the effect upon the fate and future of us all. However undemocratic it may sound, the reality is that there is among us an elite; there always has been; there always will be. And the rest of us are very much dependent upon it.

In ages past of entrenched privilege, when schooling was confined to the well born, we cheated ourselves by denying an adequate education to the gifted if they appeared elsewhere than among the privileged caste. How many Einsteins we missed we will never know. Now, however, we have found a new way to cheat ourselves. We deny the gifted the education they need because we insist upon educating everybody, including the largely uneducable. We miss our Einsteins because the money we should have spent teaching them the increasingly complex elements of nuclear physics was spent instead trying to force them into the minds of people like me.

Moreover, buried also in the *Herald's* thinking, is the pernicious assumption that academic success or failure is something that can be decided socially. We the People will decide whether Tommy Smith knows what a sentence is, or has mastered trigonometry, or can be declared able to handle first-year computer engineering. But We the People cannot decide this. What must decide it is what Tommy Smith can actually do. And if we advance Tommy Smith into first-year computer engineering, purely out of the necessities of Tommy's frail psychology and the *Herald's* mush-minded philosophy, we will in the end do no great service to Tommy Smith and a great disservice to computer engineering. Put enough Tommy Smiths in the class and there won't be any computer engineering. This, anyway, is what many in the universities keep warning us.

There is, in other words, an educational reality. It is no more possible to set standards of competence by democratic consensus than it would be possible to decide scientific fact or moral truth by democratic consensus. If nearly all men in a given society agree that the world is flat, this will not flatten the world. The fact that in given societies nearly all men agreed that slavery was good, or Jews were evil, or abortion was right doesn't make these things so. And the fact that a democratically elected minister of education declares that all of us are to experience "success and satisfaction" in education doesn't mean that we will achieve either one. We will simply have set fantasy before fact, a very dangerous thing to do. - *June 2, 1986*

Again the educators have used children as their guinea pigs

About 150 years ago, the philosopher Ludwig Feuerbach propounded the theory that since the highest known entity is the human self, then "self-actualization" should be the ultimate goal of education. If the taxpayers and parents of British Columbia and Alberta wonder what this has to do with them, the answer is that it has a great deal to do with them. Indeed, they have just spent millions of dollars and disrupted the whole structure of their elementary school systems to discover whether Feuerbach's ideas make sense. The answer, announced by implication last week in Alberta, and all but assured in B.C., is that they don't. And tens of thousands of youngsters in both provinces have lost at least two years of their educational lives finding out. They have been the guinea pigs in what increasingly appears a failed experiment.

How an educational theory descends from nineteenth century Bavaria to late twentieth century western Canada - in B.C., it is the basis of what is known as the Year 2000 Program - is a revealing story. It demonstrates, among other things, how little control politicians exert over educational bureaucracies. In both provinces the Feuerbach philosophy was adopted without debate, in Alberta without even a press release. It was done, in other words, without public knowledge until the media had discovered it.

Feuerbach's ideas were passed on in the twentieth century to the four founding fathers of twentieth century "selfist" psychology: Erich Fromm, Rollo May, Carl Rogers and Abraham Maslow. Fromm, a German psychoanalyst who abandoned Freudianism before coming to the U.S. in 1933, taught that "not self-renunciation, but the affirmation of the truly human self is the supreme value of humanistic ethics." Fulfilling "one's potential," said May, depends upon "the self's choosing its own course." The American born Rogers became the father of the "encounter group" in which the instructor "sits, as in a seminar, taking no part unless invited," the prototype for the progressive teacher, while the groups themselves became the model for the modern "pupil-centred" classroom where the object is to develop "unconditional self-regard." Maslow most influenced the modern schools. He taught that the competitive element in human nature is the source of man's miseries. If children could be raised free of all competition, he said, the aggressive element in humanity could be eradicated.

All four shared a common antipathy towards Christianity, which recommends self-abnegation rather than self-aggrandizement. But their teaching encountered other critics as well. Psychoanalysis and psychiatry challenged it because they found human destructiveness to be innate not acquired. The noted animal behaviourist Konrad Lorenz accepted aggression as a quality basic to all animals, but especially the primates and very especially man. Naturalistic philosophy challenged it by asking: what if some men achieve "self-actualization" by ruthlessly exploiting other men? How can this be "wrong" unless some standard of conduct is presupposed to which the self should adhere? And if such a standard exists, how can the "self" be considered paramount?

But such difficulties were swept aside in the education faculties of the 1960s, where "selfism" carried all before it. Far from Bavaria, for instance at the University of Alberta, a graduate student named Susan Alice Therrien became one of Maslow's disciples and wrote a thesis predicting "profound changes" in the schools when selfism was introduced. This she would assure twenty years later as Alberta's associate director of curriculum design.

Under selfism the teacher would no longer be "boss" in the class, wrote Miss Therrien. Rather than forcing information into the child, the teacher must "be concerned by the child's ability to learn about himself, about his own strengths and weaknesses." What the child does must depend on the child's goals, not those imposed by the teacher. Each child must proceed at his own rate of learning. "No child will have to keep pace with another," and evaluation of his progress must depend "not on his rank in the group, but on his own goals, his own needs, his own capabilities."

Such ideas as these simmered within the bureaucracies of both provinces throughout the 1980s. In B.C., they reached a triumphant culmination in the Sullivan Report on Education. Then simultaneous events at the political level gave bureaucrats in both provinces their chance to spring them. Peter Lougheed, who had long resisted the educrats' creative innovations, retired as premier of Alberta. In B.C. the Vander Zalm government arrived with zeal for educational reform and the selfist-laden Sullivan report at hand with schemes aplenty for radical revision. The result: drastic plans for school changes in both provinces in 1989.

Under these schemes, the whole concept of "imposed" standards of performance for various grade levels was to be abandoned. Each child must proceed "at his own pace." Children must never be promoted on the basis of comparison with other children, or class standards, or school system or provincial standards. In B.C., even the grades were to disappear, while in Alberta they signified little more than how long a youngster had been in school.

Critics raised doubts, of course. How could one teacher adequately contend with children in a class who were at a score or more of different learning levels? How could any standard of performance be maintained? Was there no legitimate role for an element of healthy competition? Did not simple fear of "failing the grade" positively motivate many children? How could such a system produce people able to meet the increasing competition of societies beyond the Pacific, all of which have tough schools? And where had these selfist ideas actually been tried out, anyway? (Answer, though the departments didn't admit it: nowhere.)

Last month after two years of mounting chaos in the schools, Alberta Education Minister James Dinning quietly disclosed that the plan was being scrapped. He told the legislature (as Abraham Maslow no doubt twirled in his grave): "In a world that awaits our students, the race will be won by the swift and the battle be won by the strong." To a reporter he elaborated: competition is to be restored. Standards are being strengthened. "We're not ready to take on the world. Yet that is what Alberta has to do."

In B.C., ministerial misgivings with Year 2000 have not yet become quite so specific. But Minister Stan Hagen's doubts about it, which he has expressed from the time he assumed the portfolio, took concrete form when the "gradeless" concept was suddenly ordered arrested at the primary level. Year 2000, it appeared certain, would live nowhere long enough to see the dawn of the year 2000 in B.C.

- May 31, 1991

Do our newfound ideas on children
maybe explain the fact we can't control them?

The same scene was repeated hundreds of times: the parent or parents whose urgency of voice betrayed sheer desperation; their indolent, 13- or 14-year-old, striving to affect boredom but exuding anxiety. His school work, it seemed, was steadily declining; three words - "Could Do Better" - appeared on every report card; he had become lazy, disobedient, mean to his siblings; every parental suggestion brought a sneer; he had acquired decidedly unsavoury associates. Could "St John's" be the answer?

St. John's was a church boys' school near Winnipeg, named for the Anglican cathedral out of whose youth program it has emerged. I was one of a half-dozen lay people who had established it in 1962 in an abandoned Indian hospital. Everything about it was what could be called "traditional." Mathematics was taught from pre-Second World War textbooks which advanced from arithmetic to calculus, relentlessly testing progress with pass-or-fail rigour. English grammar was drawn from texts even more venerable, requiring detailed examination of sentences with six or more subordinate clauses. History required hundreds of pages of reading from Thomas Costain to Francis Parkman. The school taught its own French course, developed from French-Canadian history and reinforced orally by various requirements. If you wanted to watch the hockey game, for instance, you had to do it on the French channel.

The outdoor program also echoed the past. Every winter, to make real the hypothetical values implicit in the academic curriculum, there were weekly snowshoe treks of 25 miles or so across the windswept, trackless prairie. Summer expeditions in big seven-man canoes traced the old routes of the fur trade, following its regimen: up at 4:30, break camp at 6:00; lunch stop at noon; make camp at 8:00; fifty- or sixty-pound packs on the portages; out three to four weeks; distances covered, anywhere up to 1,300 miles.

Most traditional of all was the discipline. Rules were enforced with a flat stick across the seat of the pants - failure to complete an assignment, four swats; late for a work detail, three swats; caught smoking, six swats. Compared with what would follow over the next three decades, it was barbarous. Compared with what had gone before, over the previous two to three millennia of human history, it was unremarkable.

So they came, and you watched the change. Not always, but nearly always. First the shock. Rules were rules; assignments were assignments; chores were chores. You could have your opinions, but no one was interested in them. Realization rapidly dawned that here was reality, and it wasn't so bad. You might fail, but could try again. You could work without shame. You could trust the guy beside you as never before. Soon the eyes would clear. The head would lift. The boy, by realizing himself to be a boy, had begun the process of becoming a man.

They came and they left - some after a year, some after two, some after three or four. Did it work? By the changes we saw, we were persuaded it did. And when they returned as men, they almost always reassured us that St. John's was the best thing that ever happened to them. Without it, goodness knows where they would have wound up. But how much of this, you had to wonder, was true, and how much simply generosity?

Probably the only detailed study was provided by, of all people, the Canadian Broadcasting Corporation. About seven years ago the CBC at Winnipeg, understandably suspicious that here might be yet another church residential school scandal, exhaustively interviewed about sixty St. John's alumni for evidence of "sexual abuse." They failed to discover a single instance of it.

They found instead that all but one of the interviewees supported the school program with varying degrees of enthusiasm, many extravagantly. So the CBC had a story: "Victims" of "barbarous" school overwhelmingly endorse and recommend it. But this was not the story they wanted - it backed the wrong case. If the CBC were operated by journalists, of course, they would have run it anyway. Since our government network is in fact operated by propagandists, however, they put a different spin on it. By judicious editing they produced a supposed "controversy." The sole critic was juxtaposed against the myriad of defenders, so that a 59-1 verdict was made to appear closer to 30-30. Exhibitions like this have endeared the CBC to a whole generation of Canadians - which is why they now quietly cheer as the government cuts it to pieces.

What brought all this to mind last week were two news stories. The Canadian Pediatric Association declared that most parents no longer spank their children, and proceeded to officially condemn the practice. And *The Economist* disclosed that across the western world boys have slipped behind girls at every educational level, that female students now outnumber males in university, and there is gathering around us an increasing mass of unemployable young men, psychologically alienated form the social order. To this may be added the rapid rise in juvenile crime, almost all of which is committed by males.

What we did not learn, naturally, is to what degree the first of the above disclosures accounts for the other. Is our new "non-violent" attitude towards children producing a population of increasingly undisciplined and unsocialized males?

How many marriages fail because one parent or the other, having followed all the directives of the experts, discovers that he or she simply can't stand living with the children?

One would expect that as our society rejected "violence" as a means of discipline - on the basis of the unsubstantiated dogma that "violence creates violence" - we would find ourselves, as we had been assured, living in a world in which males became increasingly serene, unaggressive, cooperative, and ready to assume all social responsibilities and civilities.

Instead we discover ourselves in precisely the opposite condition where more and more young males opt out of the system, refuse to work in school, becoming uncontrollably aggressive and far more violent than anything we have hitherto encountered. The obvious conclusion - that what we've been doing just doesn't work - is never reached, however, because the question is never allowed to arise.

But we should recognize what's happening. The educator who eliminated "coercion" from the schools was not warring with the previous generation, but with all previous generations. Neither was the criminologist who eliminated retribution, prevention and deterrence as factors in a criminal sentence warring with his immediate predecessors. He was warring with all his predecessors back to the time the first man was arrested for the first crime. And the expert who warns the parent against "spanking," of course, does not challenge the grandparent. He challenges all parents back to the beginning of man.

What we're watching, in other words, is a generation standing before all prior generations and declaring: "We know better than you do." The arrogance is monumental. So too may be the consequences.
- *October 21, 1996*

Chapter Six

Sex and its Consequences

"The abortionist trains himself, no doubt, not to observe that human eye staring at him as it is scraped off into the garbage bag. If the mere mention of these things is reprehensible, then what of the deed itself?"

- Ted Byfield, 1980

Ted and Virginia Byfield with (l-r) Mike, Phillipa and Link in 1955.

The Playboy revolution's bitter legacy of 'freedom'

The western world learned last week, with a yawn, that one of the great revolutionary figures of the late twentieth century was ill, perhaps mortally ill. How callous we are. The news itself merited only a tiny squib in the back pages of the papers. Nobody, in other words, gave much of a damn. However this yesteryear revolutionary was not a person. It was, in fact, a magazine - *Playboy* by name. It is going very broke, and may fold. But, after all, nonchalant indifference to the historical moment - and to just about everything else, for that matter - was the *sine qua non* of the *Playboy* view of life was it not? "What kind of man reads *Playboy*?" its promotion ads used to ask. The answer was an empty-headed ass, but it has taken thirty terrible years to figure that out, and the price has been beyond description.

To lay all the ills of our sick and sickening era on a single magazine and its publisher is, of course, a bit much. Hugh Hefner was nothing more nor less than a perceptive merchandiser, the man with the right product for the right market at the right moment. The moment was the mid-Fifties whose inhabitants for at least two generations had been hearing the liberal whining about fetters and censorship and taboos and "the personal freedom to choose." But the fetters, as Mr. Hefner well knew, had already gone. Religion had been debunked by secularism, inhibition had been debunked by psychology, decency had been debunked by cynicism, and human responsibility had quietly retired in favour of something called human rights. The market was the middle-income, middle-aging male who was, as always, resentful of the social bond under which he laboured and endowed with an extraordinary capacity to feel sorry for himself. The product was as ancient as the species. It is called sex.

I was there when Mr. Hefner's half-clad ladies appeared in the Fifties, followed in the Sixties by ladies not clad at all. To denounce it as disgusting would be, I'm sure, the right thing to do. It would also be a lie. Certainly the conscience put up its case, but the case was lost in the raw extravaganza of the event. The grand no-no, the thing one dast not see, the curtained delight that lay hidden behind every smock, bodice and tight sweater, there it was, all of it, for a mere buck, on every newsstand every month, a veritable seraglio of the most awesome pulchritude the imagination could possibly ask. How had that earthy Mr. Donne described it?

Full nakedness! All joys are due to thee,
As souls unbodied, bodies uncloth'd must be,
To taste whole joys.

There were the foreseeable prosecutions as the law of the state struggled in vain to replace the law of human nature and failed, as usual, to do so, as it has been failing ever since. Mr. Hefner, duteous defender of the Right to Choose, piously made his way to the bank.

There were, however, problems, chief among them the fact that the product was a fraud, the ultimate fraud of the unfulfillable fantasy. Pictures, unhappily, are not people. Mr. Hefner was not as it turned out actually in the business of sex. He was in the business of thrill. Thrill required novelty, and novelty required an inexorable slide into the slime. It was a descent Mr. Hefner, something of a romantic, one suspects, decided to forgo. Others, less inhibited began stealing his customers with the kind of photography we, as enterprising 12-year-olds in Washington, D.C., used to secretly seek out in the human anatomy section of the Smithsonian Institute. Thrill, however, demanded more yet. So the revolution went from there into the candid depravities that are now on sale in the magazine shelves of every corner store.

Pornography, however, is not the worst disaster occasioned by the *Playboy* revolution. It is the mere companion of another consequence of far graver dimension. For the appearance in the Fifties of Mr. Hefner's seemingly abandoned ladies was a signal to the simple-minded male of the day that the old rules had at last been lifted. Life-long vows no longer obtained. Familial obligation was now negotiable. Fidelity had been repealed. To walk out, to choose one's "freedom," was no longer disreputable. It had become you might say, almost noble.

The term "single parent" entered the vocabulary, and the single parent was nearly always a single mother.

The woman's reaction to this new-found male enlightenment was prompt, understandable and devastating. By the Sixties feminism had burst in all its fury. If the man would not sustain his share of the marital contract, then why should the woman? She, too, had her rights. She, too, would have a "career." She called it freedom from servitude to the man. But it soon became clear that her worst oppressor was not the man. It was the child. It was from the child that she really sought escape. If need be, she would deny it the right to live, even if its life had already begun within her.

So now in the Eighties we have a stand-off between the two halves of the species. Since vows are considered worthless, we have trial marriages. We have public schoolrooms in which two out of three children are being raised by one parent. We have the highest divorce rate in history, a suicide rate that defies explanation, and a birth rate so low that a number of western nations fear virtual extinction within three generations. Finally, we have tens of thousands of bitter people, facing old age alone and in crescent despair. They are, that is, "free", free of every human bond, of anything, in fact, that ultimately makes the difference between a life of all-encompassing purpose and one of total futility. Moreover they have produced to support them an alarmingly diminished generation. They discover themselves dependent on the children they did not have.

To attribute all this to poor faltering Mr. Hefner is, as I say, absurd. But to attribute it to the spirit and attitude of the age that produced him, and that he and his magazine eloquently espoused, is altogether accurate. He called it the "Playboy Philosophy." That philosophy has failed us, and miserably. - *December 2, 1985*

The question that got me thrown off a TV program

Here is a problem in "values" of the type that modern social studies teachers are encouraged to pose. Several men are out in the woods hunting. Suddenly one of them sees something move in the bush. At last, he rejoices, a deer. Then a warning flashes through his mind. That might not be a deer. That might be one of the other hunters. Question for the class: Should the hunter fire at the thing if there's a chance it's another human being? The approved answer is no.

I encountered serious trouble once by asking this question on a CBC television program. In fact, the tape was killed, the program was never run, and I was never invited back. For the man I asked the question of was the celebrated Dr. Henry Morgentaler, who was currently making his appeal of a conviction for performing abortions. He was one of the current heroes of the CBC and I was supposed to know that you therefore did not ask him questions that were "hypothetical" or "unfair."

The question may be hypothetical but it is certainly not unfair. The doctor, along with other liberals who defend this hideous practice, in effect argue as follows: we do not know at what point during pregnancy a fetus or an embryo becomes, in fact, a human being - whether at the instant of conception, or at the instant of birth, or at some intervening stage. Because of this uncertainty, abortion may be permitted at some elementary phase of growth. In other words, since we do not know whether the thing is human or it isn't, then it is all right to kill it, the very reverse of the conclusion that sane people would reach in the case of the hunter. The moral principle must surely be: if you don't know, you don't kill it. The abortionist argues: if you don't know, you may.

It is necessary to understand that all this is highly relevant. Abortion in Alberta is no rare occurrence. The demand for abortion is increasing alarmingly, much to the disgust of the doctors who perform it. (You cannot say who *have* to perform it because no doctor has to perform it.) Foothills Hospital in Calgary and the Royal Alexandra in

Edmonton, institutions designed for the saving of human life and well respected for their success thereat, are in this case gaining an undesired reputation for the destruction of life. And the presence of a congenial hospital in Ponoka produces statistics which give that centre the humiliating title of "Abortion Capital of Alberta."

Lay people are not encouraged to know the repulsive details of these "operations." One anti-abortion group some years ago distributed photographs of the process, too obscene to describe. Suffice it to say, it is not a picturesque affair. The essentials of personality, we are told, are carried like a computer program in the original cell. The eye forms early on, reflecting, as it always will something of the personality. The abortionist trains himself, no doubt, not to observe that human eye staring at him as it is scraped off into the garbage bag. If the mere mention of these things is reprehensible, then what of the deed itself?

We look to the moral authorities of our age for help in this regard and we get none, save as usual from the Catholic and fundamentalist churches which tell us unequivocally that it is a form of murder. My church, the Anglican, is acting on this question with accustomed inscrutability. Several of the bishops said they were dead set against it. A priestess from one of our temples in Vancouver said that she didn't care what the bishops or the church said, she was going to keep on recommending it anyway. And a bishop declared boldly that he favored "compassion," presumably for the mother. For the baby he apparently favored the garbage bag. So it went back to committee while the church waits for values to "clarify." One suspects, of course, that what we are really waiting for is to see which side proves most popular and wins. We will then come out strongly for that side. Thus we Anglicans have resolved the old question of whether the church or the Bible is infallible. Actually it turned out to be the Gallup Poll.

And finally we have the newspapers. *The Edmonton Journal*, that fearless defender of safe causes, has been predictably silent about this cause. It likes to blame the frequency of abortion on the minister of education who refuses to give little girls lessons in sex and the pill. But as to abortion itself, the *Journal* prefers to leave this, no doubt, to the "conscience of the individual." Like the bishop, it presumably means the individual mother, not the individual in the garbage bag. The *Journal* of course knows that if it declared itself wholly in favor of abortion, that might cause a spate of subscription cancellations or other unprofitable things. We have thereby reached the point at which the *Journal* becomes profoundly objective. The *Calgary Herald* is similarly discreet.

So we allow the practice to become rampant. We ignore it. We tell ourselves that since it happens so frequently it must be acceptable. We are assured too by the scientific ethos which enfolds it. It takes place in the most sensible and hygienic way, surrounded by technology, authorized by committees, advocated by respectable political activists. We do not suspect that another age may recoil in horror at the whole spectacle of what we are doing, and condemn it as we condemn the grand scale slaughters worked by other establishments in other days who were equally confident of what they were doing. That would be a time when the mere mention of a grandfather who worked in such-and-such a hospital would occasion an awkward silence in the conversation, and when the name of a town called Ponoka would carry with it the same connotation as that of another town called Auschwitz.
- *July 25, 1980*

O Canada, where we celebrate freedom by ripping up a baby

The word is macabre. The little baby - now 22 weeks on the way, sucking its thumb, stretching, yawning, blinking, with fully formed feet and toenails, hands and kicking legs - is not wanted. Not by its mother anyway. There are about ten thousand couples in Quebec who do want it, and can't have a baby because there are none to adopt. But that is irrelevant. What matters is "choice," meaning the mother's. The baby doesn't have one.

This is, in fact, the mother's third choice. First, she chose to cohabit with the father. When she discovered she was pregnant, she chose not to have an abortion. Three months later, she chose again, this time to destroy the child. The father intervened and the Quebec courts concurred with him. The mother - calm, noble, caring, the media assure us - now decides to act. She goes secretly to Boston where the little one is "therapeutically" ripped to pieces, limb by limb, by a suction machine. Was it a girl or a boy? The therapeuticians know. They had to place the pieces in a bag. But they dast not say. That's "confidential." Hasn't the poor woman been through enough? The media solemnly agree. There are no further inquiries. Back in Canada, her heroic "choice" is proudly proclaimed to the Supreme Court which has hastily assembled to hear her case. It's true that, in aborting the child, she defied a court injunction. In Vancouver, that is a dreadful thing to do, as the judges so gravely aver every time they slam the abortuary rescuers into jail for doing it. The mother receives no such admonition. She has been through enough, the judges decide. So we see how law is administered in Canada. If you defy an injunction in opposing abortion, you are a wretched criminal and must go to jail. If you defy an injunction in having an abortion, you are a national hero, and warmly commended. The following day, a grateful Supreme Court, relieved of the necessity of itself authorizing the butchering of the child, solves everything by quashing the Quebec injunction. Why it did this it will one day explain, says the chief justice.

In the streets, pandemonium breaks loose. People dance. By

having this little creature torn to pieces, the mother has struck a great blow for human liberty, says the establishment. Virtually every newspaper tells how wonderful it all is. The Southam company's western hen houses cackle in particular glee.* "Further dilatory attempts to use the courts to exert power and control over a woman's right to choose must now be given short shrift," exalts the *Calgary Herald*. "This country cannot go on victimizing pregnant women," declares the Vancouver *Province*. This is "a signal to women that the state should not be peering into their bedrooms," avows *The Vancouver Sun*. Canada, where the right to abortion is now the widest in the western world, has been saved from barbarism. We can kill unborn children any time we want.

Meanwhile the media delicately approach the heroine herself. Will she now tell her whole story, describe her entire ordeal? Really, says her lawyer, has she not suffered enough? Can they not leave her alone? It later develops that she was prepared to suffer just a little more, and tell her whole story to a London tabloid for $8,000, on the condition she not talk to anyone else first. No one writes any editorials about this.

The scene now shifts to the cabinet chamber where the divided Tories struggle to patch together a law that will shut people up. The prime minister declares himself boldly. He is "personally" opposed to abortion, he says, but unwilling to "impose" his views. (What does this mean? Will he "impose" a no-abortion law on the country? Certainly not. On his own family, wife, daughters? No. Well then to whom does it apply? To himself obviously. He is telling us that he will never have an abortion. You'd have thought him too old to get pregnant.)

---

* The editorial pages of two of the four big Southam dailies in the west, the *Calgary Herald* and the Vancouver *Province*, are edited by strident feminists whose offerings, like the so-called "judgement" of Madam Justice Bertha Wilson in the Morgentaler case, tend to read like something you might be handed on a street corner.

What is to go into this law? Already, you see a plot unfolding. What the government will put forward is a "gestational" abortion law, permitting unlimited access to abortion in the first, say, twenty weeks of pregnancy when 95 per cent of abortions occur anyway. The gestational approach is, in other words, simply abortion on demand. But it will be set forth as a "compromise." It is anything but. Moreover, it is neither scientific nor moral. As the Constitutional Court of West Germany declared:

> *Life, in the sense of the historical existence of a human individual, exists according to definite biological-physiological knowledge, from the fourteenth day after conception...The process of development which has begun at that point is a continuing process which exhibits no sharp demarcation and does not allow a precise division on various steps of development of the human life. The process does not end even with birth; the phenomena of consciousness which are specific to the human personality, for example, appear for the first time a rather long time after birth.*

The court concluded: "The right to life is guaranteed to everyone who 'lives'; no distinction can be made between individual stages of developing life, or between prenatal and postnatal life." Equally irrelevant is the criterion of viability, where abortion is prohibited if medical science could sustain the child apart from its mother. For one thing, this point continually recedes, so the law would have to be amended annually. For another, it is illogical: why should the life or death of a human being depend on such a condition? If somebody else can save the child, then the mother should be required to save it herself. Where is the rationale for such a principle?

What the government will produce in favour of its supposed "compromise," however, will more likely be a blatant lie. It will say that the Supreme Court, in its decision on the Morgentaler case, has left no option but a gestational law. This, as Professor Gerry Ferguson, assistant dean of the University of Victoria law school, has pointed out, is simply not true. Only Madam Justice Bertha Wilson made such a stipulation. The majority of the court did not. So when our supposedly pro-life MPs try telling us this, we should reply that only a demonstrable threat to the physical health of the mother should justify abortion. Nothing else. Allowing people to be killed because some party in power has deemed them "subhuman" is surely something this century has seen all it wants of. - *August 21, 1989*

Why this magazine ran that 'disgusting' story on Gay Pride

The cover story that ran in the August 16th edition, on the Gay Pride parade in Vancouver and the related question of whether homosexuality is a condition that can be changed, stirred more public furore than anything we have printed since the wars over the National Energy Program thirteen years ago. Our ostensible bigotry was featured three times on television, once nationally. It was the subject of a column-long story in *The Globe and Mail*. We received 67 telephone calls at the Edmonton office, all but two supportive. Thirty-seven people ordered subscriptions in a six-hour period. At the Vancouver office there were fewer calls, one of which was pitiable. "I'm gay," said the caller. "I've been like this since I was 17. If there was anything I could do about it, I would. But I have found nothing." His gentleness and sincerity were indisputable and heart-rending. Even he, however, took no exception to the story.

Nevertheless, to conclude that reader reaction was one of unanimous accord would be a grave error. Undoubtedly many, although they did not phone, were appalled by the story. Not because they are homosexual, indeed they might feel inwardly repelled by it, but because of Ken, or Charles, or Gloria, whom they know well, whom they respect and pity, and whom they saw being held up to scorn. For whether homosexuals number one in ten, or the more probable one in fifty, which of us does not know one or two or four or five men or women covered by the words "gay" or "lesbian?" They are talented generous, sometimes devout - and often dying, bewildered and despairing, as a direct consequence of this proclivity. In 65 years I've probably known ten. I've never known one I did not like, and there are several whom I hold in fond affection. Those who were our employees were without exception loyal and diligent.

So why, then, run such a story?

Because the issue is no longer one of Ken and Charles and Gloria. What is being sought by the homosexual lobbies is not mere tolerance. Homosexuality has become a missionary cause. It is now advocated as a "lifestyle," something all children should be familiar with and encouraged to investigate. If this seems exaggerated, then consider what is going on right now in the Toronto public school system, and is being proposed for B.C. and Alberta.

In 1985, five Toronto teenagers beat to death a school librarian who was perceived as homosexual. In response, the Toronto Board of Education called for a new sex education course that would foster tolerance. No parents objected, although some became suspicious when the committee charged with drawing it up included homosexual representatives but no parents. However, the psychiatrist on the committee was Dr. Joseph Berger, an Orthodox Jew. Last year the first draft of the course emerged. It seemed unbelievable. For page after page, homosexual practice was openly urged upon students. Story followed story on how this or that youngster had successfully "come out." Videos had been made illustrating and advocating the gay lifestyle. The names of some eighty organizations were appended with which students could consult. At least seventy of these were gay groups, one of them sado-masochistic.

The course also vehemently attacked the traditional family, contending that wife and child abuse inevitably make the heterosexual home "the most dangerous place for a woman and child." True/false questions directed students to detect intolerance and bigotry in their homes.

This program was designed for 13- to 18-year-olds and is to be followed by something similar for elementary school children. Dr. Berger exploded. The committee's recommendations, he declared, had been "hijacked." He demanded changes. The board made only minor revisions (the recommended sado-masochistic group was replaced by a prostitutes' aid organization) and it was implemented in Toronto schools last January.

Meanwhile, Sue Careless, mother of four teenagers, organized a parents' group called CURE (Citizens United for Responsible Education) which vigorously protested. They were dismissed as "right-wing" and "bigoted." CURE held one meeting in the school board's offices but further use of school property was denied because, the parents were told, "gay-bashing" violated school board policy.

Two counsellors on the staff of the Toronto Board of Education, one a declared gay and the other a lesbian, thereupon began making class-by-class presentations, sometimes distributing pamphlets with illustrations and advice on homosexual sex practices. There was no mention that anal sex is the most dangerous of sexual practices, nor of the fact that the life expectancy of male homosexuals is nearly thirty years below the national average. (Smoking, by comparison, is practically harmless.) In six months, the male counsellor alone had made 150 presentations.

Homosexuality, the pair proclaim, is irreversible. To this point the parents' group takes particular exception, since it includes several people who were once homosexual and are now married with children. Could these people make classroom presentations too? No, said one school trustee, because "such people do not exist." The CBC likewise refused air time to the former homosexuals.

Then the parents began hearing another kind of story. Several students declared in class that they believed homosexual behaviour to be unhealthy. Each was required to make a public apology for disseminating "hatred." The parents made a detailed presentation to the board asking for major changes. All were refused.

Mrs. Careless says opposing the course is legally dangerous. Criticism on the basis of sexual orientation is illegal under Ontario's human rights code. This should be of particular note to Albertans, whose human rights code does not yet prohibit "discrimination" on the basis of sexual orientation. The new minister, however, says he wants it in there. If he succeeds, any school trustee opposing such a curriculum could face prosecution. And in the provincial election, the NDP leader said he favoured adopting the Toronto curriculum. The situation in B.C. has already gone far beyond this. Under the new Harcourt government legislation, public criticism of any sexual lifestyle whatever is prohibited by law.

As will be evident, hardly any of this information has been carried by the news media in Alberta or B.C. All four major Southam newspapers are unanimously pro-gay. Therefore, although our advertisers are being attacked by the concerted effort of the gay lobbies, we believe it is our responsibility to convey these facts to our readers. On that ground we stand, and we do not propose to retreat from it one iota.
- *August 30, 1993*

And then in '94 we began to question our 'intolerance and bigotry' over pedophilia

Imagine if you can the following scenario. The year is, let us say, 2010. A new government has taken office at Ottawa and has finally overridden the prejudice and bigotry in its own caucus and in that of the preceding administration. Therefore, says the new Justice minister, it is with profound satisfaction that he is now able to introduce amendments to the Criminal Code striking out those clauses which made it illegal to love children sexually.

His speech is memorable. The ancient taboo against the sexual love of children is rooted in the prejudices of the past, he says. The same religious proscriptions that once condemned sex outside marriage, contraception, abortion and homosexuality had also discriminated against those who sexually expressed their fondness for children. "Even to this day," he declares, "there are those who continue their campaign of hate against these tender, caring people for whom the love of children exceeds all other." Eying the Alberta benches he adds significantly: "Pedophobia is still among us."

The minister traces the difficult struggle to gain this new human right. There had been the "pedophile hunts" back in the 1980s "when scores of innocent teachers were brutally thrown in jail." He lists early martyrs like Robert Noyes, the B.C. schoolteacher whose only crime had been to show fondness for children as he was hounded by bigotry from one school division to the next. And there was also the tragic story of the Christian Brothers, whose affection for youngsters aroused such mob rage that many had been sentenced to long terms in prison.

(These have long since been released, and the government is considering adequate compensation payments for the pain and undeserved suffering inflicted upon them. The thinly disguised documentary film, portraying these gentle brothers as perverted monsters and known as *The Boys of St. Vincent*, has of course been banned by the human rights commission as "hate literature" and withdrawn by the National Film Board. It is still studied at film schools, however, as an example of public hysteria.)

Unhappily even the church joined in relentless persecution of these men, although many professed Christianity and asked: "How can our love for children be wrong? Since we find it as a strong desire within ourselves, God must have put it there." Needless to say, the more backward elements in the church persisted in their rejection of "pedophilia," a word whose public usage has since been prohibited by several human rights commissions. Less intolerant clergy naturally defended it, however, and the Canadian Conference of Catholic Bishops has issued the usual apologies.

Tribute must also be paid, says the minister, to the North American Man/Boy Love Association (NAMBLA) which moved into Canada in the 1980s. In its early years it suffered deplorable abuse and contempt, until the celebrated *Regina v Langer* case that began to stem the tide of hatred and allow child lovers "out of the closet."

The whole child-love movement understandably reveres the name of Eli Langer (the Eli Langer Gallery of Child Love, the Eli Langer Child Love Foundation, the Eli Langer Chair of Child Love Studies at the University of Toronto, etc.). Mr. Langer was the artist who fearlessly celebrated child love in his famous show in December 1993 at Mercer Union Art Gallery in Toronto.

The pictures should have been inoffensive to any mind but one steeped in prejudice, bigotry and intolerance. His drawings showed children innocently performing oral and anal sex acts, a naked little girl sitting on the lap of an old man, another naked little girl straddling an old man's neck, he in a state of erotic arousal.

But to the police, these works were mere pornography and they laid charges under a section of the Criminal Code passed at the height of the pedophile hunt. Mr. Langer, of course, objected forcefully. "My art is the product of my imagination," he said. "I do not use models. Some people said I should have disclaimed any approval of the act they think is depicted in my work. I disagree."

Sensitive people spoke out. "Art World, Activists Rally Around Artist Facing Porn Charges," said one headline. Most deplored the legal provision under which the charges were laid. "They made a terrible mistake when they passed this legislation," said the aging liberal activist June Callwood. "We've lost sight of the difference between the imaginary world and the real world," said CBC producer Max Allen. "What this law does is outlaw any sexual depiction of anyone under the age of 18."

But the strongest support for Mr. Langer came from *The Globe and Mail*, which said the prosecution represented the thinking behind the Spanish Inquisition. "We persist in bringing the sanction of the state against those whose craft is to record their imaginings on paper," a *Globe* editorial protested. "Mr. Langer's prosecution is only the most recent example of this timeless impulse." While Mr. Langer's work might be "deeply disturbing," it could hardly be called pornography because Mr. Langer did not use models. The *Globe* concluded: "Whether or not his work is edifying, or even good, it was executed with artistic intent. Unless there is definite evidence that exhibiting it could cause real harm, that should be enough to keep the hands of the police off it."

From there on the story is familiar. The Supreme Court threw out the child pornography law. Urged on by the Law Reform Commission, the age of consent was steadily reduced - by 1993 it was down from 16 to 14. The next "stride forward" reduced it from 14 to 12, then to 10. Now, with the amendment of 2010, it is eliminated completely.

When the cause appeared safe enough, the Southam newspapers became outspoken in their support. Story after story portrayed "loving relationships" between this man and that boy, or these adults and those children. Soon the "thinking people" in the community came to see it not only as harmless, but as a beautiful thing, long forbidden by the "rigidities" of religion, but now claiming admiration and respect, and taught in every sex-ed class. Everyone seemingly knew at least one person who had a "loving relationship" with a child. In that atmosphere, the minister of Justice now feels secure in changing the law.

But has public opinion really changed? Curiously, no. Even in this enlightened year 2010, the polls show some 75 per cent of Canadians clinging to their bigoted belief that sex with children is wrong. Fortunately, however, we live in a society where the mob doesn't rule, where the courts make the real decisions, and where the state has no place in the bedrooms of the nation. - *January 17, 1994*

Chapter Seven

The Second Sex

"Something in her nature that all the propaganda has not been able to extinguish insists that if she does not have children some essential experience in her life will be lacking."

- Ted Byfield, 1980

Ted and Virginia in 1968.

The feminine dilemma: things versus people

The 1980s, one might expect, should prove a great decade for women. Never before they have been accorded such opportunity and recognition. Job prospects undreamed of by their grandmothers are now, in theory anyway, everywhere at hand. A woman can become a prime minister, or an airline pilot, or a Santa Claus. She can drink, smoke and swear with as much abandon as any man. Science has largely removed both the worst drudgery of housework and the horror of unwanted pregnancy. And even when the latter occurs there is abortion, something that used to be a crime and is now subsidized by the government. Sex outside marriage is not only safe and permissible but widely advocated. The loathsome male prejudice is disappearing from the language which is being enriched by such elegant manifestations as *chairperson, alderperson*, and that charming appellation "mizz," which generally designates the unmarried or de-married female person. Even the name of our species has been changed. We are no longer man but person. Welcome to the *huperson* race.

One might reasonably expect therefore that women would hail this golden new potential with unreserved and unalloyed delight. Yet they don't. Not all of them anyway. I'm thinking of one young woman in particular. She is not an Albertan and she may not be typical, though I suspect that many share her problem or part of it. She is about 23 years old, intelligent, charming and gifted. Moreover she has a trade and a good one. She has learned to be a custom book-binder. That is she can take a valuable old book, retrim and reassemble its pages, then rebind it handsomely between new hard covers. The men who have taught her to do this say that if she perserveres she will become a master of the craft which pays well and offers much aesthetic satisfaction. In short, she has it made. But she is not happy.

The trouble is that she allowed herself to fall in love. Very deeply, it appears, and with a young man about three years older who like her has never married, who also has a career, and whose career increasingly conflicts with her own. His job will take him to another city. Hers requires her to stay. He would like to have children. She sometimes concurs, but this prospect too throws her into a dilemma. The same perfectionism that makes her a good bookbinder would also make her an excellent mother - so excellent that she would not be content to delegate much of her responsibility to a daycare centre or a baby sitter. Motherhood therefore would cost her perhaps fifteen years of book-binding. Others in the trade with whom she is implicitly in competition won't lose that fifteen years. So she can't have both a full work career and a marriage and she's smart enough to know it.

And that's by no means all. The fate of at least three of her friends who did get married is far from reassuring. All three are divorced, though all were doubtless as confident as she of permanence when they married. Two have been left with children, one with no assistance from the husband who deserted her. This is a statutory offence at which the law winks where it ought to prescribe something more substantial. Like a horsewhipping.

Finally, almost every propaganda force around this young woman urges her away from motherhood and into the work force. Fashionable magazines require that she have a career. Newspaper columnists and TV commentators constantly demand that she asserts herself. The movies and TV drama portray all smart young women in work roles. The government through various "rights" laws strives to open every professional door. The only opposing propaganda influence is that of television advertising in which the housewife invariably appears as a domesticated moron, living in permanent anxiety over the effectiveness of floor polish and dish detergent. The observation that this appeal, however demented, nevertheless sells the soap does not enhance the prospect of motherhood. Maybe she will actually get like that herself. She does not notice that men's deodorant and shampoo commercials appeal to the same vegetable mentality.

All this therefore seems overwhelming. So she resolves against the marriage. Yet it is not that simple and she realizes it. There are vague disquietudes. For one thing, something in her nature that all the propaganda has not been able to extinguish insists that if she does not have children some essential experience in her life will be lacking. A life that consists very much of diapers and detergents may seem empty but so, too, does the prospect of what the new age calls career womanhood and a less flattering age called spinsterhood. The year 1985 may look golden, what about the year 2025 when her own parents will be gone and her own children will not exist?

And this leads to another reflection. Somebody may ask her in 2025 why she never married. "Because," she will say, "I wanted to do something important with my life." "Such as what?" they will ask. "Such as putting covers on books," she will reply. But then a disturbing thought follows: by what wild illogicality has she ever concluded that binding a book is important, while raising a human being is unimportant? A book may be a wonderful thing. Beside a human being it amounts to nothing at all. Yet she had chosen books over people, and it had all seemed so reasonable at the time.

I don't know how this young woman will resolve the problem. I don't know how tens of thousands like her will resolve the same problem. But I do know that if many of them decide that making things is important while raising people is unimportant, then this is going to be a very unpleasant world in 2025. Particularly if the profession of motherhood - the most important trade in the world - is denied such women as this, the talented, the resolute, the imaginative, the realistic, the people best qualified for the job. - *January 11, 1980*

Behind every successful rapist stands a host of caring women

The phenomenon of the habitual rapist, often with an accompanying penchant for murder, is becoming alarmingly familiar. As this is written, the Calgary police are coping with one in the Spruce Cliff district where women are terrified in their own homes at night. He is, the police say, the seventh they've had to contend with in the last twelve years, two of whom were killers. Other cities have had similar experiences, particularly Edmonton, and rapes are now so familiar to police forces everywhere that many are not reported except as statistics.

At the same time we note an extraordinary youthfulness among rapists. When the attack upon a New York woman by a gang of 12- to 14-year-olds shocked that city this year, the American networks discovered that in the same week there were about a dozen other cases of rape by young teenaged boys in various American cities. What, people ask, is going on? Why are so many sex crimes being committed by mere youngsters? Such things were almost unheard-of thirty years ago. What has changed?

The answer is that many things have changed in the whole upbringing of young boys, not only in their education, but in their home life, their social life and in the cultural influences upon them. Most notable of all has been the change in the adults around them. It is a change of gender. For hundreds of thousands of young Canadian boys up to the age of about 12 or 13, almost the only adults with whom they routinely have any contact are, in point of fact, women.

They are raised by single mothers. Almost all their teachers up to senior high school are women. Their counsellors are women; their sports coaches are often women; women supervise them in their summer jobs, and when they join the Cubs or Scouts there is a good chance they will have a woman Cub or Scoutmistress. Little of this can be blamed on women themselves. In many cases, women are doing these things because men cannot be found to do them. What man would want to teach a class of eight-year-olds? Sure, the school would like to have a male swimming coach but it can't find one. And as for Mrs. So-

and-So, she became the Cubmistress because of the impossibility of finding a Cubmaster.

However other things have changed which are far more deliberate. Not only does the young boy have a woman teacher, but what he is taught has been realigned in those thirty years to remove a perceived "sexism." The male is by nature far more outwardly competitive than the female. He loves contests, races, matches of skill and strength. Who can run the fastest? Who's got the biggest arm muscles? Who can walk that fence rail and not fall off? Who can spit the farthest and with the greatest volume and splatter? It's all terribly important to the young male nature, while regarded by the female nature as pointless and absurd (unless, of course, the exercise is being conducted to impress females, especially one particular female, which is frequently the case, and which changes everything).

In the modern curriculum, however, every effort is being made to eliminate the competitive factor. Even academic contests are being taken away; such things as classroom tests are discouraged because they incite competition between the pupils. Field days in elementary schools are often so designed that no individual ever loses because losing is felt to be too disheartening. As for fist fighting, well that is absolutely forbidden. Fighting is "violence," and we all know how awful violence is. That's why stories of war, heroism and villainy are taken from the course of studies. They encourage "violence." Instead, boys are urged to be caring, sharing, loving, gentle and nice. Yet the fact is the young male rather enjoys violence, and many are certainly prone to indulge in it. In the perfect university, says an Ontario feminist educator, there will be no football because the game is too expensive. However, she adds, there will be much interest in the girls' touch-football team. She means that if girls can't play the game, then the game should not be played. Similarly, what is meant by non-sexist education is feminine education. We teach little boys as though they were little girls, and we use women teachers to do it.

Then, having deprived boys of almost all significant adult male influence throughout the first twelve or fourteen years of their lives, having systematically thwarted most of their instinctive male inclinations, having given them nothing at all to feed their natural appetite for struggle, adventure, and risk, why should we be so surprised to suddenly find them responding with the kind of rage and fury that must seethe within the soul of a rapist? This surely, is exactly what we should have expected. It is no accident that something like four out of five disturbed children are boys.

Moreover, other warning signs were there. What does the little boy do when he leaves his namby-pamby classroom and arrives home? Answer: he watches rock videos which show women being beaten, mauled and raped, reads comic books that celebrate sado-masochism, listens to music that pounds his hearing into insensibility, and sees movies which combine make-believe science with barbarian carnage and show females being dragged about by the hair. That is his entertainment. His instinctive appetites having been starved all day, are now fed with poison. Consider this, and you stop wondering why there is so much sex crime. You begin wondering why there isn't more.

There is of course, another way of educating boys. It consists of first realizing that they are not girls, and should not be treated as though they were. It means bringing a great many more men onto the staffs of elementary and junior high schools. It involves restoring controlled competition to the school curricula, both indoors and out, with pass or fail, top marks and bottom marks in the classroom, and real winners and losers outside. But it also requires teaching that all games must have rules, that without rules games are no longer fun, that in the game of life the rules are called the law, and the central purpose of the law is to protect those who are weak against those who are strong. It means teaching the story of mankind as it came down to us, not censored and sanitized to fulfil some social planner's fantasy, but with all the violence, wars and horror that darken our past. However, with the villainous must come the heroic. We must glorify those who shine through the darkness as beacons to humanity, as lights along our path. For such there be, and we ought not to shrink from saying so.

Teach boys as boys, and they will become men not monsters. In

the meantime we should cease to be amazed at what we're beholding in our cities. We are reaping the harvest that we sowed.
- *August 14, 1989*

I've been convicted of murder but I'd like to make a point

The blame, it appears, has now been assigned for the shooting death of fourteen young women last month at the University of Montreal. The killer himself who committed suicide was not the real culprit. Rather, it was the conservative anti-feminists of the country whose views incited the man to do what he did. This has apparently become the official feminist explanation for the tragedy.

Thus, when I was at Golden, B.C., west of Banff, last week, I was accosted by a grim, formidable woman of about 50 who said that she had read two recent columns in which I had criticized the feminist revolution. Fixing me with a cold eye, she added something like this. "Fourteen young women have died in Montreal at the hands of a man who hated feminists. I think you should know that the difference between you and the man who killed them is merely a matter of degree."

In precisely the same vein, Thomas Walkom, a columnist in the *Toronto Star*, declared that Ted and Link Byfield on the one hand, and Montreal killer Marc Lepine on the other, "are disparate parts of the same phenomenon." Lepine, says Mr. Walkom, "represents the crazy edge of anti-feminism" while the Byfields "articulate a version which is more acceptable," but both are pursuing the same end.

The case against us, of course, is never stated in full. It is made by innuendo in a kind of sweeping generality that is intended for unexamined acceptance. That's because it will not bear much examination. Stated in full, it would go something like this:

Many men harbour a deep, subconscious hatred and fear of women. Males have given vent to this hatred by creating a society in which women are subjugated into drudgery, made to serve male masters, rear children, and tend the home. They are denied any significant social, economic or political role. The feminist movement seeks to deliver women from this servitude, and establish instead a social system in which both sexes share power. Feminism is therefore a threat to the male power establishment. People who oppose feminism, know-

*ingly or not, are inciting this male hatred of women into violent reali-
ty, causing unrestrained males to explode in the kind of incident we see
at Montreal. Conclusion: since opposing the feminist movement subjects women to physical violence, one must not criticize or oppose the
feminist revolution.*

Now let's apply the same reasoning to other instances of mass
mayhem - for instance to the appearance of a gunman several years
ago in the Quebec National Assembly who also took a considerable toll
of life. One would reason as follows:

*Many people have an inherent resistance to the coercive author-
ity of government. Politicians represent government in the popular
mind. People who criticize politicans are, knowingly or unknowingly,
inciting this inherent hatred of authority into violent reality, causing
the kind of incident we saw at Quebec. To criticize the government,
therefore, is to subject politicians to physical violence. Conclusion: one
must not criticize government.*

Or in the attempted assassination of President Ronald Reagan:

*Many people have an inherent resistance to the constituted
authority of government. The president of the United States symbol-
izes government in the popular mind. People who criticize the president, knowingly or unknowingly, are inciting this inherent resentment
of government into violent reality, as in the attempted assassination of
president Reagan. Conclusion: one must not criticize president
Reagan.*

Now Mr. Walkom (I do not doubt) was a persistent critic of president Reagan. By his own reasoning, he and the man who tried to
assassinate the president are "disparate parts of the same phenomenon." Similarly, the woman at Golden who resents male domination,
and that woman at Vancouver who, apparently out of the same sentiment, last month murdered her husband and children before killing
herself, are "separated only by degree."

Now it is possible to construct a very different explanation, if
not for the specific tragedy at Montreal, at least for the situation in
which women now find themselves, namely one of extreme danger and

increasing vulnerability to violence at the hands of males. It is an ironic thing that the modern young career woman probably has a thousand freedoms her grandmother did not share. But her grandmother was safe on the streets at night, and she is not. Like the case against the Byfields, this one too must go back to root causes.

Point 1: The chief cause of the subjugation of woman is not the man. It is the child. Because the woman had to nurture and rear young children, she has never had the freedom available to the man.

Point 2: Since all animals lay this responsibility upon the female, one must conclude that it is not the result of some male conspiracy, but an act of nature itself. (That is, unless male dogs at some prehistoric time conspired to enslave female dogs, boars to enslave sows, drakes to enslave ducks, and stallions to enslave mares, then men didn't enslave women; God did.)

Point 3: Humanity, however, developed a device to ease the burden upon women, notably the family, an institution in which the woman cares for the children and the man cares for the woman. Out of the family came the tribe, and out of the tribe came successive civilizations which rise and fall throughout human history. None is permanent. The higher the civilization the greater the freedom of women. Feminism is a product of the current civilization and will end when it ends.

Point 4: Hence, the best protection for the woman is the civil order. Anything that threatens the civil order threatens pre-eminently the woman, and when the civil order fails, as it has in parts of many modern cities, women are the first casualties. The basis of the civil order is the family, and any threat to the family is a direct threat to the safety and freedom of women.

Point 5: The greatest threat to the family today is posed by feminism which has resolved to either abolish the family, or change it into something else entirely. By attacking the foundation of the social order, therefore, feminism threatens, rather than enhances, the lot of women, and destroys the very basis upon which women have won such freedom as they now enjoy.

Conclusion: Both men and women should resist and oppose the feminist revolution insofar as it threatens the family, and if people like Mr. Walkom want to find the real source of violence against women, they might look a little more closely at what they have been writing themselves. - January 22, 1990

Ms. Justice Wilson will now tell us about human destiny

It's an old, well-justified practice in the news business that you don't call judges for comment on contemporary events because it's a waste of time. No proper judge will say anything because it is not the place of the judiciary to do so, and any reporter who prevailed on a judge for comment would only be disclosing his own ignorance.

A judge's opinion on a case before him is rendered in his decision. He does not deliver it in newspaper interviews or speeches before the Rotary Club. He is reticent to discuss any public issue because he never knows when he will be called upon to preside over a case that raises it. If he mouths off his views in advance, he disqualifies himself as an arbiter. To a provincial judge, the rule is important. To a Supreme Court of Canada judge, it's crucial. Many of the cases he will hear involve issues of public controversy. Moreover, from his decision there is no appeal.

Consider, then, the astonishing speech made last week by Ms. Justice Bertha Wilson of the Supreme Court of Canada, speaking at Osgoode Hall, a Toronto law school, now torn by sexist controversy. Said Ms. Justice Wilson, as quoted by Southam News:

• Some Canadian laws are so biased in favour of men they are "ludicrous."

• More women judges should be appointed to bring a "new humanity" to the law.

• Some areas of the law reflect a "male perspective" and "should be revisited as and when the opportunity presents itself."

• "Some aspects of the criminal law in particular cry out for change since they are based on presuppositions about the nature of women and women's sexuality that in this day and age are little short of ludicrous."

• "If women lawyers and women judges, through their differing perspectives on life, can bring a new humanity to bear on the decision-making process, perhaps they will make a difference. Perhaps they will succeed in infusing the law with an understanding of what it means to be fully human."

Now if you or I, ordinary tax-paying citizens, were to express such views, there would be nothing amiss. That's democracy. Similarly if a member of parliament were to express them, or a candidate, that would be entirely in order. We can elect or defeat them. That's also democracy. But if a Supreme Court judge makes such pronouncements, that is a very different matter. It is grounds enough, one would think, for impeachment. For what she has done is to gravely weaken the perceived impartiality, and therefore the integrity, of the whole court.

If that seems extreme, consider this: suppose a case were to come before the court challenging the constitutionality of, say, pay equity, the legislation that seeks to eliminate "systematic discrimination" by requiring certain pay levels in private industry for jobs usually done by women. Surely the people opposing pay equity have the right to expect a fair and impartial hearing from the highest court in the land. That is, they look to the court for an interpretation of law, not for expositions on human destiny from the private philosophy of the judges.

What they will in fact encounter, however, is Ms. Justice Wilson, their declared opponent before the first argument is heard. She is, she has told us, replete with a catalogue of the historic wrongs against women, and eager to confer upon us all the dubious benefits of her "New Humanity." For her, this is no legal case. It is yet another occasion to transform into the "fully human" those of us who are running maybe only fifty per cent. Some of us may feel we're human enough already, or that our perception of humanity is fuller than hers. No matter. What's there on the bench in front of us is not a judge but an ermine-robed social engineer, waiting to do a little "revisiting" now that "the opportunity has presented itself."

In short, instead of a court what we have is a kind of judicial cabal that has arrogated unto itself responsibility for social improvement. Anyone who disagrees with Ms. Justice Wilson's ambitions for humanity has about as much chance of impartiality before her as the fly has before the spider. The credibility of such a cover, as a chamber of objectively dispassionate justice, has been destroyed.

Something else is surely of note, and that is the fact that this woman's astounding behaviour meets with so little response. Where is the chief justice? Are we to infer from his silence that he fully approves of the members of his bench stumping the country with their views on the New Humanity and how they intend to shape the laws to conform with them? Are judges, in other words, now to become unelected politicians, decreeing the future of the human race, and divulging to us all how far our laws fall short of its "fulness?"

And where, one wonders, are all those yakking jackals from the Southam newspapers, the ones who write the editorials about the "outrageous" premier of British Columbia trying to "impose" his moral views on everybody? He at least expressed those views prior to his election, and the people did elect him. Who elected Ms. Justice Wilson? Nobody. But now we have her vigorously declaring an intention to impose her New Humanity and Human Fulness and heaven knows what all else. And from the Southam newspapers, either dead silence, or actual approval. What this tells us, of course, is that they approve of Ms. Justice Wilson's moral views, so she can go ahead and impose them all she likes. But they don't approve of Bill Vander Zalm's, so when he does it that's intolerable.

The wider implications boggle the mind. We have delivered ourselves into the hands of nine people, whom we do not elect, into whose views when they are appointed we are not permitted to inquire, and who now go about the land lecturing us about some New Humanity and Human Fulness, and how we are about to have all this thrust upon us. And our newspapers, our supposed defenders of democracy, utter not a whisper of protest. Thus do our freedoms perish.
- *February 26, 1990*

Sagacious liberaldom will now enlighten those lesser breeds without the pill

The controversy raging at Cairo this month would seem, judging by the Canadian media, to have a side that is self-evidently right and one that is patently wrong. Third World populations, we're assured, are exploding so rapidly we can't possibly feed everybody. So the United Nations called a conference at Cairo to develop a world consensus on what should be done about it.

Two camps emerged. In the one, we have the sane, caring, good people, represented by feminists, western technology, and the American and European media. In the other are the deluded, self-interested bad people, represented by what the media call the "fundamentalists," meaning the Muslims, Catholics and evangelical Protestants. These are intent upon sustaining the enslavement of women, are zealous to return the world to the darkness of religious superstition and ignorance, and (so we are left to assume) are rather fond of the idea of world starvation.

Fortunately, the bad people lost. Armies of "health workers" will now go forth bearing tons of condoms, diaphragms, birth control pills, abortionware and books by Gloria Steinem, invading the dungeons of despair in which Third World women find themselves, and introducing them to the shining paradise of modern secular feminism. Thus the media.

What's envisioned, in other words, is the massive imposition of one culture upon others. And that's surely odd. Because I thought we of liberaldom also believed that all cultures are equally "valid," that cultural "genocide" is one of the vilest deeds of the Christian past for which churches today swarm to apologize. How does this projected cultural onslaught differ, you wonder, from the ones we're currently apologizing for? Will we be apologizing for this one as well? Could we perhaps save time by sending the apologies along with the condoms? None of my liberal friends seem to have noticed this inconsistency. But then of course they rarely do. And anyway, the feminists have explained that logical consistency is another devious device of the patriarchy.

Nevertheless, you have to wonder how all this must look to the Third World. What would happen if the typically "backward" Third World woman, sitting in her mud hut, surrounded by her children while her husband worked the fields, were able to interview the typical North American woman, sitting at her key-punching station, surrounded by her Tylenol pills. Let's listen in:

Third World Woman: So you want to liberate me from my miserable and oppressed life and give me the advantages that you enjoy?

Modern Emancipated Woman: Exactly. When we see the horribly exploitive conditions you live under, we want to educate you, give you a career, free you from the miserable drudgery of your long arduous day.

TWW: Well it's true I have to be a cook, and feed the children and my husband, and be a doctor when they're sick, and wash their clothes, and clean the hut, and feed the chickens and tend the garden. And I have to tell stories to the children, and help teach them the ways of our tribe. It's quite a bit all right. But what do you do all day?

MEW: Oh, I work with computers.

TWW: What's that mean?

MEW: I work this machine, you see. People bring me pieces of paper with things written on them. And I type those things into this machine.

TWW: All day?

MEW: Yes. It's so much more challenging than what you're doing.

TWW: But how do you take care of your children?

MEW: Oh I pay somebody else to do that at a professional day-care centre. I see them for a good hour in the evening, except I'm pretty tired, of course.

TWW: What do you do then?

MEW: Oh I cook dinner, feed the children, tend them if they're sick, do the wash, clean the apartment, put them to bed.

TWW: Don't you tell them any stories?

MEW: I try to, but there's so little time. Anyway, the daycare workers do that.

TWW: You let other people tell stories to your children?

MEW: Of course. They're professionals.

TWW: But they're your children, and how do you know what stories they're telling? And what about the tribe? Who teaches them the ways of your tribe? Does your husband do that?

MEW: Well actually I don't have any tribe, and no husband either.

TWW: No tribe? No husband?

MEW: I used to have a husband. Two of them in fact.

TWW: They both died? How sad.

MEW: Not exactly, no. Charles, that's the first one, he left for this other woman. And David, well David was useless anyway, and he said he wanted to find himself.

TWW: You mean he was lost?

MEW: You're not kidding.

TWW: So now you're alone?

MEW: No, Bill's with us. Bill's a wonderful guy. He drives me home from work. Which is very comforting. It's not safe in that district now, you know.

TWW: You're not safe in your own village?

MEW: I don't live in a village, but no, it isn't safe at all. Four women have been raped in our neighbourhood. There are muggers, hookers, pimps, creeps all over the place these days.

TWW: How can the children be safe?

MEW: Actually, many of them carry knives when they go to school.

TWW: Don't your menfolk protect you and them?

MEW: No, we've got beyond all that. And that's what I'm trying to show you. We're modern, We're independent. We take care of ourselves. And we want to share with you all these wonderful things...

And so, of course, they will. Unless those evil fundamentalists somehow prevent them. - *September 19, 1994*

Chapter Eight

God and the Godless

"If adultery or homosexuality is wrong in the sight of God, then all the task forces in Christendom aren't going to make it right. If God is timeless and changeless, then human conduct considered wrong in the eighth century is just as wrong in the twentieth."

- Ted Byfield, 1980

'Alberta Report On The Air' in 1980.

The United Church on sex: revelation or mere treason?

In the mid-Sixties the Anglican church was flush with the funds it had collected from the postwar religious boom. Nevertheless there was within it a certain unrest. It therefore commissioned Pierre Berton to write an appraisal of the church from the viewpoint of a media man and an agnostic. Mr. Berton in the resulting book, *The Comfortable Pew*, was unstinting in both observations and remedies. The church, he said, was weak because in essence it was old-fashioned. It was hewing to dead dogmas and obsolete moral rules. To save itself, it should catch up with the times, forget all the old doctrines about sin and hell and concentrate instead on leftwing social causes. Especially, it should join the sexual revolution, get rid of its primitive taboos and remember that "love" is the only rule that really matters. Ever since then, most leading Protestant churches have been heeding such advice. The latest installment appeared last week in the form of the United Church task force report on sexual morality. This document proposes that what or with whom one copulates doesn't matter provided there is "a real though not permanent commitment" and that it is done in a responsible, joyous way. This, wrote one editor, is a "courageous" report. He did not really explain why. Responding to all those speaking engagements, requests for television interviews, newspaper articles, invitations to write books and opportunities to make money that will inevitably accrue to the report's authors will, no doubt, require untold fortitude. But they are not too likely to be burned at the stake.

Behind both Mr. Berton's 15-year-old book and the United Church's 15-day-old task force report lie two huge and false assumptions. Mr. Berton can be forgiven for them because, after all, he was hired specifically as an agnostic. He believed in neither God nor the Christian faith. One would presume this defence inapplicable to the ladies and gentlemen of the United Church task force, though they are far from reassuring on that point.

The first assumption is that if the rules and membership requirements of an organization are limp and pliable this will give it an immediate appeal to the general public. If an "Everybody Welcome" sign hangs, as it were, above every church door - and everybody of course must include the scoundrel, the whoremonger, the rapist, the pilferer and the oppressor of widows and orphans - then everybody will be extremely keen to join. That is the assumption and it is false. The old rule - easy in, easy out - still holds true. An organization that has no rules will soon have no members. And the consistent decline in church memberships since the enlightened theologies have taken hold eloquently testifies to that fact.

What the new morality does accomplish however is to vastly relieve the task of the clergy. These are usually pleasant people. They don't mind condemning the sins of Exxon because they don't have to face Exxon. But if the chairman of the board of stewards persists in cohabiting with the choirmistress, condemnation tends to complicate parish life. Thank goodness there need be no more mention of "notorious and evil living." Henceforth the minister need only ask, "Tell me, was there commitment? Was it joyous? Splendid. We'll be seeing you on Sunday, then, will we?" He can forget that being unpleasant from time to time is part of being Christian, in particular of being a Christian minister. One need look no farther than the New Testament for evidence of that.

The second false assumption is more serious. Mr. Berton and the United Church task force - and to the list I could add another dozen task forces and the like from my own church, the Anglican - all of them seem to assume that the church can teach anything it likes provided that it has the approval of its senior governing bodies, confirmed in some instances by its general assemblies. They regard the church as a kind of ecclesiastical General Motors. Doctrines and moral teachings can be added, subtracted or altered beyond recognition in the same way that new models can be manufactured for the showroom. Adultery, so to speak, went out in '77 like the Vega. We're pushing sodomy this year like the Impala. The management has decided to eliminate the real presence of Christ in the eucharist just as the management might decide to eliminate rear spring supersuspension in the half-ton pickup. We're recalling marital fidelity because it's proving unpopular and sometimes dangerous. All that's required is the recommendation of a management committee or task force okayed by the board of directors.

But the church is not like General Motors. If adultery or homosexuality is wrong in the sight of God, then all the task forces in Christendom aren't going to make it right. If God is timeless and changeless, then human conduct considered wrong in the eighth century is just as wrong in the twentieth. The day and age has nothing to do with it. Whether it is popular or unpopular at any given time is equally irrelevant because the church is not out to win popularity contests, but to win souls. If the Bible and the traditions of the church through the ages say that something is so, then some panel of sociologists and theologians are not going to discredit it through some report, however august the ratifications. What they will discredit is themselves, both in the eyes of God and in the eyes of history.

Is it not possible, for instance, that the much publicized new moralities of the twentieth century may be viewed very differently even as early as the twenty-first? They may not then be seen as "courageous declarations that confront the new spectrums of human potential" but as compromise and manipulation of self-evident moral truth, as tawdry evasion of clear responsibility, as treasonous betrayal, as desertion of the sheep by shepherds too cowardly or too gullible to meet the demands of the job. - *April 4, 1980*

What does B.J. Thomas have in common with T.S. Eliot?

Ten years ago next month when I was a teacher in the St. John's schools, I led a canoe expedition of youngsters from a point near Winnipeg to York Factory on Hudson Bay. We were dogged by rain and, as the boys paddled on wet and cold, they sang a currently popular song called "Rain Drops Keep Fallin' on My Head." Though the style was contemporary, the message could hardly be more traditional. It was a simple appeal for fortitude in the face of adversity. The man who made it popular, my students tolerantly explained, was Mr. B.J. Thomas. Ever since then I have felt indebted to Mr. Thomas. Whatever else he might have accomplished, he helped to get us to York Factory, raindrops or no raindrops.

I was interested to learn therefore that B.J. Thomas was in Calgary last month for a concert and then disappointed to see him panned mercilessly by the Calgary critics. His failing, it appears, was not in his music but in the fact that he had "got religion" and then made his religion the dominant theme of his performance. "There's a time and a place for everything," wrote Mr. Brian Brennan in the *Calgary Herald*, "and a commercial pop concert, which has more to do with making money than anything else, is hardly the place for public proclamation of religious beliefs that should be the private concern of the individual involved."

Now this is a very odd thing. Apparently if one is a devotee of pacifism, or left-wing political causes, and makes these the dominant theme of his music - Bob Dylan, Joan Baez, Arlo Guthrie, Buffy St. Marie are suggested to me as examples - one is thereby considered brave, outspoken, even heroic. But if one does the same thing with a religious cause, one becomes downright offensive. Mr. Thomas' transgression is not that he had religion. But he is viewed as a man without a sense of fitness or decency when he allows his religion to intrude, to trespass, onto the hallowed ground of a commercial rock concert. This is beyond endurance. Mr. Brennan simply had to speak up.

Similar outrage was expressed last year by another writer for the *Herald*. Miss Catherine Ford noted that the woman who is president of the Mormon Relief Fund had on the grounds of religion, actually been crusading against the Equal Rights Amendment. Wrote Miss Ford: "Formalized religion belongs in your heart, in your home, and in your church. It does not belong in the marketplace." Christians apparently should disenfranchise themselves wherever their religion has anything to say about politics.

Now Mr. Thomas no doubt knows that he is in some very distinguished company. In the 1920s, for instance, Mr. Thomas Stearns Eliot was a perfectly acceptable poet and writer. He was respectably cynical and an orthodox nihilist. Then, sadly, he went through the same sort of thing as B. J. Thomas. His next play, "Murder in the Cathedral," demonstrated a suspicious credulity if not an outright faith. And after the war came "The Cocktail Party," a blatant witness to Christian commitment. Naturally the critics were appalled. Surely, they said, the public stage was no place for religious testimonial. Or, as Mr. Brennan observed in the Thomas case: "It seems that every entertainer who has been saved from a life of sin feels the need to lay his particular religious trip on those who come to hear him perform."

The intriguing question is why? Not why should religion be ordered to stay in the closet? But why does its mere public appearance so incense the critic in a way that social or political commentary does not?

The answer is certainly not obvious. Possibly it lies somewhere along the following lines. Social or political commentary is not only acceptable in the arts, but actively commendable, because social commentary in an age of tolerance is both inoffensive and safe. Either it aims at a distinct minority - the rich, the powerful, the supposedly comfortable - or at institutions and concepts so vague as to represent nothing at all. Who is to blame for such and such a social condition? Society is to blame, wails the popular singer. And who is society? Society is everybody and therefore nobody. We can all so easily confess to being part of the social evil because there is scarcely a single thing we need to do about it. There is no conscience quite so trouble-free as the social conscience.

But religion, especially the Christian religion, concerns itself primarily not with the sins of society, which are so conveniently unspecific, but with the sins of the individual which can become very specific indeed. When Mr. Thomas sings about religion, he makes me think about the way I treat my wife or children or parents, the acceptability of my lifestyle, the possible purposelessness of my whole existence, and all the other things that I would prefer to forget about. I become uncomfortable. So get off the stage, Mr. Thomas, and keep your religion to yourself.

All of this is no doubt appreciated by B.J. Thomas. If he persists in this practice he could damage, possibly wreck, his career. Two thousand years of Christian history and fifteen hundred of Jewish history before that, however, should forewarn him that religion, true religion, has never been universally popular. So a lot more than raindrops could fall on the head of B.J. Thomas before he reaches his own York Factory. Apparently he considers the trip worth it nevertheless. Because he has been given the fortitude to make it, and he does not travel alone.

- *May 23, 1980*

Did Christ really live? Historical scholars say yes

Apropos the enunciated credos of your ten apostles, "Did Easter Happen," would any of them care to provide us unbelievers with three references to Jesus or his teachings, or to his having lived, never mind having risen from the dead, in the profane literature of the first century? And would the scientists among your group say how much credence they would put in an uncorroborated report of a scientific discovery that was written two hundred years after the event being described. - James H. Gray*

No one has done more to acquaint western Canada with its own history than the author of the above letter. His books have preserved our past in a way that will certainly help shape our future. His historical views of the west, born of a deep love for it, are therefore indispensable. However, his historical views of Christianity, born of a different emotion, are altogether dispensable. Among the historians of biblical literature, in fact, they were dispensed with at the turn of this century. But in the popular media, or among some ex-clergymen (or clergymen who should be ex), they continue to enjoy wide acceptance, all founded upon a school of criticism pronounced dead some 85 years ago.

Mr. Gray wrote the above to refute the testimony of ten western scientists and scholars, carried in our Easter edition, setting forth why they believed Christ rose from the dead. Against them Mr. Gray makes two points. The New Testament books, he says, were written about two hundred years after Christ's death. This, if it were true, would destroy their credibility. The stories would have been preserved orally for about six generations, far too long for reliability. He contends as well that there is no mention of Christ in the secular literature of his day, suggesting that his historicity was entirely a Christian concoction.

This same criticism of Christian beginnings was made in the 1940s by the Anglican bishop of Birmingham, and again more recently by the Anglican bishop of Durham. In 1948 it drew a formal refutation from a remarkable quarter. Sir Frederic G. Kenyon, director of the British Museum and in his lifetime one of the world's foremost authorities on papyrological manuscripts, prepared a paper summarizing the implications of twentieth-century biblical archeology and criticism to the credibility of the New Testament. "I believe the time has come," he explained, "to shake off the excessive scepticism characteristic of much biblical scholarship in the latter part of the 19th century." This scepticism, he said, began in 1831 with the writings of one F.C. Baur who founded what became known as the Tubingen school of biblical criticism. In general it declared all the books of the New Testament unauthentic. Only the epistles to the Romans, Corinthians and Galatians could have been written by St. Paul. A late second century origin was assigned to the gospel of St. John. The other three gospels were dated in the first half of the second century, about a hundred years after Christ's death. A later Dutch school assigned even later dates to all four gospels. And now, apparently, we have the James H. Gray school that dates them later still.

By the end of the century, however, a reaction was well under way. English scholars, using the same methods that Baur had used, demonstrated him grievously in error and in 1897 the most respected scholar of the age, Adolf Harnack, wrote: "In all main points and in most details the earliest literature of the church is, from a literary-historical point of view, trustworthy and dependable. In the whole of the New Testament there is apparently only a single writing which can be called pseudonymous in the strictest sense of the term, namely the Second Epistle of Peter. The assumptions of the school of Baur, one can almost say, are wholly abandoned."

Abandoned, that is, by scholarship, but not by the popular press nor by "advanced" clergymen who have continued to periodically excite headlines by trotting the whole thing out again, though nothing has turned up to justify its disinterment. In fact, the contribution of the present century argues very much the reverse. The King James Bible, for instance, was translated in the seventeenth century from texts dating back to the ninth. By 1900 much earlier texts dating back to the fourth century had turned up, though they showed no theological variation from those used for the King James. In 1931 a whole collection of New Testament writings was found, some dating from the second century. Finally, in 1920, a tiny fragment of the Gospel of St. John, about 2 1/4 by 3 1/2 inches, was found in central Egypt, whose date papyrological experts have placed at about 130 A.D.

If the Gospel of St. John was circulating in central Egypt at that time, many miles from its place of origin, the scholars therefore concluded that it seemed entirely likely the date traditionally assigned to its origin, i.e. about 90 A.D., was undoubtedly the date when it was written. The other three gospels were indisputably written before it, beginning with Mark in about 65 A.D., followed by Luke and Matthew in the 70s. This means that they could reliably represent the memory of witnesses. Moreover, the Pauline epistles, the earliest Christian literature, would then have been written in the 50s and 60s. Indeed, the current edition of the Encyclopedia Britannica dates them earlier still, i.e. 40 to 60 A.D.

As for references to Christianity in secular history, such there certainly are. We have Tacitus' account of the Neronian persecution of the Christians in 64 A.D., Suetonius' account of their expulsion from Rome in 52 A.D., and further references to them in Suetonius' *Life of Nero*. Then we have Pliny the Younger's famous *Letter to Trajan* in 112 A.D., detailing measures to control the sect, and Trajan's reply predicting its imminent demise because, he says, Christianity is "out of keeping with the age."

Which, of course, it always was, and this has been a common reason for rejecting it - Pliny's, Trajan's and (one suspects) James Gray's. But lack of historical credibility is not a reason. Here the foundations are very strong, and the man and events described are better documented than anyone else who lived at that place and at that time.
- *May 5, 1986*

If the new agers get grants, why not the Presbyterians?

In Edmonton next week a group of teachers, educational bureaucrats and other forward thinkers of the New Age will get down to the serious business of what their hosts call "intuitive thinking." The less kind might call it dingbat occultism. Their conference, entitled "Thinking...For a Change," will, according to its advance publicity, "use the tools of the Age of Intelligence, Mind Mapping, Multi-Layered Six-Hat thinking and the Deep Fluid Mind State" to "put people in touch with their intuitive thinking." Far be it from me to challenge the credibility of any of this, but I think somebody ought to ask one question. How many of these conferees are there on a government or school board expense account, and how can this be justified in a society that insists on a clear divorce between the public school system and religion?

For whatever else such gatherings may be called, they dabble sooner or later in the "supra-natural," in other words, the religious. And if tax money pays public educators to attend such affairs, then why shouldn't it likewise be used to send teachers to the annual meeting of, say, the Presbyterian Church of Canada? Is eastern mysticism the only kind of religion public money can support? It's an issue public school administrators must soon resolve, because the so-called New Age Movement already penetrates deep into the public school program.

I had never heard of this phenomenon until last year when some unusual subjects began turning up on western teachers' convention agendas. They concerned things like "self-exploration," "self-promotion," "whole-brain thinking" and the "holistic view of life." The speakers usually came from Los Angeles or San Francisco. It seemed absurd. Here we have a system that cannot teach children to read, or do elementary mathematics, yet it's into stuff like this - going, as it were, from mere incompetence to abject lunacy.

I next noticed that one Desmond E. Berghofer, assistant deputy minister of Advanced Education for Alberta, was advertising on his office stationery "the Alberta Catalyst Forum" which was to "create the future for Alberta" at a conference in Edmonton on "possibility thinking." Was the government endorsing this thing while chopping the grants to university libraries?

No, said the Advanced Education Department. Yes, said the conference's chief speaker and organizer. The question was left obscure, as no doubt was the future of Alberta. What became much more concrete, however, was the future of Dr. Berghofer. By January of this year he had ceased to be assistant deputy minister, and now thinks intuitively for a living. He is sponsoring next week's meeting in Edmonton.

Last December, a cover story in *Time* magazine began to explain all this. What we had noticed were merely the local manifestations of the New Age movement, which *Time* described as "a combination of spirituality and superstition, fad and farce, about which the only thing certain is that it is not new." Faith healing, in its current form, has been around for at least a century, and pantheism which makes God and nature virtually the same thing was much older than Christianity. It has, however, several discernible doctrines, such as: everybody is God and a co-creator of the universe...you can be whatever you want to be...pain is perception, not a reality...spirituality is profitable.

In its more respectable manifestations the movement sponsors such things as management conferences for executives of companies like IBM, General Motors and AT&T, who in four-day seminars, costing their companies $15,000 per participant, discuss how metaphysics, the occult and Hindu mysticism might help them "compete in the world marketplace."

Similarly, at its respectable level, we find the City of Edmonton paying $25,000 to enable parks and cultural groups to "engage in inventing the future of culture in Edmonton" by such methods as "deep listening." An *Edmonton Journal* columnist, John Geiger, who gets wiser as he gets older, did some investigating and reported a vision of his own: an idyllic city council which was not sap enough to throw away $25,000 on the utterly screwball. For beneath the respectable veneer, the New Age descends rapidly into the crackpot. Last August twenty thousand devotees assembled, for instance, at places like Mount

Shasta in California to chant the Hindu "OM," uniting believers in everything from the I Ching and crystals to astral travel and Tarot reading in one vast "harmonic convergence." The high priestess of the movement is, we are told, the actress Shirley MacLaine whose five books on her New Age experiences and insights have sold eight million copies. Other gurus have been doing nicely with seminars on such topics as "Healing Yourself with Crystals," "American Indian Magic Can Work for You," and "How to Use a Green Candle to Gain Money."

All this success, says *Time*, has a single explanation. There is among modern people a "profound cry for meaning in life." They "want a living experience of spirituality." This conclusion accords precisely with the findings of Dr. Reginald Bibby of Lethbridge who notes that, though the churches are emptying, all people, the young in particular, yearn for an experience of God.

And where, meanwhile, are the churches' leaders? Most have abandoned religion in favour of politics. Bishops prate on about farm economics and archdeacons demand sanctions against South Africa. Deans denounce the sinister militarism of church parades and moderators proclaim the virtues of selective sodomy. They have become, in effect, a farce - in religion irrelevant and in politics a joke - while the quack and the scoundrel ravage the flocks entrusted to them.

One of the New Age manifestations in Canada is called the "Transformation Research Network," known as the TRN. "From our meditation and celebration," says a TRN press release, "we will shape new rituals to embody our mystery and equality in the circle of life." TRN has some distinguished sponsors: David Crombie, Marcel Masse, Marion Dewar, David King and also former United Church moderator Lois Wilson and the Most Reverend Edward E. Scott, former primate of the Anglican Church of Canada. "God," says Archbishop Scott, "is speaking to his church in new ways." The possibility that it might not be God who is speaking does not seem to have crossed his mind.

"If we can ever bring [humanity]," says the devil Screwtape in C.S. Lewis' famous *Screwtape Letters,* "to believe in 'forces' while not believing in 'spirits,' our whole great work will be nearing fulfilment." Well it's getting there. - *August 15, 1988*

**Before deciding Christianity has had it,
check out the Christmas of 995 A.D.**

Five Christmases remain in the second millennium of the Christian Era (cherished by the politically correct as "the Common Era," so as not to give offence, although the only thing common to it is Christianity). We are, that is, just five Christmases away from year 2000.

There is the usual deluge of bad news, of course - sensitive school principals who forbid the singing of Christian carols on their public premises, aggrieved citizens who don't want "Away in a Manger" played in City Hall, zealous human rights advocates who harken to the herald angels by requiring them to shut up. Most recently, there's the discovery by a Southam News-Angus Reid poll that where in 1987 some 27 per cent of Canadians thought Christmas primarily a time to reflect on the birth of Jesus, this number has now declined to 21 per cent. However, 55 per cent of Canadians still plan to go to church - 71 per cent in the religiously fervid Atlantic Provinces, barely 43 per cent in pagan British Columbia.

So let's consider how we're doing after nearly two thousand years. One measure might be to examine our situation at the end of the first millennium - back in 995. Our prospects then could hardly have looked more grim. Christianity had been largely driven out of its birthplace in Palestine. The whole of the Middle East and North Africa, entirely Christian three hundred years earlier, had been forcibly converted to Islam by Arab armies. Spain too was Muslim except for a forlorn Christian element holding out in the northern mountains. Even France would have fallen to Islamic invaders had they not been stopped in a bloody battle at Tours in 732. The Christian bastion of Constantinople was constantly threatened from the south by the Muslims, and from the east by the waves of tribesmen from the steppes. Russia and most of the Slavic peoples were still pagan. Conversion of the fiercely anti-Christian Vikings of northern Europe had barely begun. The Nestorian churches, which had spread

Christianity through Asia and into China, had nearly all been wiped out.

Christianity, in other words, had been reduced to an impoverished remnant in western and central Europe, besieged on all sides, and challenged in particular by the militant new religion of Islam. If anyone had predicted that in the next ten centuries this bedraggled faith would spread across the six continents and become the largest religion and dominant moral influence in the world, he would have been dismissed as mad.

Look back a hundred years, however, and a very different picture appears. By 1895, all over the world, Christianity seemed established and utterly secure. Five-hundred-year-old cathedrals dominated the skylines of every city in eastern and western Europe. Every village and town was built around a parish church. The laws of every country except France were rooted in Christian assumptions, and all the crowns of Europe were centred upon a cross. Beyond the seas, the nations of both North and South America would call themselves Christian, and Christian missions were active in nearly every Asian country. Africa, south of the Sahara, was signed in every locale with the cross.

But beneath this confident Christian exterior many things were going wrong. Charles Darwin had persuaded the scientific and intellectual world that God did not create the myriad species of nature; rather, they occurred accidentally over millions of years through the process of natural selection - the survival of the fittest. The German devotees of a discipline called the higher criticism had discredited the New Testament by "proving" much of it was written as late as one hundred years after the events it purports to describe, making it little better than legend. Knowledgeable people, emancipated from the shackles of religious dogma, were assuring us that the applied sciences would soon produce the perfect society, and we could look forward to a twentieth century in which wars would be unknown and humanity, rising on the wings of science and socialist enlightenment, would achieve an enduring Utopia.

The knowledgeable turned out to be only half right. As the century unfolded we were certainly emancipated from the shackles of religious dogma. Decade by decade, Christianity was progressively removed as an influencing element in the primary and secondary public schools, and ceased altogether to gain serious consideration in the universities. By the Sixties the news and entertainment media changed, and by the Eighties movies and television rather specialized in bizarre attacks upon all things Christian. Every priest or minister was dependably characterized by buffoonery, skulduggery, or villainy. Amazingly, however, at Christmas 1995, those 55 per cent of Canadians still doggedly insist upon attending church.

Yet perhaps not so amazingly. True enough, the new era went far to eradicate the old faith. But it has nothing adequate to replace that faith, a fact which is becoming disconcertingly evident and has long since begun to take its toll. Failed marriages, neglected children running wild, laws that cannot be enforced, governments that cannot cope and are heading for bankruptcy, faltering education - all these spread a deepening sense of futility and purposelessness.

Meanwhile, science has proved woefully two-sided. While we can travel at hitherto unimaginable speeds and have even made it to the moon, while we can bring right into our living rooms entertainment that was once available only to the most privileged, while we can stifle pain, and talk across whole oceans and continents, we have also discovered ways to blow everything to smithereens by pushing a button, and our envisioned century of peace has featured the two most horrible wars in human history.

But other things have been taking place too, just as they were a hundred years ago, things that have not yet gained wide recognition, least of all in the media. Darwin's theory, for instance, is in real trouble. Although it is still preached as dogma in most public school science courses, in fact required by ministerial order in British Columbia, it has been rejected by reputable scientists, who have recognized that the fossil records simply do not confirm it. Indeed, in many ways, they refute it. It seems that all the essential transitional creatures, through which one species was supposed to evolve into another, just aren't there. And how did the eye come about, or the wing? As one scientist wondered,"What would be the evolutionary advantage of a creature with five per cent of an eye?"

A similar reversal of scholarly view has taken place on the New Testament. New manuscript discoveries and literary research have driven the dates of the books ever earlier. Many scholars now consider they were written within twenty years of the events they describe, thereby vitally endorsing their credibility. But this, too, remains unknown to the media most of whose religion writers are still back in the nineteenth century.

We may begin therefore to bid farewell to the second Christian millennium with far more confidence than we could possibly have had at the end of the first. Yes, we have problems. But things have been a whole lot worse.

Merry Christmas! - *December 18, 1995*

Artistic Nonsense

"The first rule of any kind of creativity is, surely, that you do not achieve originality by striving for originality, and you cannot become unique by trying to be unique."

- Ted Byfield, 1988.

Byfield in 1973, at the time of the
creation of St. John's Edmonton Report.

Why can't the the CBC leave a nice guy like me alone?

One of the penalties you pay as proprietor of the last domestically owned general news publication in western Canada is the necessity of being recurrently "explained" by the CBC. Twice, in the last couple of years I have been featured on CBC programs. I was the subject of a half-hour television documentary (dangerous ideologue) and a lengthy "treatment" on the national radio show, *Sunday Morning* (religious fanatic). Now I notice that the CBC is prominent among the sponsors, and plans a national review on television, of yet another explanation, this one a stage play about this magazine called *Prairie Report* where I am once again featured (peevishly pompous bore). Now, I have it from no less an authority than my wife that I am really none of these awful things, that I am actually a very sweet person and do not deserve all this abuse from the Canadian Broadcasting Corporation, especially after all the nice things I've said about them.

Anyway, there I was the other night, right in front of myself so to speak, at Edmonton's Kaasa Theatre, where I appeared at centre stage as Dick Bennington, a man of cultured tones (true enough), impeccable language (absolutely), and constricted views (now how can they say that?). Distracted by his yacht, Mr. Bennington querulously agonizes through about ninety minutes of lachrymose dialogue with his staff of endlessly whining editors. At issue is the sale of this priceless treasure, i.e. the magazine, to a vicious horror figure, i.e. an eastern businessman who has made a fortune manufacturing paper bags. In the end the bag man gets it, and runs it under the nominal direction of my semi-moronic son who has been rendered clueless, oafish, inarticulate and dazed by the two insurmountable disabilities that have wrecked his life, they being (a) farming and (b) me. The staff is your typical newsroom mix: the usual imported Brit editor (right-wing and therefore ruthless, obscene, cynical, lying, self-serving and unvaryingly treacherous), a lady editor (left-wing, and therefore caring, noble, perceptive, honest and courageously outspoken) along, of course, with your indispensable homosexual (also a woman, gifted, victimized, pathetic and given to bursting into tears that provide the lady socialist with a chance to be tender, and the Brit conservative with a chance to be rotten). Both the right and the left are pounded in this play, say its promoters, an assertion which is exactly half true.

Now the author of this wallow of self-doubt and dire declamation is, I'm sorry to say, Mr. Frank Moher, who for four years ran the "Books" section of this magazine. He is a fine writer. He has since moved to live among the retired millionaires and aging hippies on Gabriola Island in the Georgia Strait. (I was going to say "retired hippies," but that would be inaccurate, it being impossible to retire if you've never worked.) Here, Mr. Moher lives with his wife and two children and writes plays to "explain" the west to Toronto, which in turn explains it back to us.

One gains the impression that Mr. Moher was not happy on this magazine. Certainly nobody in his play is, and one result of his ordeal-of-conscience for having dwelt so long among the Philistines is what can only be described as an unsuccessful play. It is billed as a comedy with a message. To write polemic is difficult, to write comedy is even more difficult, and to write polemical comedy is very difficult indeed. Shaw could do it, and so could Dickens, but it obviously requires a strict discipline of proportion. Shaw, for instance, used to get some of the philosophy off his chest by writing gargantuan prefaces to his plays. The play itself must keep people laughing throughout the whole performance. If your script runs about ninety per cent jokes and ten per cent message, you can do this. If you offer ninety per cent message and ten per cent jokes, what emerges is one hundred per cent boring. This, unhappily, is the pitfall into which Mr. Moher has unguardedly plunged. I went there expecting to see something like Ben Hecht's *Front Page*. What I saw instead was an attempt to use a dash of Neil Simon as a kind of jocular introduction to the book of the prophet Jeremiah. Somehow it doesn't seem to work.

Moreover, Mr. Jeremiah at least knew what his message was, and you get the impression that Mr. Moher does not. It is nowhere made clear, for instance, why any publication produced by such a passel of wailing willies and their stuffed-shirt pooh-bah could possibly be worth saving. Saved for what? In order to establish the same kind of pinko press in the west that we are already overfed with from the east? Are caring western liberals somehow to be distinguished from caring Toronto liberals? Does the air west of the Lakehead have some mystical regenerative effect on the social conscience? Why strive so tirelessly to preserve the indigenous press, or the indigenous arts community, or the indigenous anything else, if the only thing it's going to tell us is what the CBC, the National Film Board, Can-Lit and all the other precious artsies are already pouring upon us night and day out of Toronto? Maybe there is some mysterious difference in western liberalism, but I sure didn't hear any in Mr. Moher's play. It was pure Bay-and-Bloor and that's why the CBC helped pay for it.

There is a point to be made here and it is this. If Mr. Moher, whose talents are many, discerns his role in life as developing a unique western Canadian identity within the arts, then he is going to waste those many talents. Because the first rule of any kind of creativity is, surely, that you do not achieve originality by striving for originality, and you cannot become unique by trying to be unique. If our western playwrights, artists, composers, and, heaven help us, publishers, want to accomplish a western Canadian school of anything then the very first thing we must do is forget about being western Canadians. There are a thousand dilemmas and problems facing humanity in the late twentieth century that have never faced us before. They are as pressing in Paris as they are in Pincher Creek, and if we have things to say about them, then we should say them, not in order to establish our uniqueness, but because we think they should be heard. And if they are valid and well stated, then we shall certainly discover ourselves to have been unique, though that had been the farthest thing from our minds.

We are already enduring the offerings of, and paying the costs of one pampered ghetto of "Canadianism" in the east. We don't need another one in the west. And if the only reason to sustain *Prairie Report* is the fact that it's owned on the Prairies, then by all means sell the damned thing. - *November 7, 1988*

Alberta's genuine culture

It is a very odd thing that at the time of the great flowering of the English language, Elizabethan and early Stuart England, there was no English word for culture. Which is to say, when the English were at their most cultured, they had no need to say so. They were not conscious of it. There was no distinction between the cultured crowd and the uncultured one. Shakespeare's plays were written for the masses. Donne's sermons were preached to the general rabble in the congregation, and his ribald poems were addressed to everybody. How different it is today in Alberta where we have:

a) The "cultured," who account for perhaps five percent of the population, those who patronize our great theatres, concert halls, and art galleries, along with the maybe one tenth of one percent who actually buy the books that are funded by the Canada Council and known on the university courses as "Can-Lit." Then there is:

b) The uncultured, who patronise chiefly television, the Coliseum, the Saddledome, McMahon and Commonwealth stadiums and, in much larger numbers, those centres of what in fact is the only real culture of Alberta, places like the Beverly Crest Hotel.

What's that? You've never heard of the Beverly Crest Hotel? Well that is perhaps because you are not part of Alberta's genuine culture, the unsubsidized one, the one that exists, not because some bureaucrat or the artsy-crafties among us think it should exist, but because the mass of the people make it exist. It does not represent what we would like people to think we are. It represents what we are. In seventeenth century London, you had the Globe, and in twentieth century Edmonton you have the Beverly Crest. And all across the province, everywhere from Milk River to High Level, you have places that are like the Beverly Crest.

Should you doubt me, ask yourself this: if someone were to write a description of how the great mass of Albertans lived in the 1980s, how they entertained themselves, what they believed in, what in short was their culture, do you really think he would be accurate to describe the crowd and program at the Citadel Theatre or the Calgary Centre for the Performing Arts? The point is that for every Albertan who attends such places there are a thousand others who attend the province's various Beverly Crests. Therefore, in a real sense, and whether we like it or not, the latter far better represents the true culture of Alberta. It may not be an altogether elegant culture, but it is us. That's why any description of the true culture of Alberta, as distinct from the artificial one, must make its way sooner or later to the Beverly Crest.

I myself came to know the Beverly Crest through an accident of geography. It is located on 118th Avenue in northeast Edmonton. It happens to be five hours on foot, my foot, from Lessard in southwest Edmonton where I live, via the city's beautiful river valley park system. As an addict of walking, I have in old age controlled my habit at one five-hour jaunt per week. Any less and I don't get the proper jag. Any more and I would probably collapse. Five hours in a northeasterly direction lands me just outside the Beverly Crest with beer and rye whisky just inside, and a wife willing to drive out there and, so to speak, pick me up. Hence, for the last six years I have walked pretty well every week the seventeen miles from Lessard to the Beverly Crest, where I spend perhaps an hour or two researching the culture of Alberta.

Now it is true that we of the Beverly Crest crowd do not actually produce plays. They blamed us for producing a murder last year, but that was untrue. The murder was not in the hotel, only in the parking lot, and the victim had actually been patronizing another place down the street. But the incident was, I admit, an embarrassment to us, and not at all typical of our behaviour. We do not kill people in the Beverly Crest. Fights, yes, but not murder. In fact, our conduct has become almost what you could call sedate - ever since we got rid of the bikers, or at least they decided to go somewhere else. That was about five years ago, and was beneficial because people no longer arrive in the beverage room on motorcycles.

The dance, however, does figure prominently in the culture of the Beverly Crest, and it comes in two distinct modes. In one section, known most recently as "Cheers," you have a sort of interpretive and highly stylized performance dancing, usually by female artists. These follow a strict choreography, much associated with costume and the progressive subtraction therefrom. Characteristically, this dance begins with a kind of demure and delicate tiptoe about a central stage, then increases rapidly in vigour to a climax in which the performer is customarily upside down, or lying on her back and peering between her thighs with her feet behind her neck, the costume by now having been subtracted entirely. Obviously this type of dance is not for everyone. The male equivalent of it must sometimes be abruptly discontinued because the audience, wholly female and given to clutching and shrieking, has become uncontrollable. My own study of this aspect of the Beverly Crest was also abruptly discontinued after my chauffeur allowed that if I wanted to sit watching that kind of thing, I could find someone else to go and get me. Which just goes to show how much she cares about culture.

In another section of the Beverly Crest, known as the saloon, one encounters another kind of dancing. It is participatory, and could be called freestyle, very freestyle, representing, in fact, almost every choreographic fashion known to man. It is performed by couples dancing together, and punctuated often by shouts of encouragement to the musicians who accompany it. The costumes are equally varied. Though denim predominates, there is also a profligacy of a garment known as the muscle shirt. The management, in a sudden surge into the respectable, is said to have once shocked the clientele by insisting that people wear shoes. It didn't last. The steps themselves are similarly diverse. In one, the participants leap ecstatically into the air as though the flooring were of hot coals. In another, much less energetic, in fact bordering on total somnolence, the couple drift about dreamily, leaning on one another like a pair of table knives set on end. It is, of course, a very disciplined dance, since if one party makes an unexpected move, the other can fall flat on his face on the floor. This happens, but the management does not like it.

As for the music, this too is entirely original. We have various groups with names like "The Dust Dogs," none of which, so far as I know, is supported by the Canada Council.

There are other aspects to the Beverly Crest culture. In one corner, for instance, on several televisions, we lustily follow the sporting events, voicing our opinions of the game as developments occur. Prominent in these expressions of opinion is what Waugh called the indispensable repeating participle of the British Army without which no communication is possible. "Did you see that — idiot? Where was the — referee? That — Montreal. They get away with it every — time."

We are also very big on conversation at the Beverly Crest, usually spirited, of course, and plunging frequently into controversy. When it becomes too spirited, the management intervenes. Large people appear from nowhere with broad suggestions and broader shoulders. They propose that this topic might better be continued outside. Such a suggestion, if resisted, is generally followed by a sort of sweeping movement in which the conversationalist finds himself suddenly leaving his chair in midsentence and flying, still in a seated position, across the hall and out the door, to sit instead in the middle of the street. But the whole thing is done quietly, swiftly, deftly and happens no more than three or four times in the course of a typical evening.

Such is the culture of the Beverly Crest which is to say, therefore, of most of Alberta. Now there is surely a distinct detriment when a country has two cultures - a real one which consists of the mass of the people doing whatever they like doing, and the contrived one which consists of a coterie of the effete, putting on little exhibitions for one another and requiring the rest of us to help pay for them. I think there are three reasons why this dichotomy ought not to be. For one, it is unjust. For another, it is untrue. And finally, it is unproductive.

It is unjust because it is predicated upon a supposed and unproven superiority. Why, after all, should a plotless, pointless, largely incomprehensible theatrical offering, staged for the select set who watch such things in some oh-so-quaint downtown theatre, have claim upon the public purse, while "The Dust Dogs" are supposed to package, promote and produce their works on their own? Why not make them both do it on their own? Why not say that if so few people are interested in "Can-Theatre" that it cannot possibly support itself, this is persuasive that it ought not to exist. Oh, I know the argument: Franz Josef Haydn was subsidized by the count of Esterhazy, so why shouldn't this or that playwright be subsidized by Alberta Culture? But Haydn had to appeal at least to the count, who was human, rather than to a bureaucracy which isn't. Moreover, the subsequent market for his work has continued strong for the last two hundred years. I don't see such a market for most of the precious products of Canadian theatre, nor heaven knows for the works of Can-Lit. The fact is that nobody wants them, and you can't give them away. So why the subsidies? It's not fair.

Neither is it true. I mean it is simply false to say that Can-Lit, or Can-Theatre, or Can-this, or Can-that in fact reflects what the mass of Canadians do, think, espouse, eat, drink, enjoy and believe in. The mass of Canadians don't even know such things exist. And if they did they wouldn't have anything to do with them. I can't pretend to have seen a great many Canadian plays, and I have not exactly immersed myself in Can-Lit, but I have read many reviews of both, and I can tell you right now that none of it would go down well at the Beverly Crest. And this is not because we of the Beverly Crest don't appreciate art. In fact, it's because we do appreciate it, that we would certainly watch plays and even read books that reflected ourselves, or anybody we've ever met. But most of these things don't. The people who appear in them are very much like the people who write them, and we don't know anyone like that. So on with "The Dust Dogs" and get that junk out of here. It's a lie.

Finally, it is unproductive. Counter-productive would be a better term. The fact that our gifted people can somehow make a living turning out that which is essentially fraudulent prevents them from producing that which is essentially good. We should be in no doubt about this, incidentally. John Metcalf, in his hilarious commentary on the Canada Council, *Freedom From Culture* (William Hoffer, Vancouver,

1987), discloses that though publishers, literary printers, magazines, writers, critics, translators, publicity agents, distributors and the writers unions are all subsidized, the fact remains that a well-reviewed Canadian novel is lucky to sell eight hundred to twelve hundred copies. Only one Canadian in twenty-six thousand buys it, an audience of .00385 percent. "That figure means," says Metcalf, "that if you chose someone at random on the street, they'd be just as likely to have AIDS as to have bought a Canadian novel this year."

But need that be so? If playwrights who produce meaningless twaddle in the name of "theatre art," or authors who composed mere bafflegab in the name of "Can-Lit," discovered themselves starving because nobody would buy what they wrote, then one of two things would happen. Either they would be forced to make a living some other way, or they would change that which they produced so that people would take an interest in it - the people, that is, at the Beverly Crest.

Now this, of course, would serve two purposes. First, we would have real culture instead of artificial culture. And second, we of the Beverly Crest might get some idea of who we are. For the Beverly Crest needs the artist as much as the artist needs the Beverly Crest. A people who do not know what they stand for, what they believe in, what characteristics and qualities make them and their society distinct from other societies is a very impoverished people. That, unhappily, is our state right now. It has become our state in part because our artists are so busy enthralling one another that they forgot about us, their real responsibility.

One great heresy of the age is encapsulated by the slogan, "Art for art's sake." Art does not exist for its own sake. It exists for my sake, and your sake, and for the sake of the people in the Beverly Crest. You and I, that is, may see the sunset. So does the painter. But the painter sees in the sunset that which you and I cannot see, and his responsibility as a painter is to show that to us. The novelist or the playwright can, like me, visit the Beverly Crest. But he can see things there that we of the Beverly Crest do not see about ourselves. Pointing those things out to us is his responsibility as an artist. If he fails to do so, he fails us, he fails himself, and he fails his art. Art is no more for art's sake than plumbing is for plumbing's sake. The end of all work is to serve God by serving the brethren, and no work matters more than that of the artist. His job is to tell us who we are.

When he does not do this, and we do not know who we are, then of course we must soon perish. How this will happen is altogether evident. Because we do not know who we are, we do not now produce children. Our birth rate is dropping steadily and is already far below the level of population replacement. Hence we must open our doors to immigration on a scale that exceeds everything in our past, and as new people arrive we properly urge upon them the need to sustain their hereditary culture. But what of our own? What of the one they themselves have opted to embrace. That, unfortunately, we are prepared to neither defend nor even state. We're not even sure what it is, and its values seem to change from year to year with every fad in the media, or decision of the Supreme Court. This is not a healthy situation. It is time our artists abandoned their cozy little enclaves, and came down to the Beverly Crest. We know we have a culture here, and a real one. All we need is that somebody tell us what it is.

- Reprinted from Alberta: Studies in the Arts and Sciences, Vol. 11, no.1 *(University of Alberta Press, 1989.)*

Chapter Ten

The 'Authorized Version'

"So then to whom does the CBC belong? Why, it belongs
to Pierre Berton, of course, to Pierre Berton and everyone else
in the select little Toronto in-group that runs it, and has used it
to promote the Authorized Version of Canada for all these years."

- Ted Byfield, 1991

Byfield at the wheel of the *Credimus*, off
San Francisco in 1986.

Strange that Canadian broadcasting
turns out to have so few 'friends?'

I got an intimate personal letter from Pierre Berton last week - I and several hundred thousand others got it. It was addressed, "Dear Fellow Canadian," and wanted me to join "the Friends of Canadian Broadcasting" and "unite with 25,000 other Canadians" in "fighting to preserve our national dream and beyond that our country itself."

Our "twentieth century national dream," says Mr. Berton, is the Canadian Broadcasting Corporation. It is "an electronic ribbon of steel from Twillingate to Tofino." He was likening the CBC, of course, to the Canadian Pacific Railway, the subject of his best known book, *The National Dream.* (To equate anything with the CPR as a means of praising it measures how far from western Canada Mr. Berton now lives. But then again, probably as many westerners have mentioned "the damned CBC" in the last half of the century as mentioned "the damned CPR" in the first half.)

Anyway, our latest national dream, Mr. Berton explains, is being destroyed by "a callous government." When that government cut the CBC's budget back by ten per cent (so now they only have something like one thousand million dollars a year left to run it on, plus all the television advertising revenue) that was the last spike ... er, straw. So now, says Mr. Berton, "we may become a nation of strangers. We won't share our hopes and fears, our history and our dreams. We may cease to be a country at all."

Now this is a revealing letter. When the budget cuts came, the CBC made it a top item on its newscasts for two or three days. (That this warping of the news to focus attention on oneself might constitute a "conflict of interest" - a favourite CBC topic when it concerns other interests than its own - does not seem to have inhibited it.) In other words, they are the biggest, costliest media organ in the country, and they pulled out every stop. They called in all their IOUs from the likes of Mr. Berton and others of the lib-left persuasion. They launched a massive direct-mail campaign. Now, after nine months of this, even by their own figures, the best they can come up with is 25,000 supporters coast to coast. That's far less than the population of Fort McMurray. Moreover, this "Friends" group existed long before the cuts were made. It's been around since 1985. Six years, and they still aren't up to Fort McMurray.

What we're being told, then, is that the bugles are sounding as loud as the CBC can blow them and practically nobody's turning out for the parade. They run up the flag and almost no one even notices, let alone salutes. The Friends of Canadian Broadcasting have discovered Canadian broadcasting to be virtually friendless.

I think I know why, and perhaps I should tell Mr. Berton and his Friends. His letter contains a curious sentence. "The CBC does not belong to the government," he writes. "It belongs to the people of Canada - to you and me." He's exactly two-thirds right on this. The CBC indeed does not belong to the government. The government is forbidden by law to directly influence the contents of any of its programs. But neither, heaven help us, does it belong to me, because if it did I would put the half of its programming, the missing half, on the air - meaning, of course, the conservative side of any issue it undertakes to report, discuss or laboriously portray on one of its awful dramatic efforts.

So then to whom does the CBC belong? Why, it belongs to Pierre Berton, of course, to Pierre Berton and everyone else in the select little Toronto in-group that runs it, and has used it to promote the Authorized Version of Canada for all these years. That is the Canada that Mr. Berton sees threatened if the CBC were to disappear - and in this he's perfectly right. But it is also why the CBC with all this massive effort over six years, can find only 25,000 friends. The message of Mr. Berton's letter is really this: "We at the CBC know what Canada is supposed to be. We understand its distinctions, history, sensitivities, moral imperatives, political idiosyncrasies, everything. You need us to tell you these things hour by hour, day by day. And these dreadful politicians, whom you elected, are trying to prevent us from doing this. So stop them. By saving us you will save Canada."

Many people have trouble swallowing this, and they're all "fellow Canadians." I asked one what he thought of the ten per cent cut in the CBC budget and he answered: "I'll see their ten and raise it twenty!" And then we had the letter writer in last week's magazine whose response to the closing of the CBC station in Calgary was: "Calgary gets all the breaks." Are these *enemies* of Canadian broadcasting? No, they are not. But they are enemies of what's being *done* with Canadian broadcasting by the CBC, and what's being *done* with Canada by means of the CBC. Of that, they are very truly enemies, and I venture to say if they formed themselves into a club and had one-tenth of the publicity potential of this Friends group, they would very rapidly get ten times its membership. But their voice is rarely heard, least of all on the CBC. To the Pierre Bertons of the country, they are "un-Canadian."

Yet, one thing more needs be said. No one can read his books without realizing that this same Pierre Berton passionately believes in Canada. He is the genuine patriot, certainly one of the greatest Canadian writers of the century, a person without whose books we would lack even such feeble acquaintance with our own past as most of us possess. He has done us a magnificent service and he is owed an unpayable debt. He has been as good for the country as the CBC has been bad.

And yet, through many of his books (save, of course, *The Comfortable Pew*, which reads now as though it were written by the lilies at Anglican Church House in Toronto) there runs the same strange dichotomy. The people he so plainly admires - the Donald Smiths, George Stephens and Clifford Siftons who put the country together - in no sense resemble or fulfil the political ideals he purports to espouse. They were tough, rugged, two-fisted individualists, for whom things like medicare and the "sharing" and "sensitive" society would be the ultimate wimp-out, an object of contempt, loathing and horror. The resolute, steel-hard, "Galician" settlers, who so clearly commanded his respect, came here to escape the very kinds of government control that he now fervently recommends. Mr. Berton, in short, should read his own histories, and tell *that* to the CBC. Then maybe they'd have more Friends. - *September 2, 1991*

A rule we of the media would be well advised to observe

Anyone peering back upon late twentieth century Canada from the vantage of the next century or beyond will no doubt be astonished at the extraordinary power of the media. Certainly, we have always been strong beyond anything we deserved or earned. But never before have spectacles like the following become quite so routine. All have occurred within the last week or so:

• A Greenpeace vessel ties up beside a Vancouver chlorine plant. A banner is raised. A young lady is chained to a fence. Shipments from the plant are arrested by a human blockade. The three television stations arrive, and the two daily papers. Photographs and news footage are ritually taken. The young lady is unchained. The banner is taken down. The following day an injunction is obtained and the blockade disappears.

• The CBC camera crew arrives at the Peigan reserve in southern Alberta. A bulldozer that for weeks has been labouring to open a diversion channel and thereby obstruct an undesired irrigation dam - something that would have taken a determined construction crew about three days - is persuaded to cough back into action. The indispensable footage is acquired that shows the machine hard at work, along with interviews that show the iron determination of the Indians. The CBC crew departs. The bulldozer stops. Everybody settles down until the next news crew arrives. It becomes evident, even to the CBC, that the Peigans know far more about working the media than they know about working bulldozers.

• At Oka the "Warriors," utterly determined, as they keep assuring us, to fight to the death defending the inalienable rights of the Mohawks to nobody seems sure just what, continue to meet the army face to face. It's Warrior against soldier, jaw to jaw, a sort of single psychological combat in a romantic isolation marred only by the immediate presence of six TV cameras and crews, fourteen microphones, yards of underfoot camera cable, a host of technicians and a dozen or two gawking reporters getting it all down for posterity's sake. In the meantime, it is disclosed that some of the Mohawk Warriors are not Mohawks, nor even Indians, and that one of their most eloquent spokesmen is a white man from Brooklyn. Needless to say, no Warriors have actually died, and even their liberal defenders wish they would clean up their language a little, because it is difficult to conceive of these gents as the rapturous defenders of a pristine innocence when their every second words starts with F. One Warrior, it is true, got beaten up a bit while the nation fittingly brayed, deplored, and tried to forget that being beaten up is something that happens to eighty or ninety Canadians pretty well every night elsewhere in the country. However, since the usual cause, i.e., mugging, is not very noble, nobody writes anything about it.

Now the word to describe all this is "phony." The sham and hollowness is obvious and exacts a frightful price. It conveys to the citizenry the message that those things their leaders would have them believe are at the core contrived and artificial, that government itself is phony, and that ultimately the whole country and everything it is supposed to stand for is a manufactured concoction dreamt up by advertising experts and hucksters.

Why is it, we are repeatedly asked, that more and more people seem to have given up on Canada and the whole democratic process? They don't read newspapers; they don't vote; they ignore the whole modus and rationale of our system. The answer is plain. They have concluded it's wholly spurious, that everything that smacks of government and the laws is some kind of charade being staged by those in power to keep them in power. They're reassured of this every night. First they get Roseanne and then they get the news. Both are produced and directed. Moreover, the whole spectacle of defiance erodes the credibility of the state. People know that protestors do these things only because they are certain those entrusted to enforce the law do not have the conviction and fortitude to do it. Why? Because the supposed enforcers are terrified of the media. They know that any politician who authorized determined enforcement would be hounded, deplored, pilloried, maligned, castigated and condemned for months by the columnists and the commentators and the academics and the gurus until he himself went to jail instead of the protestors. So the law goes unenforced, and the system that stands behind it becomes a mockery. Again, it's the power of the media.

It does not take much imagination to see the danger in all this. First, we are creating a vast bloc within the electorate that has opted out of the whole system. It has been alienated. As long as it can be fed, housed and entertained it will pose no threat. However, as soon as these securities disappear, as eventually they must for no economy remains sound forever, it will constitute a menace, waiting for the right spellbinder to take control and lead it against the system it has come to despise and blame for its misfortunes.

Second, what it would take to set this off is an "incident," and such an eventuality is always only too possible in the current climate. For the device used by the protestors is thrill. The "media event" must promise to entertain. The great problem with thrill is that you need to go ever farther to sustain the same effect. At first by merely blockading an office, you could provide it. Then you must blockade a country road, then a main highway or rail line, then an integral metropolitan bridge. Each time you do this, you risk the unforeseeable. Introduce one itchy trigger finger, an uncontrollable crowd, a deranged mind, and your calculations can go disastrously awry. The skull of the girl chained to the fence is cracked by a police billy club. The corpses of the warriors hang as burnt meat on their barricades. Then, if the conditions are right, what began as an incident becomes a revolution. Third, the surest safeguard against such a development, the media, are increasingly discrediting themselves by championing one dubious cause after another, and by allowing themselves to be drawn into exhibitions that are staged solely for their benefit. If the young lady will only be chained to the fence if the media come to take her picture, then this argues against taking it. As the fable goes, every time we cry wolf when there isn't one, our cries of wolf become that much less compelling when there is. There will be a day when the media had better be heard. Its present appalling irresponsibility weakens it against that day. Surely, it's time we adopted a rule: If it won't happen unless we're there, then let's not go. - *September 24, 1990*

Check the McKenna case and see why the media lose credibility

Power corrupts, said Lord Acton, and he was not stating a tendency but a principle. It's hard to imagine a better instance of that principle than what's happened to the media, and it's hard to imagine a better instance of media corruption than last week's imbroglio over the CBC-National Firm Board "docu-drama" called *The Valour and the Horror.*

The series represents "advocacy journalism." That is, the producers, Brian and Terence McKenna, use the events of the Second World War to advocate a social theory - on the futility of war, how it enables sadistic militarists to dupe gullible young men into fighting purposeless battles and killing tens of thousands of innocent people, all to aggrandize military reputations and satisfy the natural blood lust of your typical general or air marshal. Expected conclusion: no war is worth fighting, and we must all strive to create a world socialist state in which human conflicts are resolved by rational rather than physical means.

The McKenna brothers said they also produced the series out of "sympathy" for the Canadian fighting man. That is, they wanted to cast him in the most revered role our society recognizes. He was to become a "victim." He could then join all the other "victims" - women, children, the aged, natives, people of "colour," homosexuals, the handicapped. The ungrateful veterans apparently didn't appreciate this. Being portrayed as simple-minded patsies, lured into wanton destruction of human life by twisted and incompetent militarist monsters, did not sound to them like sympathy. They would rather continue to think of themselves as heroes.

Their protest set off two inquiries. One was by a Senate committee. This, of course, could be discounted. After all, the senators making it were themselves veterans. The other was more serious. It was the CBC's "ombudsman," himself a television journalist. Last week he tore the McKenna work to shreds, as historically slipshod and blatantly contrived. CBC president Gerard Veilleux apologized for the production and said it would not be broadcast again without changes. It is very much to the credit of the CBC that this report was both made and made public.

What's more noteworthy, however, is the media's reaction. "How dare they criticize us!" demanded a host of editorialists, columnists and commentators. The sacred "arms-length principle" between the corporation and the politicians had been violated, said a spokesman for the Writers Guild of Canada. The CBC had "alarmed its staff, appalled its friends, and saddened its supporters." Worst of all, the ombudsman had betrayed "a host of men and women who selflessly served this country by going to war." (Notice the reasoning: First by discrediting the suggestion that they were chumps and suckers for having fought in the war in which they needlessly killed women and children, the ombudsman has somehow betrayed the veterans. Second, what they were fighting for was the right of a coterie of avant-garde left-wing flacks to peddle their personal propaganda at public expense with neither question nor criticism from the representatives of the people whose money they're spending. According to the Writers Guild of Canada, that's what the Second World War was all about.)

To see what is really happening here, put the CBC in its historical context. From the start, it represented the deliberate suspension of the central principle of Canadian democracy, i.e., "responsible government." By that principle, the civil service must answer to the cabinet, the cabinet to parliament, and parliament to the electorate. In the usual democratic process, every detail of the CBC's work would be subject to ministerial direction, amendment and control. Parliamentary committees would routinely examine it, and ministers would be expected to "interfere" in what the CBC did. However, in the case of the CBC, a major exception was made. The elected representatives must stay "at arm's length" from what the CBC does.

Behind this decision, of course, lay a large assumption. Politicians must not be allowed to control the CBC because politicians might abuse this power and use the CBC to serve party interests, or ride the hobbyhorses of the minister. The assumption was that journalists would never do this. They would have no personal visions, and if they did they would never dream of using the CBC to further them. So we established a government agency that was in effect a law unto itself. It was responsible to nobody. Our reasoning seems to have been: power might corrupt all manner of men, but not journalists. Lord Acton was wrong in the case of journalists.

Was this wise? For many years, it seemed to be. CBC reporting was a model of objectivity. But then about 25 years ago, the CBC changed. Gradually, it moved into "advocacy journalism." It began to advance its own views of Canada, of the world, of life, of morality and, most lately, of the Second World War. Programming that accorded with the CBC was furthered; programming that disaccorded was suppressed. The CBC has been doing this for years, and whenever a politician questions the practice he is instantly assailed for violating the sacred "arm's-length principle."

The other device the CBC did not shrink from using is the "docu-drama," a type of program said to combine the documentary and the drama. But in so doing, it becomes the very essence of journalistic fraud. The documentary producer is limited by his documents. He can withhold but he cannot invent. The drama producer can invent, but the viewer realizes he's inventing. It's fiction and everybody knows it. The "docu-dramatist" can do both. He can begin with a social theory, use whatever documents support it, ignore those that don't, and invent "facts" to fill in the gaps, even invent people to say them. The viewer, having no way of knowing what's document and what's drama - in other words, what's fact and what's fake - can be led in any direction the producer cares to lead him. The McKennas are "professionals" in docu-drama, and this is the journalistic "professionalism" that we are being exhorted to defend. Indeed, it was to defend this "freedom" that men and women "selflessly served this country by going to war" - or so we are told. It will no doubt come as a surprise to them.

The media have lost much credibility of late. On October 26th, the whole force of their editorialists and most of their commentators urged us with one voice to rise up and vote yes for the Charlottetown

Accord. We rose up all right, but most of us voted no. We ignored the media because we now correctly recognize the media as at the centre of the Establishment. The media have power. And we know that power, once again, has corrupted. - *November 23, 1992*

A case history from the annals of Southam and Gomorrah

That Southam Inc. should become sensitive to criticism these days is certainly understandable. It already owns the four biggest newspapers in Alberta and British Columbia, both the dailies in Vancouver, and is currently under federal combines inquiry because it has also swallowed many of the community weeklies in the Vancouver area as well.

Mr. Ian Haysom, editor of the Vancouver *Province,* for instance, takes umbrage at the criticism levelled by Rafe Mair, a Vancouver talk show host, who, says Mr. Haysom, "has been compounding a sad and common mistake."

He goes on: "Mair would have his listeners believe that the editors of *The Vancouver Sun* and the *Province* take their daily editorial marching orders from Southam's head office in Toronto. Let me put Mr. Mair straight. Southam is an enlightened newspaper group with a hands-off editorial policy. In short, it believes each newspaper knows its own market, its own readers, better than someone ensconced in a highrise on Bloor Street."

From Catherine Ford, editor of Southam's *Calgary Herald*, we get a similar avowal. She is quoted in a recent issue of *Media West* magazine: "Any person who has ever met me, who thinks for one instant that editorial direction of this newspaper is set by Toronto, is beyond all hope. People think that because it's convenient. It's easier to think that than it is to recognize that we all have an independent voice."

Such literal minds these Southam people have. Frankly, I have never heard anyone suggest that some sort of daily communication issues forth from a kind of control centre at Southam's head office, conveying the positions to be taken by the corporation's various editorial pages throughout the country. Such an arrangement, apart from being impossible, would also be unnecessary. The way you exercise control is not by telling an editor what to say, but by picking an editor in the first place who will say what you want without your telling him.

Toronto needs only let it be known that it wants as editors people of a particular style, a particular mindset, a particular way of looking at things, a particular set of values, people whose views are advanced, uninhibited by the rooted prejudices of the past, free, liberal, marching forward with mankind. How this works in practice Miss Ford (apparently unconscious of the inconsistency) was good enough to describe for me in the same *Media West* interview. She is quoted:

"There are too many people in the media who don't want to be here (i.e. in the west). They want to be in Toronto. That really irritates me because if you want to be in Toronto, what do you have to do - attract the attention of someone in Toronto? So how do you do that? You suck up to what Toronto thinks you should be doing." (Vancouver *Province*: please copy.)

As an explanation of what I mean, I can't improve on that. But there is at hand an even better illustration of this method in action, a veritable case history. Fourteen years ago, a talented editor on the *Brampton Daily Times* wrote an amazing editorial. It was headed, "Hey Quebec, Suck a Lemon." Here are some excerpts:

"Hey, Quebec, go suck a lemon. Better still, give me a divorce. A no-fault, no-contest, you keep your property and I'll keep mine, split. I don't want to be married to you any more...Please take your Olympic deficit, Jean Drapeau, tainted meat, past corruptions and future graft; the sewage polluted St. Lawrence; Mirabel airport; your air traffic controllers, the James Bay project and your language, and move out of the house. This reconciliation which the federal government is calling bilingualism and biculturalism, just isn't working, no matter how many marriage counsellors are on the civil service staff. I won't let you dominate the house. Share, yes. But control? Forget it!" It concludes: "I quite simply don't want you any more. I don't want your language, your customs, your problems and your whining voice grating in my ears."

Now contrast all this bigoted bombast with the calm, studied Southamistic liberal view of Miss Ford's *Calgary Herald* editorial page. "There is an absurd and cruel irony," that paper intoned last February in reference to the Sault Ste. Marie no-French decision "in the fact that a city founded by French-speaking missionaries and still bearing a French name should serve itself as a symbol to pig-headedness and blinkered intolerance." The Soo made "thinking, caring and tolerant Canadians shake their heads in bafflement." The *Herald* lamented: "Just what hope does Canada have of staying together as a bilingual nation?"

Nine days later, we heard from Miss Ford again: "Passions and prejudices on the language question in this country run deep. Those emotions have been subject to intermittent flare-ups, and when the insults fly, calm and sensible leadership is needed." She deplored Canadians who "willingly fling themselves into the bearpit to flail away at their neighbours" and "the vindictiveness that permeates politics in this country" over the language question, and the "eagerness with which some English-speaking Canadians have embraced its intolerances."

Now it is surely obvious that Miss Ford's denunciations in the *Calgary Herald* are aimed squarely at the very sort of people who write editorials like the one in the Brampton Times. The problem is, however, that the author of the editorial in the *Brampton Times* was Miss Ford, now directing the pieties on the editorial page of the *Herald*. The metamorphosis is, to say the least, staggering.

How can you account for it, one wonders. Miss Ford herself felt called upon to offer an explanation after Gorde Hunter, a columnist on the Victoria *Times-Colonist*, was thoughtful enough to recount her earlier, less enlightened views. So many things have happened since she wrote that piece, she explained - The Quebec referendum, multiculturalism, the Parti Quebecois, unions, the National Energy Program - that "along the way, I became a passionate defender of bi-bi, having realized that the true threat to this country was regionalism...I am a Canadian, therefore I am of Quebec."

Along the way also, of course, she somehow impressed the Southam management in Toronto as holding the balanced viewpoint, the national outlook, the sort of person the company could depend upon to say the right thing, at the right time, in the right way, to a city that can become, well, rather extreme.

She became addicted, that is, to what could be called the sin of southamy. She was southamized, and could therefore be depended upon. So what need is there of daily phone calls from Toronto.

- September 3, 1990

Chapter Eleven

Canada & the Canadianists

*"A Canadian is a person born or naturalized in Canada.
A canadianist is somebody who makes a living describing,
defining, defending and declaiming a particular view
of this country for the benefit of the rest of the citizenry,
usually at government expense."*

- Ted Byfield, 1986

Ted in his driveway with a copy of
The Atlas of Alberta in 1987.

The case of the country that has vanished away

A Queen's University professor speaking in Edmonton late last month declared that the Canadian confederation has about five years left to live. So strong are the regional tensions in the country, he said, and so frail the adhesive factors holding it together, that it is certain to be pulled to pieces. He didn't seem to mean that the terms of confederation would be amended. He meant that Canada was a dead duck.

The intention of such talk is to condemn regionalism as destructive. On this theory Canada once stood as a healthy, united, single-purposed nation. Then along came certain nasty provinces and wrecked it by putting their own parochial interests first. In other words the rise of regional loyalties had eroded the national loyalty. That is one possible explanation for Canada's plight.

Here is another: Canada's national loyalty never has been strong. What there was of it has been starved out of existence through neglect and irresponsibility. The regional loyalties have sprung up to fill the vacuum created by its demise. People must believe in something. For many, belief in our nationhood was simply impossible. Belief in a "homeland" was not. But the homeland meant the region.

When I think of my "homeland," for instance, I get a number of pictures. I see the dazzling lights of the new Edmonton reflected by the black waters of the North Saskatchewan on a summer night. I see the green and rolling barley fields of spring. I see Calgary's awesome skyline rising defiant against the smoky line of the autumn Rockies. I see snow blowing over limitless prairie. Above all, I see the odd churches and strange little restaurants of Winnipeg's north end, where I came, desperate and destitute nearly thirty years ago. For me, they were a strange people - Ukrainians, Jews, Germans, Indians, Poles. In other words, the west. But I found myself one of them and I have been one of them ever since. So the west is home. Ask me if I'd fight for it, and the answer is definitely yes, however little use I'd be.

But ask me if I'd fight for the land of my birth, i.e., Canada, and I become confused. Few people under 40 will understand what I mean by this, but the land of my birth has, in a sense, vanished. Though I was born in Toronto, I was not born a Canadian. Like everybody else on our street (it was Courcellette Road), I was taught to think of myself as "British."

Britishness was God's gift to humanity. The British were ordained to lead, counsel and rule the world by eventually conferring upon all of it the precious gift of Britishness. All other breeds were lesser.

All this fervor for Britishness did not come about by accident. It was cultivated. Public school classes began with the pupils standing rigidly to attention to sing "God Save the King." We also learned to sing "Rule Britannia," "Land of Hope and Glory," "Hearts of Oak," and one about our own branch of the empire called "The Maple Leaf Forever." Lest anyone discern in this the seeds of a Canadian nationalism, however, the words quickly exterminate it: "In days of yore, from Britain's shore, Wolfe the dauntless hero came, and planted firm Britannia's flag, in Canada's fair domain." The song "O Canada" was known. My great aunt, who was national president of the Imperial Order of the Daughters of the Empire, once called it "contemptible." Its author, she whispered with a knowing nod, had later emigrated to the United States.

There was certainly no such thing as a Canadian flag. Our flag was the Union Jack. It consisted, we were told, of three Christian symbols - the crosses of St. George, St. Andrew and St. Patrick. This evidenced that the empire was the product of Christianity, and that behind the laws of man must lie the more fundamental laws of God. Postal trucks carried crowns and the sign "Royal Mail." We lived near "the King's Highway, No. 2." On Victoria Day (what they now call May 24, I can't even remember), almost every house on our street flew one or more Union Jacks. And in 1936, I remember waiting by the radio for the final news that the King, George V, was dead, and I wept myself to sleep. I was 7 years old. The world, I thought, must surely be in some grave danger. As a matter of fact, it was.

But that didn't matter. To be British was to be rooted in

antiquity. We were taught to identify with the past. When Simon de Montfort rode into battle at Evesham carrying with him the seeds of the parliamentary system, we rode with him. When Drake sallied forth to meet the Spaniard off the Scillies, we were there.

The childhood I have described would be unrecognizable to my youngest son. He is not British; he is Canadian. His highways are marked "Alberta," and his mail service, a subject of incessant criticism, "Canada Post." He could probably sing the words to "O Canada," though I'm not sure. He certainly knows the words to a hundred other songs, all of which emanate from California. The Christian symbolism of the Union Jack has been replaced by the pantheistic symbolism of the sugar maple, a tree that does not grow in the west. Finally, though Elizabeth II doubtless figures in the picture somewhere, government to my son is, I suspect, personified in a very different way. Where I had the regal resplendence of George V in his crown, he must somehow sustain his patriotism through the protoplasmic resplendence of Mr. Trudeau in his bathing suit.

In short, they took a working basis of patriotism in English-speaking Canada, Britishness, and replaced it with an obvious absurdity. In desperation men's loyalties turned instead to the homeland. And the homeland is the region. But to blame regionalism for the failure of Canadian confederation would be to mistake an effect for a cause. It would be like blaming the lifeboats for the shipwreck. The passengers, by the way, will not easily give up those lifeboats.
- *April 11, 1980*

The new phony Canada is a Toronto creation

It is necessary these days to be able to distinguish Canadians from what could be called canadianists. A Canadian is a person born or naturalized in Canada. A canadianist is somebody who makes a living describing, defining, defending and declaiming a particular view of this country for the benefit of the rest of the citizenry, usually at government expense. All canadianists are, of course, Canadians. But not all Canadians are canadianists, nor (I suspect) even faintly agree with them, though they had better be careful how they say so.

The great risk, I discovered last week, in criticizing the canadianists is that you will be immediately construed as attacking Canada itself. Any criticism, that is, of the image of Canada constantly emerging from Toronto's arts and media community is assumed to be a criticism of the nation and the national heritage. But as it happens, the very opposite is the case. The central fraud of the canadianist is this: the Canada he purports to show us is not the Canada that exists today. Nor did it ever exist. Nor, one hopes to heaven, will it exist in the future.

For what, when you get right down to it, is the national heritage? How did we get here? Are we not a people who crossed the seas, pushed back the forests, charted the rivers and lakes, rammed the railways through the mountains, broke the prairies, and tamed the barrens of the Arctic? Are we not a people who found gold in the Pre-Cambrian, oil in the Beaufort, and grew food for the world where men could hitherto scarcely find food enough for themselves?

Are we French? Are we English? We are both, and German, Polish, Ukrainian, Dutch, Chinese and who knows what else. Why did we come here? For most, there was a single answer: land. For land, the Carignan-Solieres Regiment established the first substantial settlement in Quebec. For land, the Loyalists came. For land, the eastern Europeans peopled the western prairie. For land, the Chinese built with their blood the railways, the Japanese opened the fishery, and the Jews of Russia created Winnipeg's north end and the thousand cultural endeavours that have flowed from it. What all these people wanted, in other words, was private property, safe from expropriation, safe from tax collectors, safe from thief and marauder. Property, that is, meant freedom, and freedom was worth life itself.

What did we believe? We believed in God. Religion was either the chief motive for, or indispensable companion of, almost every settlement. It was both puritanical and authoritarian, be it the authority of the Bible or the authority of the church. It was narrow, intolerant of non-conformity, and quick to condemn what it viewed as corruptive. But it was not anti-intellectual. Religion, in fact, established our school system. And a tough system it was, sparing neither rod nor child. It knew its goals, and against them it examined pupil and teacher remorselessly, overworking both. Indeed, work was a thing it revelled in, lots of it, with back and brain, dawn till long past darkness, men, women and children included. If a man would work, he should live. If he would not work, he should starve. If he *could* not work, it was up to the community to care for him, generously and positively with the hope that he would one day care for himself.

With the faith came the family. In families we arrived. In families we divided the land. In families we saw our children grow and prosper. In families we found companionship, purpose, comfort, warmth, guidance and an occasional clout on the ear. Was the mother of this family exploited and oppressed? She certainly was. Being exploited and oppressed was at once her burden, her privilege and her delight. That's what motherhood was about. In fact, in a sense, that's what the whole family was about. Either you believed in it, or you didn't.

We believed in it so much we quite readily fought for it, whether in the schoolyard or in the trenches. For we are indeed a fighting nation. Scarcely had the first shots been fired when we plunged into two world wars, years before the Americans, and those years we spent berating them for their backsliding cowardice. We left our blood and bones on the slopes of Vimy Ridge until we had hacked our way to the top of it, something the army of no other nation had been able to do.

We were tied to posts and bayoneted at Hong Kong. We tore through the skies in the Battle of Britain, and we littered Germany with the corpses of our bomber crews. But these were wars of justice and we won them. We do not apologize for this.

Who would have us do so? The canadianists, that's who. For the clear goal of the Toronto media propagandist is to reshape what we are, into something we are not. Every one of the values out of which the country has emerged he repudiates. He debunks our religion and he undermines our families. He tells our women that raising children is contemptible, and aborting them an act of heroism. He plumps and pleads every cause from state daycare to pansy parsons. He lets the killer stalk the streets while jailing parents who spank their children, and he has helped create governments so bloated and beyond control that more than 50 cents of every dollar we earn is required to feed and pamper them.

If sufficiently subsidized he will package and peddle our history. Mostly, however, he's ashamed of it. Our forefathers did not overcome the natural barriers of a continent, they "despoiled" them. They did not break the prairie. They seized it from its rightful owners. They were duped into fighting their wars, and most of their heroes were fakes. Our responsibility as a nation is to abandon the Americans, leave ourselves at the mercy of the Russians (who really aren't that bad, after all), let the trained professionals of government raise our children, and provide bigger and better budgets for the CBC and the National Film Board so they can continue to tell us all these wonderful things.

If we are going to have a Canada, surely the first thing we should do is dump the canadianists. The second is to realize whence we came, who we are, and what we believe. - *April 14, 1986*

Just think: half a dozen 'international' boundaries between Calgary and Vancouver

One of this country's more dangerous attributes is the expanding gulf between the views of the Ottawa bureaucracy and those of the general populace. This gulf is discernible in every area of government, from the state of the fisheries to the state of the deficit. Nowhere is it more evident than in the matter of native affairs, however, and never has it become more noticeable than it did last month, with the release of the latest royal commission report on the native question.

Without benefit of any polls or opinion surveys, I think it's possible to describe the way most Canadians view "the Indian problem." They regard these people as having been exploited. Their lands were taken from them; they were herded onto reserves and thereafter inadequately supported as the official welfare cases of the government. They often live in considerable squalor. Not always, because some reserves are model communities. But many are nests of disease, drugs, drunkenness, violence, suicide, ignorance and despair, which no amount of money can cure because the malady is deep in the souls of the people.

Even so, Canadians feel no great guilt about this. For one thing, nobody alive today was around when the system was established. And most people, whatever they may say, do not feel much responsibility for their grandparents' behaviour - or the behaviour of somebody else's grandparents. Actually, the descendants of 19th-century Canadians probably account for barely a third of the present population.

Moreover, they regard the fate of the Indians as the inevitable consequence of human progress. In the European settlement of North America, an industrial age people supplanted a Stone Age people. The latter lost just about everything. But then, what else could you expect? They must either accustom themselves to the new conditions or perish. There was no preserving the old ones. Assimilation, whether tribal or individual, is the only way to go, and assimilation therefore should always be the aim of government policy. Since the reserve system worked to obstruct assimilation, the reserve system has been a disaster.

Finally, they can also see that when assimilation occurs, the problems usually disappear. They know of native men and women leading very productive lives. They read of well run, prosperous native businesses. They see natives who marry and raise fine families in purely non-native environments. So they wonder if things would not have gone a lot better if the natives had been encouraged to mix with the white community from the beginning.

Meanwhile, the Ottawa bureaucracy, along with the "native movement" it has brought into being and financed, has been heading in the precisely the opposite direction - formulating, and then adopting as sacrosanct, principles that the public has scarcely heard of, let alone endorsed. These now suddenly burst forth in a royal commission report which reflects attitudes and assumptions wildly at variance with public perceptions.

After spending five years and $58 million, the commission proposes that native "nations" constitute another order of government in Canada with their own Parliament and their own legislative authority, whose laws need not be subject to the Charter of Rights and Freedoms. Thus we would have nations within a nation, and natives would enjoy a dual citizenship, having the rights of all Canadians off their lands, and special rights on them. Furthermore, rather than have the specific territorial boundaries of these "nations" established by negotiation, subject to ratification by provincial legislatures, they would be determined by an "independent" lands and treaties tribunal.

There are many other recommendations. Ottawa and the provinces should train ten thousand aboriginal health professionals. Federal resources should insure adequate native housing. All Canadian schools should be required to provide instruction in native languages. Governments should finance an aboriginal arts foundation and an aboriginal youth policy, all entailing an extra $1.5 to $2 billion annual charge on the federal budget.

None of this comes as any surprise in Ottawa, or to the native lawyers and bureaucrats whom Ottawa has brought into being. These are the terms in which they have been thinking for years. But to the rest of the country they sound like something out of cuckoo land. Not only are we to see Canada sundered by the imminent departure of Quebec, but the ROC, the Rest Of Canada after Quebec is gone, is now to be shattered into a myriad of native "nations," so that in driving from, say, Calgary to Vancouver one would cross several "international" boundaries, every one of which would presumably be administering its own laws and imposing its own taxes.

What's more, citizenship in these "nations" would be determined by one factor alone: race. There would presumably have to be heredity criteria to decide who is and who is not a "native," reminiscent of the tests imposed by the government of Germany in the 1930s to determine who was and who was not a Jew. Thus racism, which we have preached against for years while quietly preserving it in the Indian Act, is now to become the basis upon which we will carve up the country into independent "racist" states.

All these, we are told, will formulate their own laws. The way this would work out in practice was very perceptively observed by Trevor Lautens in *The Vancouver Sun*. Bishop Hubert O'Connor, he said, was convicted of sexually assaulting a teenaged native girl about thirty years ago. She was working in the residential school where he was principal. Whether it was an assault was debatable; she had acquiesced. The court held, however, that since he was an authority figure it amounted to assault. So he got two years in prison. Meanwhile, on one Manitoba Indian reserve where the sexual abuse of native children by native adults is known to be rampant, the band council decided to crack down, charging 48 adults with the crime. But they were tried by the new native judicial system, which involves appearing before a native "sentencing circle." All but five were sentenced to a "healing process" that involved nothing so unpleasant as incarceration. The five were jailed briefly, in several cases because they were not sufficiently enthused about being "healed."

So that's the Canada we're establishing, notes Mr. Lautens.

"The Indian goes to a healing circle, his name unreleased, the proceedings undocumented, the whole thing unreported. The non-Indian goes to court and, if found guilty, to jail - his identity clear, the trial usually fully open, his life probably ruined."

The Canadian people are only now beginning to dimly realize what their bureaucrats have been up to. The latter, cocooned as usual in their own peculiar little world, have blithely assumed that the rest of us were going right along with them. Well, we weren't. And this could be the cause of great trouble. - *December 9, 1996*

The undiscovered conservatives whose help may win the war

The CTV network's *W5* show did a fifteen-minute item on our magazines last week which, I have to admit, came as a shock. I expected the usual hatchet job which has occurred every time we have been "exposed" by the head office crews of that Other Network. Instead, the *W5* bunch asked all the hard questions, but then actually ran our answers to them, instead of their own. It was amazing and I am deeply grateful. The other thing about it is, of course, that we didn't pay for it. What really hurts when you are hanged by the CBC is the knowledge that you, as a taxpayer, are paying the hangman. It always seems a bit much.

But on *W5* we didn't get hanged at all, except insofar as we were allowed to hang ourselves. However, there was one error in the presentation - our fault, not the CTV's, but it needs to be corrected. The commentator represented us as declaring that Canada is bringing in "too many Chinese immigrants."

I don't ever remember writing that and I simply don't believe it. The observation seemed founded on a cover story we ran in *B.C. Report* which described heavy immigration from Hong Kong, but I don't think deplored it. I certainly have written that immigration must be very high because our own birth rate is very low. But that hardly constitutes a declaration that there are "too many Chinese immigrants."

I suspect the CTV people leapt to what has become a familiar but erroneous conclusion. Anybody who defends capitalism, deplores the excesses of feminism, opposes the acceptance of homosexuality as an "alternative lifestyle," advocates family values, and is generally conservative must surely also be a racist.

However, the self-evident truth is that of all the groups over all the years who have migrated to Canada, not one has better distinguished itself for hard work, honesty, intelligence, community effort, family values, free enterprise and whole-hearted acceptance of our democratic institutions than have the Chinese.

This thing gets quite personal. I have a young godson, of whom I'm very proud, who is the son of a refugee Chinese doctor. When we started up these magazines we were generously helped by a Hong Kong student who worked particularly hard to make them succeed. For years we were assisted editorially by a Chinese lady lawyer from Singapore. When we moved into B.C. one of our first reporters was the daughter of a Hong Kong immigrant. (In university, by the way, she had specialized in British medieval history.) I'm as delighted as anybody that the lieutenant-governor of British Columbia is a Hong Kong Chinese and no one has ever done that delicate job better than he is doing it.

This sentiment goes back a long way. In 1949 when I arrived flat broke to work for the paper at Timmins, Ontario, I ate for a week on the cuff at a Third Avenue cafe through the generosity of the proprietor who didn't know me from Adam. His name was Gary Fong and he could scarcely speak English. So yes I'm "prejudiced" on the question of Chinese immigration, prejudiced in favour of it. But prejudice "for" is as bad as prejudice "against." Immigration acceptability should be founded chiefly on aptitude. The person who can contribute the most to the country should be chosen first, whether the skin be yellow or black or white.

But there is one other aspect to the current change in the "complexion" of Canada that merits notice. Our immigrants are among the most conservatively-minded people in the country, in particular those from the Pacific Rim, the Middle East and the Indian subcontinent. They work very hard. They open businesses for themselves. They distrust government. And there are no better advocates of "family values" than they. The so-called "alternative lifestyles" which are now so widely advocated through the media are an incomprehensible horror to them, and represent their only misgivings about Canada. They don't want their children poisoned by these ideas.

But it has not yet dawned upon these people that an outrageous felony is being worked on their account by the politicians and bureaucrats. We are continually being reminded by the liberal media that Canada is "no longer a Christian country" because of the presence of all these newcomers. Therefore Christian values, which at one time provided a moral foundation for our law, can no longer justifiably do so. The argument is, as I say, utterly fraudulent. For the values being scrapped on behalf of these people are shared by the people themselves. Indeed many are Christians. If believing in the traditional family, in the restriction of socially acceptable sex to heterosexual unions, in parents (not the state) having the primal responsibility for children, in the virtues of hard work, and in a school system that teaches skills rather than "self esteem," if all these things make you a redneck, then whatever other colours these new Canadians might be, they're all rednecks. That is, they're conservatives.

Now the tragedy is that the political conservatives in this country - whether out of fear, ignorance, habit, sloth or stupidity - ignore them. You do not see them at Reform Party meetings, yet they should be prominent in the membership and leadership. You rarely see many of them at Social Credit gatherings in B.C., yet that is where their philosophy should be taking them. Instead many are lured into the NDP, which solicits their support and caters to them, all the while concealing from them the real implications of its agenda.

From every direction these days we are being given evidence of collapse - political, fiscal, educational, cultural and social collapse. We cannot trust most politicians. Our government cannot pay its bills without suicidal borrowing. Our economy seems verging on disaster and every week we hear of more thousands being laid off. We are becoming illiterate though we have the most expensive schools in the world. Our streets are unsafe, our marriages and families are breaking up, and much of our entertainment is depraved.

But those chiefly responsible for this calamity are not "people of colour." They have white faces and WASP names. They are well intended, but ill informed, dangerously imprudent and spout ideas whose real implications they haven't even begun to figure out. This disease did not come upon us from without. It is very definitely from within. And we may one day find that those now joining us become our strongest allies in the war to recover that which we have lost or thrown away. - *October 5, 1992*

Why my grandmother could revere even Liberals and we find it hard to respect any politician

Heaving her weary frame to the top of the front stairs of her sprawling home in Toronto, my grandmother would pause before a framed photograph. "Sir Wilfrid," she would say, as though acknowledging a presence. Which was odd, since Laurier was a Liberal and my grandmother a lifelong Conservative, indeed the sister of the seven-term Conservative mayor of Toronto, Tommy Church. Needless to say, a still larger portrait of "Sir John" was positioned on the main floor, as well as a bust of Macdonald - the man, Grandma never tired of informing us, who was our first prime minister and who "made Canada."

What brought this to mind last week was the out-of-court settlement of the Mulroney libel suit. The implication is that perhaps the former prime minister wasn't quite the sleaze the media have been portraying. Even so, I can't really envision the day when anybody - anybody outside his immediate family, that is - will admiringly install a portrait of Brian Mulroney, or display a bust of, say, Jean Chretien. We don't revere our politicians any more. It makes you wonder. Have we changed, or have they?

One might leap to the latter conclusion, and assume that Canada produced "statesmen" then, and now mere politicians. But this is nonsense. If sleaze consists of patronage, slush funds, favouritism, cronyism and just plain bribery, there was as much of it, in fact probably a whole lot more, in Sir John's day than in ours. Sleaze by that definition was so much taken for granted when the Siftons ran the west for Laurier that it scarcely called for comment. Naturally Grits got the jobs when their party won the election. What was so remarkable about that? How else could you run a government?

So it has been we, the public, who have changed, not the politicians. Today, we would no doubt tell ourselves, we are better informed; we do not play favourites; we read; on television we see these people up close; we know what's what. In my grandparents' day, unillumined electors admired their leaders because our forebears were ignorant of all the awful things politicians do.

This does not accord with the facts as I recall them, however. Dinner-table conversation at my grandparents' house, in which I spent much of my childhood, consisted of only two subjects - current politics and family gossip. Names like King, Bennett and Meighen came up at every meal and the policies of these men were discussed exhaustively. The tone was never one of adulation, the assumptions were always to say the least sceptical, and the expectations for virtuous conduct as doubtful for the politicians as for assorted members of the family. A grave pessimism always obtained. And I have every suspicion that in a still earlier era, when the names of the day were Laurier and Macdonald, the attitude was exactly the same. My grandparents' generation, in short, were not politically naive patsies for propaganda. They knew as much about politicians as we do - perhaps even more. Yet they could still revere them and proudly display their portraits. They could still have heroes. Why was this, I wonder - and why can't we?

I think it has to do with our education. In my grandparents' day, Christian assumptions still provided the foundation for moral teaching. We humans were assumed to have been created by a good God. But God gave us free will, enabling us to choose between doing good and doing ill. We are capable of both great good and great evil, and in various ways and degrees we only too frequently choose to do evil. Even so, some of us, often despite powerful adverse influences, manage to accomplish remarkable things. Laurier may have been a religious opportunist, Catholic where it paid politically and not a Catholic where it didn't. Nevertheless, he made possible modern Western Canada. Macdonald may have been a drunk. Nevertheless, he envisioned and brought to reality an entire country. So people hung their pictures and acknowledged their accomplishments, for our inheritance from them is very considerable indeed.

The modernist, however, seems able to make no such allowance for human foible. While he may never come right out and say so, he cherishes a certain impossible expectation of human conduct. For him, people are bound to be either good or bad, saints or scoundrels, famous or infamous. And since no one can ever meet his lofty standards for the good, he lives in a state of perpetual disillusionment. Thus we elect our leaders, swoon over them briefly until the flaws begin to appear, then denounce them as frauds and consign them to villainy. Since they were not entirely good, they must be entirely bad. Whether we admit it or not, that's the way we now think.

Take, for example the letter that appeared last month in Alberta's Sun newspapers, from a senior production executive of the CBC in Toronto. I had written a column for the Suns, noting how all the special documentary programs on the CBC seemed to fix upon some dreadful deed of Canadians, real or supposed: abuse of children in Catholic orphanages, callous neglect of Vancouver prostitutes, the cover-up of the murder of an Indian girl, our military record in the Second World War, how respectable Anglicans ignored the sexual abuse of choir boys, and how Catholic tradition denigrates women. Why, I had asked, can't our national broadcaster ever find anything good about us? The CBC man replied: "Mr. Byfield could find support for his opinion in a prominent twentieth-century theory which holds that drama should say only positive things about the society in which we live and the government that rules us. It's called socialist realism. Its chief proponent was Joseph Stalin." Notice the assumption: Either we must have total blackwash or total whitewash. There can be nothing in between.

This same attitude is also built immovably into the minds of the human rights policemen. Our own magazines, for instance, are repeatedly accused of "disseminating hatred" because we preserve and assert the historic principle that the practice of homosexuality is morally reprehensible. This means, say the rights people, that we must hate homosexuals. Actually it means nothing of the sort. It means that we believe this is the way some human beings go wrong. Others, ourselves very much included, go wrong in other ways, possibly worse ones. But in the modern view, to find any fault is to find total fault. People must be either admirable or contemptible. Nothing else is allowed. If you hate the sin, you must *per se* also hate the sinner.

My grandmother, raised a Methodist, would never have understood such an attitude. That's why, having at last reached the top of the great staircase, she could pause to admire Laurier. Even if he was a Liberal. Even if he was, like the rest of us, a sinner. - *January 20, 1997*

Chapter Twelve

The Deplorable Unrest in the Colonies

"Some people may actually be proud when they cheat the government. Far from regarding tax evasion as reprehensible, they consider it positively virtuous. Beating the GST is their "good turn for the day."

- Ted Byfield, 1993

The budget: a political payoff venting an unbridled hatred

People rarely collect mementoes of pivotal historic events. We may, for instance, treasure a copy of the newspaper that was published on V-E Day when the war in Europe ended, but we did not keep the paper that recorded the Battles of Alamein or Stalingrad when the outcome of the war was actually decided. Few kept papers from those fateful October days in 1929 when the worst depression of the century got under way. And the first flight of the Wright Brothers became barely a squib in the back of *The New York Times*. Yet, if we had thought to keep such things at the time, they would have been much valued later. For this reason we would be wise to keep copies of the Alberta papers from last week. History will one day record that it was on Tuesday, October 28, 1980, that a government of Canada by act of deliberate policy tried to destroy the prosperity of the one section of the country that had escaped the recession and offered the best hope for the whole nation's future. At the same time it indentured the country to the Middle East's oil producers and brought its own oil industry to a catastrophic halt. Historians will be hard pressed to find anywhere an act of government so irresponsible, so vindictive and so insane as that which was produced last week by Mr. Trudeau and his thugs at Ottawa. So save the papers. You will show them one day to your grandchildren.

What a calamitous year it has been. Think back to only last November. At that time the final touches were being put on an oil agreement between the then Conservative government of Canada and that of Alberta. Had that agreement been allowed to stand, consider what the situation would have been today. The Cold Lake and Alsands plants would have been going forward at full throttle. Exploration would have been proceeding on the whole northern and eastern rim of the continent. The pipeline construction would have been under way as would the exploration of the further reaches of the Deep Basin which hold such great promise. Oil rig operators would have been desperate for men. Investment capital, reaching across the whole west, would have been opening new jobs and new opportunities. Billions of dollars in equipment orders would have been streaming forth to central

Canadian plants, and our provinces would have been working hand in hand with the federal government towards a goal which everyone would have clearly understood - oil self-sufficiency by 1990. All that could have been.

But it was rejected by the voters of Ontario as "incompetent" policy. Instead they have wished a pestilence upon us all. They preferred government by thugs because the thugs said they would continue to supply the cheapest gasoline in the world. They voted back into power the rump of the old Liberal government which every respectable Liberal politician had long since abandoned because it was starting to smell. These sinister people - the devious Coutts, the malevolent Pitfield, the crafty Goldfarb, the turncoat Argue, the sycophantic Olson, the fevered Lalonde, the bilious MacEachen, the preposterous Axworthy - these now run the country, and what a job they're making of it. Investment capital pours across the border to the U.S. The oil rigs follow, those that can make it, because ten per cent of the drilling contractors are said to be going broke through lack of work. Hiring comes to a stop in Calgary because the explorers have lost all confidence in government. Dome Petroleum, discoverer of the Beaufort, entrepeneur of the Deep Basin and one of Canada's top two home-grown oil companies, watches its stock crash down as the thugs advance "Canadianism" in the oil patch. Instead we have the loathsome "Petrocan" spreading its bureaucratic fat all over downtown Calgary, bringing to the oil industry all the notable efficiencies of the post office. Development stops on the tar sands plants. We buy sludge in Mexico at top prices while our own low-grade plants cut down production for lack of customers. Our consumption of oil soars ever higher while that of every other industrialized country in the world goes down. More and more we enthrall ourselves to the rapacious Arab and Mr. Lalonde hastens to explain that all this represents "sound energy policy." And if we can't bring ourselves to believe him, Mr. Goldfarb will explain it for him with our money.

Why have they done this to us? Why have they made Tuesday, October 28, into the blackest day in Alberta history? There are, I believe, two reasons.

First, they must at all costs stay in power. Power comes from Ontario and Quebec. The purpose of the budget was simply to pay off Ontario and Quebec at the expense of the western provinces. But beyond this there is another reason, one that seethes in the heart of Pierre Trudeau. People say that he is indifferent to western Canada, and this may once have been true. I think it is true no longer. He now has a keen feeling about us because we have so long and so decisively told him that we want neither him nor the gang of toadies around him. For this he now hates us, and passionately. It is a hatred that runs to the roots of the man's being. It is the hatred of the socialist for the individualist, the cold fear of the high-born for the self-made, the aversion of the theorist for the pragmatist, the derision of the urbanist for the peasant, the disdain of the intellectual for the uncouth, the contempt of the Gaul for the Slav. All these hatreds have helped to dictate the posture of the Trudeau government towards the west, and on Tuesday, the 28th of October, they were paraded before the nation in the form of public policy. - *November 7, 1980*

The technique of Ottawash and how I became a victim

I learned last week that I have become a victim of a process known as Ottawash. The Ottawash technique is akin to the brainwash technique, except that it is less violent, much subtler, and has a different history. Where the brainwash process was developed by the Stalinists, the Ottawash process was developed by the Trudeauists. Where the brainwash process involves the use of drugs, usually on people who have suffered some great adversity, the Ottawash process involves the use of propaganda, usually on people who have suffered some great prosperity. Where the brainwash process operates on people who cannot help themselves, the Ottawash process operates on people who can but don't.

There are many examples of Ottawash at work - the vilification of the oil industry, the blackguarding of the Crosbie budget, the perpetration of the rights charter, and so on - but its veritable triumph occurred in what is called metrification. One would have thought that the infliction on a whole people of a hundred petty irritants every day without explanation by a coterie of remote bureaucrats acting for a government they didn't elect and obviously despise would have caused, to say the least, some sort of outrage or rebellion. Not at all. For a long time the only reaction was a contempt for those rustics considered to be "backward," and those industrialists considered too grasping to recognize the untold benefits that their far-off masters were conferring upon them. These were branded as bigots, kooks and clowns and told not to sit in high places. The explanation for this astounding public gullibility is Ottawash. And even as you read this, if you find yourself groaning, "My God, he's joined the anti-metric movement," go now and look in a mirror. You will be beholding another victim. You, too, have been Ottawashed.

Who made me aware of my afflicted condition was that woman I married. She is herself immune to Ottawash, utterly and sometimes terrifyingly immune. She disclosed my own sad condition when she suggested I do a column on the "insanity" of metrification. "Oh, come on," I said, "what's really so wrong with metrification?" She looked at me startled. "What," she asked icily, "is right about metrification?"

Now this sort of question leads to the only known antidote to Ottawash, a cure which its practitioners do everything possible to prevent their victims from discovering, namely the habit of thinking for themselves. The Ottawashers do not want their victims to ask whether any proposed policy is useful or useless, practical or impractical, affordable or unaffordable, good or bad. They want instead to concentrate our attention on whether it's the kind of policy that would be approved of by advanced people, whether it is "reflective of contemporary attitudes," whether it will be perceived as "forward-looking," whether it is "compatible with the modern world view," everything but whether or not we need it - which, of course, in the case of metric, we did not.

It is therefore difficult to recall the reasons cited for metrification because the most notable thing about the metric debate was the fact that it didn't happen. Or if it did, it was poorly covered because few seemed to have realized what we were getting into. Suddenly it was there. We were buried in kilometrage. In retrospect, however, one may surmise that two justifications were advanced. For one, it was a decimal system throughout and therefore simple. For another, everybody else was doing it. Both, however, were flawed.

It is true, no doubt, that metric is easier for a child to learn than the English system which is no system at all. Nevertheless we all seemed to have survived the learning of it. What is not at all simple is the process of changing from one system to another. Hence if simplicity is itself a value, it argues against metric, not for it. And as to the argument that we should follow the crowd, this also now appears to have been a mistake. For us, the part of the crowd that matters is the American part. So sharp has been the U.S. reaction that the programme has been shelved, depriving us of the economies of scale which U.S. participation was supposed to provide.

The positive side of metric is turning out therefore to have been an illusion. The negative side, however, is as real as ever. There are three arguments against it, and their significance is growing, not diminishing.

First, it is an appalling expense, thrust upon an economy that cannot and should not have to sustain it. Whether it's the conversion of heavy industrial gear, or the replacement of farm equipment, or the acquisition of new scales for grocery stores, the costs are both steep and senseless. They do nothing immediate to increase production. They may in fact never increase it.

The second discredit derives, not so much from what was done, but from how it was done. To slip some white paper through the commons without real assurance that the public in fact knows and approves of what is going on is typical of the slipshod deviousness which Ottawa so widely represents to this country. People didn't know, and they had a right to know. The proper answer to this kind of tyranny is defiance. We long for a grocer who simply tells Mr. Trudeau what he can do with his kilograms. The man might go to jail, but half the town might march there with him.

Finally, the programme was ill-advised because it meant one more change in an era which is already changing too much. Everywhere things which connect us to our past are vanishing. Much of this is good, of course, because much in the past was worth changing. But the process has gone too far, so that today nearly all the thousands of little elements that held society together are disappearing, and social and psychological chaos is resulting. In such an era we should change nothing we do not have to change. Miles and pounds are important simply because our parents and grandparents thought in terms of miles and pounds. We do not want to lose all touch with them because our own stability depends upon our links to our own heritage. Without roots, the tree falls. The metrification programme is severing another root. But few see this. Like me, they were Ottawashed.
- *April 12, 1982*

One question every westerner has to be ready to answer

How are we going to convince Ontario and Quebec
that it [the Triple-E Senate] is in the national interest?
- Nova Scotia MP Howard Crosley

Here we have in one single, neat question the central problem of the politics and economics of hinterland Canada. The occasion of this rhetorical inquiry was the meeting at Edmonton of the Joint Senate-Commons Committee on Senate Reform. The Alberta and Edmonton Chambers of Commerce had stated the case for the "Triple-E" Senate in Canada, that is of a Senate that would be (a) Elected, (b) Equally representative of each province, and (c) Effective, meaning that it could veto any bill passed by the Commons. Such a Senate exists in the two other great resource-producing democracies of the world - the United States and Australia. Such a Senate does not exist in Canada and the whole squalid history of exploitation by central Canada of what Manitoba Senator Duff Roblin calls "Outer Canada" is the consequence.

That consequence has continued for a century. Whether we're talking about the destruction of the economy of the Red River colony in the 19th century, or the near destruction of the Calgary oil industry in the twentieth, the fact is that neither one would have happened if Canada had a Senate like that of the United States or Australia. Discriminatory freight rates, deliberately intended to retard industrial growth in the west, could not happen. Tariffs which protect the central manufacturing sector at the expense of the western resource exporter could not happen. This was the case made by the two Chambers of Commerce and eight other presentations to the committee, and Mr. Crosley's question was the logical rejoinder. How can either Ontario or Quebec be persuaded to support such an erosion of their own overwhelming power in Canada?

The answer becomes obvious if we recognize two elementary facts of Canadian economic life:

First, just as Canada is a nation of dual cultures, French and

English, so too it is a nation of dual economies, a central manufacturing and consumer economy in the central region where most of the people live, and a hinterland resource-producing economy in the outlands where relatively few people live. If the power of government is based purely on population, therefore, the populous consumer area will always and inevitably exploit the resource producers. They will not do so because nice people live in the hinterland and nasty people in the centre; it is the unavoidable outcome of the situation. If the west and the Maritimes had most of the people, they would certainly take similar advantage of central Canada. It is simply the way human beings behave.

Therefore, when Ontario or Quebec have something to sell they automatically command either the international price of those products, or sometimes a price even greater than the international price. But when the west wants to sell oil in a time of shortage, it is compelled by the same centrally controlled government to sell at far less than the international price.

Various constitutional guarantees provided for the smaller provinces means, as it turns out, nothing at all. Mr. Trudeau has set the precedent of legislating into law an outright invasion of provincial revenues, thereby demonstrating that no one can stop a determined central government. If you or I break the law, the police can arrest us. If the federal government breaks the law, who can arrest it? And now that a blatant invasion of provincial rights has succeeded, any successive government, whether Tory, Liberal or NDP, can be expected to do the same thing. That is one of the sad rules of life. Successful behaviour repeats itself. Just as we lost control of the grain industry to Ottawa in the Thirties, and the oil industry to Ottawa in the Eighties, so now we are being warned that we are about to lose control of our livestock industry to Toronto and Montreal, and the way is paved for the loss of the coal, hydro-electric and the forest products industries in the future. The precedents are there. That is the first fact to be absorbed.

The second is this: while the west can prosper without central

Canada, central Canada cannot survive without the west. Alone, southern Ontario and Quebec are a mere adjunct to the eastern American industrial complex, much of their manufacturing facilities in fact obsolete. Without the resources and markets of the west, Toronto or Montreal have the economic potential of a Harrisburg, Pennsylvania, or a Syracuse, New York. The west on the other hand has grain, livestock, oil, gas, metals, timber, fish, fruit, every resource an economy requires. It has the technical expertise to manage these resources, and - once liberated from the interminable and frequently irresponsible interference of Ottawa - it would have access to the foreign capital necessary to develop them. In other words, to put it crudely but accurately, we do not need central Canada and they very much need us. That is the second fact to absorb.

How, then, can we persuade Ontario and Quebec to approve the Triple-E Senate? The answer is that we must first make every westerner thoroughly conversant with these two facts of our economic life. From these, he will rapidly come to see that three choices lie before us: we can turn Canada into a true federation like the United States and Australia by instituting a proper Senate to protect the hinterland regions. Or we can opt for an independent country in the west. Or we can go through the twenty-first century, as we did through the twentieth, as an economic colony of that crowded tiny triangle that lies between Toronto, Ottawa and Montreal. Once they see this, I suspect, most western Canadians will assign their priorities in precisely that order. First they would prefer to be Canadians in a true federal system. Failing that, they would choose independence. The one thing they would not abide is the perpetuation of the present injustice.

If that thinking even begins to take root in the west, central Canada's approval of the Triple-E Senate will be both certain and swift. They dare not risk our secession. - *October 10, 1983*

Hire your five hundred auditors, Ottawa, but spare us the moral appeals

When Victoria MP David Anderson took office as Canada's minister of National Revenue back in November, he embarked on a kind of conscience-raising mission. The "underground economy," he said, now totals as much as $56 billion a year. "It is no longer mom and pop. It is becoming very major."

True enough, Mr. Anderson announced that the government was hiring five hundred more auditors to crack down on tax-evading Canadians. These would be added to the existing departmental staff of 33,000. However, the minister's remarks at the time were not exactly threatening. They were more in the nature of a moral appeal. "We've got to change the attitude that tax avoidance is tolerable behaviour," he declared. He plainly wanted Canadians to feel guilty about it.

But they obviously don't. So twelve days later Mr. Anderson's tone changed. He now spoke more menacingly. His department, he said, is planning a big crackdown. He wants some "high-profile cases," prominent people who have failed to pay the tax on goods or services they've bought. He wants to make an example of somebody. Which is, of course, the old formula used to stifle rebellion in the navy: "Hang one man."

Now this failure of Canadians to feel guilty about tax evasion is not merely part of Mr. Anderson's problem. It is the very heart of it. The minister says tax evasion is growing worse, which can only mean that more and more Canadians find it "tolerable."

Indeed, it may go farther than that. Some people may actually be proud when they cheat the government. Far from regarding tax evasion as reprehensible, they consider it positively virtuous. Beating the GST is their "good turn for the day." Denying the government money becomes their contribution to the prosperity and well-being of Canada. An otherwise law-abiding citizen might acquire a carton of smuggled cigarettes, calculate the tax on it, and send this sum to his favourite charity, just to demonstrate to himself his motive is not pecuniary. Even though the purchase price goes to the underworld, he reasons, it will do far less harm there than if it were to fall into the hands of the government.

The point I'm trying to convey is this. If Mr. Anderson tries to terrify us into paying our taxes, he may superficially succeed. He will no doubt catch some people, although the high cost of extra auditors will sadly diminish the return to the treasury. But if he attempts to shame us into compliance with appeals on behalf of "our government," his task is frankly hopeless. It has been years since what goes on in Ottawa could claim to be "ours." It's "theirs," they being the collective bureaucracy, lobby groups and media liberals who manipulate and run it. The role government fulfils for us ordinary people, if any, is closer to that of an enemy.

For though Mr. Anderson himself has spent most of his life in government, and no doubt believes in it wholeheartedly, many of the rest of us do not. We do not think government is a good thing. We do not believe government on anything like the present scale is even a necessary thing. We believe government, or what it has turned into, to be an actively evil thing. Therefore the less money it gets, the better off the country. In such a circumstance evading taxes becomes a public-spirited gesture, an act of benevolence for the common good. Instead of putting tax evaders in jail, maybe we should give them the Order of Canada.

Now this view is admittedly extreme, and yet I suspect it is not far removed from the common, if unarticulated, perception. Look at the results of the referendum of 1992, for instance, wherein all the governments in the country told us to vote yes, and we voted no. Look at the results of the federal election, when a party dedicated to the division of Canada swept one province, and a party dedicated to a total top-to-bottom change in government, including an awesome reduction in its scale, swept two others. These things evidence scorn.

There need be no mystery about why this scorn exists, and why government has become so odious to those who are required to pay for it. Many of us can look back thirty years to a time and condition when the scale of government was astonishingly less. Things worked all right then, we think. We had medicare. We had UI. We paid our way. We had almost no debt. But since then government has swollen grotesquely, driving us into more than half a trillion dollars in debt, much of it owed to foreign bankers. People who won't be born for another twenty years will, as adults, still be paying for what government has spent in these disastrous thirty years.

And for what? What do we have to show for it? What is government doing now that it didn't do then? What single thing did we get out of the whole Trudeau-Mulroney era that we couldn't have done without? The answer, it seems, is very little. True, we have hundreds of new services, but most of us didn't ask for them, few of us want them, and the majority of us would unquestionably have refused them if we'd ever had a chance to vote on them - especially if we knew their eventual price.

The result is the subconscious but keen resentment of a people who sense themselves defrauded. And this resentment is what works against Mr. Anderson, or anybody else who takes on his thankless job. However many auditors he hires, that resentment will continue. Governments can collect taxes if the people who pay them consider those taxes to have been levied fairly, that we are paying for what we ordered. But in Canada there is a growing discernment that we have been ripped off, that things were done "for our own good" by people who assumed they knew better than we what we need. So we were simply saddled with these unwanted "services." Suddenly there they were: sought by the lobby groups; contrived by bureaucrats; and expounded, defended and extolled by the liberal media.

Now Mr. Anderson protests that we sense no shame when some of us defiantly seek to escape paying for them. He wants us to feel guilt. This is a bit much. Let him thrash us into line with his augmented army of auditors. Let him find his high profile cases. Let him hang his one man. But spare us all the high moral appeals. If some of us seek to avoid paying for what most of us never ordered anyway, we do not feel guilty, not in the least. - *December 20, 1993*

Chapter Thirteen

The Distinct Society

"In the coming year when we are again assailed over the 'rising spectre of separatism in Quebec,' maybe we should adopt a new attitude. We could call it the 'Bon Voyage Movement.' We love you, we might say to Quebec, but we are not prepared to bribe you anymore. If you want to stay in, then be satisfied with what you've got. Otherwise, best of luck. Have a great trip."

\- Ted Byfield, 1989.

With Premier Don Getty in 1989.

The 'racism' of Olds-Didsbury and what it actually means

It was informative to learn last month how our prime minister explains the victory of a separatist in an Alberta by-election. You and I might have thought it was because of federal energy policy, or agricultural policy, or transportation policy, or a hundred other outrages inflicted upon that half of the country which refuses so steadfastly to vote for him. But apparently we were mistaken. The celebrated prime ministerial power of perception has already discerned that the vast majority of voters in Olds-Didsbury are what he calls "racists." They hate French Canadians. Observations like this no doubt explain why so many Toronto and Montreal intellectuals increasingly regard this man as a sage. They also explain why so many western farmers and oilmen increasingly regard him as a jackass.

Let us therefore explain to this man (if he should ever read it) what is the attitude of many of us in western Canada on three subjects: French Canadians, bilingualism and the bilingual policy of his misbegotten government. We regard these three entities quite distinctly.

To begin with if we westerners were to "hate" French Canadians we would have to do so as a man would "hate" his own body - his hand, or his arm, or his eye. They are part of us, and among us, and have written some of the great pages in our story. It was their ancestors who beat the first paths out here. With scores of other groups, they broke the sod of the prairie, weathered its bitter winters, and grew the first grain. Lacombe is a patron saint, and a century after Riel we begin to sense what he sensed and confront the same insensitivity eastward. They watched dismayed as their own interests were sacrificed to those of Quebec, and it was the electors of that province who doomed the French schools of western Canada. Still, they persevered and grew with the west, giving us some of our best jurists, our best clergy, our best physicians and our best entrepreneurs. To say that we "hate" them is to talk lunacy. There is a drycleaner in Edmonton with 22 branches named "Trudeau's." If money can be made in Alberta with that kind of handicap, then this surely bespeaks tolerance. (One assumes the relationship is distant.)

On the second issue, that of bilinguality, we are far less enthused than we were a dozen years ago. Fluency in a second language is an enviable advantage, though some would prefer German or Ukrainian to French. Nevertheless, I'm told that no province outside Quebec invests more per capital in bilingual instruction than this one, and French immersion courses are so popular they sometimes disrupt public school routine. But all this dates from another era when federal governments felt they had to "sell," rather than legislate, bilingualism. We were easily sold; we wanted to believe. I remember when the little town of Warburg exchanged visits with students from a similar little town near Quebec City. So endeared were the Warburg farmers to their visitors that some shed tears as the latter departed for home. And I know a teacher who spent eight years developing a specifically Canadian French course for English-Canadian pupils, its whole ethos based on Canadian, rather than Parisien, usage. If we speak English with a Canadian accent, he argued, then why shouldn't we speak French with a Canadian accent? He recruited the help of western French radio broadcasters in making hundreds of tapes for youngsters to listen to until they understood and he travelled to Quebec to find them summer jobs in a French environment. It was a task born out of an irresistible affection for French Canadians. (Who could drink beer better?) I know this because I was that teacher.

Then came The Sage. We are told out here that he incarnates the Gallic. What he incarnates is the Cynic. He has no more in common with the warmth and resolute faith of rural Quebec than he has with the same qualities as they appear in rural Alberta. He is as far removed from the habitant as he is from the cowboy, but unhappily neither knows it. To him, of course, all this falderal of weeping Warburg farmers, student exchanges, and summer employment was a silly waste of time. The idea was to legislate, to hammer it into us, to accomplish in five or ten years what would otherwise take a century. If the western rubes objected, he would scream "racist" and all the lily-white liberals would gasp, raise their eyes heavenward, and pronounce, "Amen." Thus we entered the new era, the era of bilingualism by jackboot. It is to this that the west objects with great vigour and with great reason.

There are, in fact, two reasons. The first is the essential difference between central and western Canada. If the whole country consisted of two provinces, one French and one English, each with a great city, and a capital city between them reflecting both, then perhaps a case could be made for compulsory bilingualism. Such, of course, was once the case. It is so no longer. Of the six or seven major cities in the west, only one has a French tradition at all, and even there it has all but vanished. If a government suddenly tries to impose on these an official and compulsory language that is not spoken widely within two to four thousand miles that government will quickly come to be viewed by the local populace as "foreign." This does not prove the populace racist, only human. Suppose some government tried to force Montreal to speak, say, Cantonese on the grounds that the Chinese played such an important part in the development of Vancouver. What, the Montrealers would ask, has that got to do with us? That's what people are asking in Vancouver. Mr. Trudeau says it makes them all racists.

Our second objection is this. It effectively places the possibility of senior office in the federal administration virtually beyond us. The English youngster growing up, in say, Calgary simply does not now, nor will he ever, have the same opportunity to learn French that the French youngster growing up in Montreal has to learn English. The only possible outcome of this therefore is to remove the federal civil service ever farther away from people in the west. Again, the operative word is "foreign." More and more you sense that attitude towards Ottawa. It is not because we are racists. It is because we do not like being discriminated against, and we do not like being pushed around.
- *March 8, 1982*

Here are a few percentages Mr. Masse hasn't mentioned

If politics are, as they say, the art of compromise, well the west certainly has a bevy of artistic beauties in the House of Commons. Consider, for instance, the illustrative story of Bill C-72, Mr. Mulroney's most recent gift to Quebec, passed earlier this month with thunderous applause from all parties over the negative votes of nine Tory members. Four of these are slated for retirement, the other five for undoubted political execution at the earliest possible moment.

The purpose of this bill was to further fulfil the bilingualization of Canada in general and the Canadian government in particular. Its opponents, originally forty but bludgeoned down to nine by the time the bill came to a vote, had an incontestable argument against it: if fluency in both languages is an essential of all senior civil service positions, then the top echelon of the civil service must of necessity come from Quebec.

This need not be the result of francophone chauvinism, but the inescapable consequence of our cultural geography. It is an incontestable fact that people raised in places like Montreal become bilingual as a matter of course, whereas people raised in the west can only learn a second language with great effort and skill, exercised from the earliest years and constantly practised. Since only one in eighteen Alberta youngsters, for instance, is now registered in "immersion" courses, and half of them will drop out before they're finished, this means that twenty years hence only one Albertan in 36 will have the same opportunity at a senior federal job as virtually any person raised in Montreal. Such is the case. How do the proponents of the bill respond to it? Very simply, they do not. They murmur about "racism," and "holding Canada together," and "the unexplored potential of French immersion," and they change the subject. With the passage of Bill C-72, the government may reflect the outlook, values and culture of one province alone, but it's a long way off, and we have an election to fight.

But is it that far off? Look at the civil service now. The francophone proportion of the population is 24.3 per cent. (Francophone, remember, does not mean someone who can speak French. It means someone for whom French is the language used at home. Many of the French-Canadian families of the west - that of Jacqueline Picard, for instance, after whose grandfather the controversial Edmonton school was named - are now deemed anglophone. Francophone, in other words, nearly always means "from Quebec.") It follows, therefore, that a fair proportion of francophones in the federal civil service would be about one in four, or 25 per cent. It now stands, in fact, at 28.2 per cent. It was 21.5 per cent in 1965. That's disproportionate but not ludicrously so. But now examine certain key areas in the public service, and a very different picture emerges.

Of deputy ministers and senior administrators the proportion is now 32 per cent francophone. The Privy Council Office is 48.2 per cent francophone. The Federal-Provincial Relations Office is 49.1 per cent, the Canadian Intergovernment Secretariat a resounding 81.8 per cent. The big-spending Department of Supply and Services, which decides whether a contract will go, say, to Montreal or Vancouver, is 41.1 per cent francophone. The Secretary of State Department, which hands out federal largesse, is 67.9 per cent. The Public Service Commission, which chiefly decides on promotions within the civil service - will the job go to Peter Black from Winnipeg or Pierre Leblanc of Trois Rivieres? - is 60.5 per cent francophone. And if the francophone proportion of the armed forces during the Second World War was somewhat lacking, the francophone proportion of the Department of Veterans Affairs compensates. It is 41.2 per cent francophone.

All of which raises another question. When the Department of Energy or Petro-Canada falls short of the 24.3 per cent francophone quota, we hear much loud protest from Mr. Masse to stop hiring Calgarians and bring that francophone proportion upward. Why are we not hearing similar yowling from the ministers in these other departments to bring it downward? Where is the watch-dog Commissioner of Official Languages? Why is he so much more sensitive to francophone under-representation than over-representation? Perhaps that's because the commission itself runs 74.1 per cent francophone.

Almost as bad as the Elections Canada Office which is 82.5 per cent francophone, but better than the Supreme Court of Canada staff which are 65.3 per cent francophone, while the court itself is 45 per cent.

What we are unquestionably beholding over the past twenty years, in other words, is a francophone takeover of the federal civil service which Bill C-72 is designed to further. Mr. Mulroney deftly sought to avoid inflammatory controversy by quietly introducing it for passage without debate in the dying hours of last fall's session before the Christmas break. The story of how a handful of MPs stopped him with midnight telephone calls and all-night car rides back to Ottawa has been told by this magazine.

The bill was thereby forced to undergo committee hearings, and 157 witnesses served notice they wanted to testify, 47 from the western provinces. The committee in fact heard 21 (a dozen the government's own witnesses) all very much in favour, and six from private groups also supporting the bill. Of 87 witnesses opposed to the bill, the committee heard three. Of the 47 western witnesses, one was allowed to speak. (All you westerners need to do to get clout in this country, Pierre Trudeau used to say, is to send government members down to Ottawa. Ho, ho, ho.)

With a few minor face-saving amendments to give the forty Tories who had declared against it something they could talk about, the bill became a law. Manitoba MP Dan McKenzie was symbolically fired from a parliamentary post for voting against it.

What does it all prove? Two things: First, the country as presently constituted is a farce. An overwhelming majority of westerners are unalterably opposed to what is taking place because they are being denied any significant role in the future government of Canada. But, as in the case of the CF-18 contract two years ago, their supposed representatives in Ottawa again prove utterly incapable of checking the influence of Quebec. Whether we are represented on the government benches or the opposition makes no difference. In the real politics of Canada, we do not matter.

Second, how did Quebec gain such power? Simply by saying

unmistakably, "Change the system, or we'll get out." Saying it and meaning it. Not until we take that lesson wholly to heart have we the slightest chance of playing any significant role within this country, or the way it is governed. - *July 25, 1988*

The next time Quebec yowls let's hear a big 'bon voyage'

Run your eye over Canada's print media last year and you will discern three current versions of what people are thinking in Quebec.

First there is the "Toronto view," meaning the one shared by the Toronto media such as *The Globe and Mail*, the *Toronto Star*, the *Calgary Herald* and *The Edmonton Journal*, along with all respectable liberal intellectuals, and those university professors and political commentators regularly quoted by the CBC.

According to the Toronto view, Quebec has at last come of age. It has abandoned its servile adherence to the Catholic Church, stopped having hordes of children, raised its educational standards, adopted a progressive, tolerant and sensible attitude on just about everything, and will - once Meech Lake is approved - accommodate itself comfortably and permanently within a bilingual and idyllically liberal Canada.

Second, you have the "Quebec view," shared by the French Canadian intelligentsia, the intellectual Quebec press and many in the new Quebec business establishment. It goes like this: some 228 years ago, when we Quebecois were a colonial people who had hacked a livelihood out of the North American wilderness in the interests of French imperialism, we saw the forces of France defeated on our own soil and ourselves abandoned to an exploitive and heretical enemy. This enemy moved in upon us, took all the best houses and jobs, and made plenty of money by the sweat of our brows. Through patience, diligence and determination we have preserved our language, institutions and culture intact, rid ourselves of most of the Anglo business establishment and replaced it with one of our own, and become a nation in every respect but the formality of political sovereignty. We now need only wait for the opportune moment to declare that sovereignty to the world. That moment will come when (a) we are economically self-sufficient, and (b) we are being required to put more into Anglo Canada than we can get out of it. In the meantime, we must strengthen our economy by every possible means, develop trade with the world and particularly with the Americans, derive anything we can from what remains of our association with the Anglos, and make sure that those elements which unite us, language foremost among them, are in no way compromised.

Third, you have the "western view," shared by Prairie yahoos, bigoted Bible-belters, fossil-minded right-wingers, intellectual dinosaurs, cattle ranchers, the oil industry, the odd surviving British imperialist, and this magazine. According to it, Quebec is not part of Canada and never has been, and it will remain in confederation only until this ceases to pay, or alternatively until Canada can be made part of Quebec. Therefore the best response to Quebec's recurrent threats to depart is to let it go.

Now the point to note about these three views is that the Quebec one and the Western one are largely the same. Both see Quebec's role in Canada as distinctly terminal and both see the Quebec position on constitutional questions as consistent with a people who seek sovereignty. The only disparate version is the starry-eyed Toronto one whose adherents cling to it for dear life as wave after wave of disconcerting evidence rolls in against them.

The latest wave is the current and utterly predictable Quebec response to the Supreme Court decision on Bill 101. First the court, reflecting, of course, the Toronto view, invokes the Charter of Rights and Freedoms, and throws out the Quebec bill. Next Quebec, correctly sensing a threat to its indispensable purity-of-language laws, opts out of the charter. Once again we have the usual weeping, wailing and lamentation in the Toronto media. Quebec has failed the vision again. How could it do this to us? How could it do this to Canada? The possibility that Quebec might do this because it doesn't give one sweet damn about Canada is not anywhere considered. That does not accord with the vision. But what it wholly accords with is the western vision, and with the Quebec one also.

Then we get the Manitoba response to Quebec's opting out of the charter. Manitoba will kill the Meech Lake accord. Since the whole point of Meech Lake was the appeasement of Quebec, and Quebec acts the way it does about minority language rights, why should Meech Lake be approved? asks Manitoba's premier. A good question. Then notice the immediate reaction of Quebec's premier. He "hates to think" what will happen if Meech Lake is turned down, says Robert Bourassa. "Canada will suffer more than Quebec will suffer." In other words, more of the old threats. Play the game our way or we'll get out. Now you've done it, wails the Toronto media to Manitoba. You've once again raised "the ugly prospect" of separatism in Quebec. Already, that is, Toronto is preparing to pay whatever price Quebec demands.

So we begin the new year with yet another "constitutional crisis" manufactured by Quebec. Well, for a change here are some different thoughts we might entertain about it:

1. A Canada without Quebec is not as unthinkable as we used to suppose. The language idiocy would end. Quebec would speak French and Canada would speak English. Quebec City would be a French-speaking capital and Ottawa would be an English-speaking capital. The Quebec police would speak French and the Mounties would go back to English, as would the post office, the CBC, the air traffic controllers and several hundred thousand other civil servants.

2. In a Canada without Quebec, the west would be the dominant partner, the Pacific would become our forefront trading area and Vancouver would gradually become the dominant financial city.

3. In a Canada without Quebec, the tax transfers which now channel billions of dollars into Quebec would channel them instead into the Atlantic provinces, the North and the Prairies.

4. In a Canada without Quebec, the railway head offices would move out of Montreal to the west where most of the railway operations are conducted. Air Canada would probably move back to Winnipeg where it was started, as would the CF-18 contract.

Now none of these things strikes me as all that disastrous for western Canada. Some might even see them as downright good. So in the coming year when we are again assailed over the "rising spectre of separatism in Quebec," maybe we should adopt a new attitude. We could call it the *"Bon Voyage* Movement." We love you, we might say to Quebec, but we are not prepared to bribe you anymore. If you want to stay in, then be satisfied with what you've got. Otherwise, best of luck. Have a great trip. - *January 2, 1989*

Odd how the federal leadership seems largely a Quebec affair

The speculation about who will succeed Mr. John Turner as leader of the Liberal party reveals what is nowadays called the *realpolitik* of Canada. That is, it shows us how Canadian politics really works, as distinct from how it is ostensibly supposed to work.

In the school textbooks, for instance, any Canadian from any part of Canada might gain the prime ministership and hang on to it. In reality, it is becoming wholly evident that a prime minster, in order to win and remain long in office, must of necessity come from one province alone, namely Quebec. This was not always so, but it has certainly been the condition for at least twenty years.

Hence the favoured candidate to succeed Mr. Turner is Mr. Chretien who comes from Quebec. His closest rival is Mr. Paul Martin Jr. who also comes from Quebec. These two will compete to decide who will oppose the Conservative Mr. Mulroney who comes from Quebec. And if Mr. Mulroney should retire before the next election, it is the accepted wisdom that the only Tory candidate who could hope to compete against either Mr. Chretien or Mr. Martin must likewise come from Quebec. That is the *realpolitik* of Canada.

Similarly there have been only two distinctly successful prime ministers since 1968. They are Mr. Trudeau and Mr. Mulroney, both from Quebec. And there have been two distinctly unsuccessful ones. One is the Conservative Mr. Clark who came from Alberta and could form only a minority government which was ousted after nine months, largely because he produced an energy policy that subverted the interests of Quebec (and Ontario) to those of the west. The other is the Liberal Mr. Turner who sat for a Vancouver constituency and was defeated after three months because Quebec turned decisively against him in a general election.

Indeed, Mr. Turner is one of the last surviving specimens of a creature that could be called Old Liberal, now otherwise extinct. Having been educated in British Columbia, practised law in Montreal, and been in business in Toronto, he would seem to fulfil the Old Liberal all-Canadian ideal. Not anymore. In the new Canada, the PM must not only be fluent in French, but he must *sound like Quebec*. Mr. Mulroney is "The Boy From Bay Comeau," and Mr. Chretien is "The Boy From Shawinigan," and Mr. Turner was "The Boy From Bay Street," which is almost as hopeless as being, as Mr. Clark used to call himself, "The Boy From High River."

Now these observations will not appear in most Canadian media. The fact that Canadian leadership campaigns have largely become contests between the citizens of a single province is not the sort of thing our pundits are prone to dwell on, or even point out. They might be called "racists" or "bigots" or "rednecks" or "illiberal" or "divisive," and that is usually enough to spook almost any one of them into quailing submission. So the issue - why always Quebec? - may never arise anywhere else.

But I don't myself think it's anti-French racism to point it out. That is, I don't think Quebec's astonishing accomplishment in making itself, as it were, the decisive arbiter of Canadian political leadership, proves anything whatsoever against Quebec. If a province, whose French element at this point accounts for about a fifth of the whole Canadian population, can so engineer things that every national policy and even national party leadership cannot be determined without its approval, then surely this calls not for contempt but for admiration. It's a Gretzky-class performance. One man dominates the game. To do anything but cheer would be churlish.

But if we're going to go on with the game ourselves, it behooves us to see how they do it. Quebec, after all, is represented in the Commons on about the same scale as the four western provinces. Why does the Canadian *realpolitik* not require that the next Liberal leader come from the west? Why Quebec? I think there are three good reasons.

First, Quebec has a national, not a provincial, identity. It has its own language, history, culture, media, even its own CBC. Its provincial legislature is called the "National Assembly." Could you imagine the reaction if B.C. renamed its legislature "The National Assembly of British Columbia?" We would think confederation had come to an end. Yet with Quebec it is accepted. It is a nation apart. It is not *in* Canada; it is *in partnership with Canada*, a very different thing, and it is now the senior partner.

Second, it always puts the nationalistic issues ahead of the political issues. That is, the first question it asks of any political leader is not, "Is he of the right or of the left?" but, "Will he stand up for *us*?" Liberalism, conservatism, NDPism, mean nothing in comparison. What matters first is Quebeckism. Mr. Clark did not answer well to that question, nor did Mr. Turner. Mr. Trudeau, whatever he said for consumption elsewhere, was never doubted. Mr. Mulroney had to prove his loyalty and did. Thus the Manitoba language decision, thus the CF-18. The west meanwhile dithers between left and right, national cause vs. provincial cause, Conservative vs. Liberal vs. NDP, hopelessly splitting our vote and rendering ourselves inconsequential on the national scene.

Finally, Quebec is one province and we are four. Therefore, where Mr. Bourassa alone speaks for Quebec, Messrs. Filmon, Devine, Getty and Vander Zalm speak for the west, each representing a somewhat different interest, and often saying quite different things. Similarly, Mr. Bourassa can choose - in fact, probably did choose - whether to use the undoubted clout of the provincial party to support or oppose his federal Liberal colleagues. That he chose to support the Mulroney Conservatives nationally is now plain. Western Tory premiers have no such option. If Mr. Mulroney whistles, party loyalty requires that party premiers jump. But Mr. Turner could whistle all he likes, and Mr. Bourassa does not have to hear him. Federal parties come second in Quebec. What comes first is us.

So what do we do about it? How do we, too, get effectively into the game? The answer, surely, is obvious. We must begin to think and vote regionally. We must develop the western view, and the western regional presence in Ottawa. Not a presence that can be fobbed off with assorted phoney "funds" and welfare programs, but one that the *realpolitik* is compelled to take into serious account. And happily, the way to do just this is already before us. It is called the Reform Party of Canada. Put forty or fifty of its people in Ottawa in the next federal election, and strange new and respectful attitudes towards us will mysteriously begin to appear. That, after all, is what Quebec taught us. Let's learn the lesson. - *May 15, 1989*

The psycho-profiles of Bouchard and Quebec
carry a vital message for the premiers

A journalist friend of mine took a job in central Canada this summer which involved working with a number of young journalists from Quebec. "You wouldn't believe these guys," he told me last week. "They assume that separation is an all-but-accomplished fact. What's more, you cannot reason with them. They've bought into a kind of cultural mystique. For them Quebec is not just their home, it's an overwhelming cause. They see themselves as 'a people' and they are very serious about this. And they see us as standing in the way of the realization of this dream."

Now my friend is given to dramatization, which makes him a very good radio and television producer but prompted me to somewhat discount his reaction - until I read precisely the same conclusion from an entirely different source. The psychological profiles of Lucien Bouchard and of Quebec nationalism, published this week over the name of Dr. Vivian Rakoff, former director and psychiatrist-in-chief at the Clarke Institute and professor emeritus at the University of Toronto, depict and explain exactly what my friend had encountered. They have crucial implications for western Canada.

Dr. Rakoff very convincingly shows us that in dealing with Quebec we no longer face the merely rational pursuit of self-interest. Nor are we contending with the irrational. We are confronting the non-rational, the Hegelian "folk culture" that can seize an entire people. Dr. Rakoff has long studied this phenomenon: its "yearnings grounded in blood, history, ancient wrongs, triumphs, martyrs, songs and the sense of a shared fate," which cause "the prickling of the skin, the tears in the eyes, the moody exaltation of a banner-waving, anthem-chanting crowd, joined in the mystical unity of a folk identity."

This fervour, he says, is not what Quebec chooses to show the world. To outsiders, it offers instead a rational case based on language alone. Canada consists of two founding peoples, Quebec argues, harnessed together out of what was once political and economic necessity, but the French one is at a permanent disadvantage. If only the two could separate, however, genuine cooperation would be assured. The new Quebec is thereupon "packaged" and presented to the world as a "late twentieth-century pluralist state that includes Haitians, Jews, allophones and anglophones, bound only by the use of French as the *lingua pura*," and with all these minorities protected by the current conventions of tolerance and understanding.

However, "when the pressure is great, the rational shell of pluralist territoriality cracks and the true impulse leaks out like involuntarily exposed lava. The French-speaking Haitians and Algerian Jews, the allophones and the anglophones are told, "We know who you are, and you are not us!"

We witness this, says Dr. Rakoff, when we see Louise Beaudoin [Quebec's minister of intergovernment affairs] "barely containing her bitter hatred, blazing anger, saying to the camera - to us in the rest of Canada - 'It isn't enough to love us. Recognize us!' " Or when we see the tipsy Jacques Parizeau, after losing the referendum by less than one per cent, bitterly blaming Quebec minorities for the defeat,

"An essential component of the politics of desire is the politics of resentment," Dr. Rakoff explains. "It grows from deep feelings of hurt. Insults, deprivation, humiliations are its nourishment. And because these insults, etc., are often as symbolic as they are real, they cannot be adequately apologized for or made to fade with recompense. The politics of desire in action is irredentist, expansionary, punitive. It must move the goal posts because it is an addictive need for something almost transcendental which cannot be fed by ordinary positive stuff."

Now if Dr. Rakoff is right, and this is the horror that Ottawa must contend with, it is no wonder that the Chretien crew seem so totally stymied by it. How do you counter it? What do you offer instead? A better than ever deal from Canada, they say. We have had Quebec prime ministers for 27 of the last 29 years. In the last House, the leader of the opposition, the leader of the Tory party and the minister of finance were all from Quebec, but this is nowhere near enough. So, now we must offer them still more - a permanent veto upon all future constitutional changes, and the constitutional designation of Quebec as a distinct society, meaning whatever the Supreme Court decides it means. This is the Ottawa "solution."

The premiers, particularly Alberta's Ralph Klein, have another idea. Mr. Klein says he knows Lucien Bouchard. He's sure he can make a deal with him. Certainly, Mr. Klein would no doubt concede, there is a certain fanaticism abroad in Quebec, but Lucien Bouchard is above all this. He might exploit it, but is not himself committed to it. Therefore, when the premiers meet in Calgary this month, Mr. Klein will press for a "Calgary Declaration" to offer to Quebec, and the pragmatically realistic Lucien Bouchard will promptly forget all about Quebec's national aspirations and accept it.

Unhappily, the Rakoff profile of Mr. Bouchard eliminates any such possibility. Mr. Bouchard not only identifies with Quebec's aspirations, he embodies them. "He is them [Quebeckers], he speaks for them. When he addresses them, starting slowly and then moving into a more rhythmic, declamatory style, he doesn't so much tell them what he thinks, as articulate more nobly and passionately what they already think and feel. He is a kind of gifted national poet who, in speaking of his own particular desires, speaks of the yearnings of the general community. And if he is at one with Quebec in his [personal] history, sentiments and loyalties, then acting in self-interest is acting in the interests of Quebec."

Put these two pieces together - the Quebec profile and the Bouchard profile - and a certain pessimistic conclusion becomes inescapable. We are not likely by further bribes to cajole Quebec into remaining very long in Canada and we could easily cripple ourselves in the attempt. If fifty per cent of Quebeckers were prepared to vote separatist even under the absurd Mr. Parizeau, and another twenty per cent voted "No" only because they thought the time had not come quite yet, then it is altogether probable Quebec will secede. And what the premiers should be primarily considering is not, "How can we get them to stay?" but far more importantly, "What will we do when they leave?" They might also remember the costly lessons learned the last time (i.e., about sixty years ago) that we had to deal with a "folk culture" on the march, namely that it regards every gesture of appeasement as weakness and every concession as an opportunity to demand more. If we forget this, the "Calgary Declaration" might better be named the "Munich Declaration."

Only the Reform Party now thinks in these terms. Mr. Bouchard calls them "dangerous" - and dangerous they indeed are, to him and "the folk" anyway. Too bad he doesn't consider the premiers dangerous as well. - *September 8, 1997*

Chapter Fourteen

The Time Has Come

"If any reader of this magazine has been haunted for the last seven years or so by the conviction that government in this country is stacked against the west, and that there's nothing we can do about it, well at last it's possible to contradict him."

-Ted Byfield, 1987.

A pariah of all the parties has a compelling proposition

These are very dark days for western Canada. Step back for a moment and consider what is happening to us. A constitution is being forced upon us over the protests of eight provincial governments which reduces our four provinces to second-class status and breaks our tenuous hold on our resources. An energy program has been thrust on us that apparently seeks to nationalize our most lucrative industry, and cuts us off from the sources of foreign capital which we used to develop that industry. In Ontario a plan is now advanced that will require us to "Buy Canadian" no matter how much cheaper we can get the same materials overseas. Every possible effort of government is being assembled to break the growing power of the western financial community and reassert the ascendancy of central Canada as the control point of the country.

We find no recourse within the present political system. The western Conservatives cannot obstruct the Liberal constitutional coup because the Ontario provincial party is supporting it. The western wing of the New Democratic Party is equally paralyzed and the pleas of the premier of Saskatchewan and a handful of courageous members of the party's federal caucus are simply ignored. As for the Liberals they have fashioned themselves into the club with which Quebec and Ontario hold us at bay. Separatism offers no hope. Not only is it unsaleable, it seems to attract unto itself a racism that is both morally wrong and historically ignorant. No group on the prairies has been more ill used by central Canada than have our western French Canadians by the province of Quebec. Yet they have become the butt of this racism and that is unconscionable.

The future looks darker. Having established the pattern with the National Energy Program, central Canada will now extend it to all the resource fields. We can expect grain to be produced "for the benefit of all Canadians," meaning of course at far less than the "artificial" world price. We can expect freight rate policies to be maintained that will assure that the food processing industry continues to move to central Canada. We can expect no trade concessions for our food and petrochemical industries because these could only be negotiated at the price of concessions to foreign manufacturers which, of course, would adversely affect Ontario and Quebec industry. So that will be that. Anyone watching the march of events in Ottawa for the past year who cannot see this happening is simply blind, richly deserving the contempt in which our prime minister so obviously holds us. There is "nil chance" of the west doing anything about it, he says, and he proves once again to be absolutely right. Or so it seems. Lately, however, something has been happening that provides a distant but very real hope.

There is in Edmonton these days a man who is proffering a solution. When I first heard his ideas I dismissed them. They were attractive but too outlandish to ever really happen. Yet the more I thought about them the sounder they seemed to be, and every development at Ottawa makes them more attractive still. I can suppress this sentiment no longer.

The man is Dr. Hu Harries, the former Edmonton Liberal MP, much deplored in conventional political circles. The NDP dislike him because he is an economist who is not left-wing. He is very much a free enterpriser, who runs a cattle business, a trucking business, and the best known consulting firm in the west. He even qualifies under Jack Horner's odd criterion for the true westerner. He can not only ride a horse; he is one of the most accomplished horsemen in Alberta. The Tories hate him because he ran three times for the Grits. He served one term and quit in disgust because, he said, the Liberal establishment is incapable of even considering western interests. He ran again because he believed one of Mr. Trudeau's early seventies recantations towards the west. He ran a third time after Mr. Trudeau promised to retire but then didn't. Finally, the Liberals hate him most of all because he has refused to go along with the farce of their much proclaimed "concern" for western problems and has become, in fact, one of their most devastating critics. He knows them inside and out.

And what does this much-despised pariah of the political

establishment envision? He sees a new party, a coalition of those who have concluded that we are in a no-win situation. He knows such a group could never form a government, but this doesn't bother him. The Grits and the Tories, he says, are bound to split the rest of the country in the next election, and a thirty- or forty-seat bloc from the west would inevitably hold the balance of power between them. That way it could barter its support to either party, and gain for the west those policies of government which otherwise we will simply never achieve.

Fanciful though this may seem, it has very impressive historic credentials. The Progressives of the twenties achieved more for western Canada than any group before or since, and they were just such a movement. Even the control of resources upon which the Alberta boom was built was an achievement of the Progressives. For once, we decided to act on our own, rather than to attach ourselves as the largely irrelevant adjunct of a political organization whose chief concerns lay in Ontario and Quebec.

Do it again, says Dr. Harries, but he declines to offer himself as the leader of such a group. Whom does he see leading it? Obviously he cannot say, though it is not too hard to imagine. He sees a major multi-partisan movement, led perhaps by a Mazankowski, or a Romanow, or a Gordon Gibson from British Columbia, or a Nystrom, or even by a Lougheed or a Blakeney or a Lyon.

I asked ten friends representing all three parties what they thought about such a plan. The result was intriguing. All ten said they didn't think it could happen. All ten said they would vote for it if it did. One of them, a hyperactive Tory who goes back to the Roblin days in Manitoba, shook his head. "Too much to even dream of," he said. "Would you vote for it?" I asked. "Vote for it!" he replied. "I'd work with every ounce of energy I have to get it elected."

Perhaps some genius will come up with a solution within the present party structure. That would be preferable. But if none appears, the chemistry is there for the kind of upheaval we have seen in the west before. - *April 17, 1981*

Five more conditions which a western party should meet

The proposal I made for a moderate western political party that was neither separatist nor radically left or right but dedicated to western objectives and the Triple-E senate seems to have achieved the remarkable feat of satisfying absolutely nobody. Western separatists say it ignores mathematical reality; Quebec and Ontario would instantly coalesce against and outnumber it in the Commons. Conventional Conservatives say that such a movement would only erode the Tory vote, thereby electing the Liberals or NDP. Liberals say the west's best interest lies in switching back and forth between themselves and the Tories, each time collecting the election bribes.

Then we have Mr. Patrick O'Callaghan who devotes most of a page in the *Calgary Herald* to the western problem, first reciting a litany of Alberta grievances, followed by a conclusion that a western party wouldn't work because Social Credit didn't, followed by warnings about western separatism. What's missing of course, is any sort of solution. An interesting response comes from the thoughtful Mr. Bruce Busby, editor of the Banff *Crag and Canyon*. He dolefully concedes that the present system doesn't work, but concludes that the Triple-E won't either because nothing does unless it serves Quebec and Ontario. His solution is to await "the natural course of political events," what he calls "evolution." Unhappily, however, we have already seen what happens in the "natural course" of political evolution in Canada. The Atlantic provinces went into confederation as the most promising region in Canada. Within a half-century they were reduced to a state of near penury, chiefly through the unbridled domination of central Canada. In the end their bare survival depended wholly on hand-outs from Ottawa. That is what is in store for the west, too, if we wait upon "evolution" to take care of us.

Finally, I have received a letter from Mr. Ernie Jamieson, the independent candidate in the Pembina, Alberta, federal by-election and a former Tory MLA whose election would do more for the western cause right now than all our provincial governments put together. Anyway,

Mr. Jamieson wants me to dream on. What sort of a western party would I accept as "credible," he asks. Very well, I will try to tell him.

First, I think it should consist, as do most populist movements, largely of people of no previous political identity. Populism, that is, springs up like grass in a bare field; hence, I suppose, the term "grass-roots movement." It should not represent an amalgam of also-rans from previous elections and old parties. It should be fresh, untried, naive, gullible, clumsy, unpolished, chaotic, honest and wholly convinced that it is right.

Second, it ought to have trouble finding a leader, not because no one is convinced enough, or able enough, to do the job, but because of the humility of the membership. No one wants to push himself forward because all are alert to the dangers of internal division and strife. This also characterizes populism. William Aberhart did not advance himself as Social Credit leader until he had been in fact leading that movement through all its formative stages. In the farm movements of the Twenties whole parties were elected leaderless to majority control of provincial legislatures.

Third, when a leader is finally chosen he ought to meet two qualifications. For one, he would best not be an Albertan, since the reputation of Alberta for producing extremism hopelessly prejudices his chances in the other provinces. For the other, he would be Jewish. Not only do Jewish people have a fine, and much merited, reputation for effective bargaining, and bargaining would be the central function of this party, but the fact of a Jewish leader would discourage the weirdo element that seems so inevitably to attach itself to such movements in Alberta. The James Keegstras of the province would not feel impelled to join.

Fourth, this party should not - in its initial stages anyway - run provincially, only federally. There are a number of reasons for this. In the tension natural to Canadian politics (because there is no Senate), provincial governments invariably find themselves opposing federal governments. If this party did not invade the provincial area it would soon attract the the tacit sympathy and support of provincial governments, even though their federal wings might be in power at Ottawa. Again, if it did run provincially and did come to power in one province, it would promptly become known as the party of that province, where in order to succeed it must be the party of the whole west. Only in the later stages, when the constitutional amendment supporting the Triple-E senate had gained parliamentary passage through its coalition with a major party, ought it to turn its attention to provincial politics, and then only if a provincial government threatened to oppose the amendment. In short, I think such a party could soon become the expression of provincial governments at the federal level, the first step in securing the Triple-E.

Finally, I do not conceive of such a party as having permanence. Its mission would be to change the system. When the system was changed, it should fade into history, its work done.

Has such a party any chance whatever of occurring? Curiously the man who writes against such a chance, Mr. Busby in the *Crag and Canyon*, sets forth the one condition upon which it could happen. "Nothing except a trauma equivalent to the Depression of the Thirties will trigger a populist party of the kind Byfield envisions," he writes. And I entirely agree with him. He, however, obviously thinks that such a depression is highly unlikely.

I wish I could agree, but I don't. You do not need a degree in economics to see that we seem to be entering a period of vast surplus in everything we produce out here, whether grain, or oil and gas, or minerals, or coal, or even forest products whose usefulness is constantly narrowed by other materials. We must do everything we can to avoid it, but it seems blind optimism to conclude that it cannot happen.
- *September 15, 1986*

The time for talk has departed, the time for action has arrived

If any reader of this magazine has been haunted for the last seven years or so by the conviction that government in this country is stacked against the west, and that there's nothing we can do about it, well at last it's possible to contradict him. There is something we can do about it, something very definite. And if we miss the opportunity, our children and theirs will suffer the consequences of our omission.

The "Western Assembly on Canada's Economic and Political Future," called for May 29th to 31st in the Hyatt Regency Hotel in Vancouver, may well prove a turning point in the history of the west and of the country. I've heard a lot about it, and have had a very small part in the planning. Everything I've heard and seen has been reassuring. For instance:

• The three people so far announced for its steering committee are all of solid accomplishment: Mr. Preston Manning, son of the former Alberta premier, is a reputable business consultant and economist. Mr. Stan Roberts is a former Manitoba MLA, former vice-president of Simon Fraser University, former president of the Canadian Chamber of Commerce and of the Canada West Foundation. Mr. Robert Muir is past president of the Canadian Petroleum Law Foundation and former general counsel for Dome Petroleum. The names of the other five steering committee members have not been announced, but there is every reason to believe they will be of the same calibre.

• They are putting policy before politics. Their plan, that is, calls for specific proposals on senate reform and other constitutional change, federal contractual spending policies, resource control, freight rates, research and development, and changes to the banking system. They want these proposals developed by people of unchallengeable authority. They want them responsibly debated, amended if need be and adopted, so that a program for change emerges that can be both widely advocated and articulately defended.

• They are screening the delegates to the Assembly. The reason is obvious. It is both unfair and inaccurate to dismiss earlier movements for western change as irresponsibly led. Some in these movements certainly deserved such criticism. But the vast majority were capable people of genuine concern for the west. However, it is these very people who today favour the screening process. Delegates are to be nominated by citizens and reviewed by nomination committees in each province. They want sixty delegates from each of the four with sixty more chosen at large.

• They have at this stage no specific plan for direct political action. For a number of reasons this is wise. First, many people in the established parties would feel treasonous in attending if an intention to form another party had been declared. Second, all three parties can, if they want to, present their own proposals to the Assembly. Finally, the decision follows established precedent. The great farm movement of the First World War era, for example, long refused to "go political." It felt the established parties should take up its cause. When it finally did form a party, however, its accomplishments during its decade-long regime were awesome. It won for the prairie provinces control over their resources. It won the statutory freight rate on grain. It forced the removal of the tariff on farm equipment. That's why anyone who contends today that a western party can't do anything has an argument with history. But the political initiative came last. First came the policies. And policies are what this Assembly hopes to formulate.

• They have stayed away from provincial politics. All their policy propositions are in the federal field. This, again, is sound. It means that provincial governments, all of which by the very nature of the Canadian system are pitted against Ottawa, will naturally look upon this movement as an ally, rather than a threat. It means that provincial Tories in Manitoba, Saskatchewan or Alberta, and Social Crediters in B.C., can freely take part in the Assembly. It means that provincial governments can furnish it with information. (Indeed by merely mentioning its existence, and implying support for it if it should "go political," the provinces can themselves use the movement to their own advantage in all negotiations with Ottawa.)

Where the Assembly could go from the Hyatt Regency is already clear. After a summer of refining and spelling out its program, it can call another, bigger meeting for October. At this one, it could name an "advocate" in every western constituency. The advocate's job would be to put the assembly program before every municipal council, constituency organization, service club, community league and chamber of commerce in the west, explaining, arguing, and selling. Since he would represent no political party, giving him a hearing would not pose problems of precedent. This process would take a year. If by the end of it, some federal party seemed to have unreservedly embraced the Assembly's program, then its work would have arrived. But if none had responded, then the time for politics would be there. Every "advocate" would suddenly become a candidate.

Neither is it altogether unforeseeable that some of these advocates may be sitting MPs. As this is written, Mr. David Kilgour of Edmonton has appeared in the Sun newspapers declaring his disenchantment with the federal Tories. He is the first western MP to do this. One doubts he will be the last. But he isn't sure where he belongs - whether in another party, whether as an independent, or whether out of politics altogether. I know where he belongs. He belongs at the Hyatt Regency on May 29th.

So what can we do? First, talk about it. Tell your neighbours, your business associates and friends that the Assembly is happening. Second, nominate delegates, persuade people you know who should participate to do so, that the west needs them urgently and now. Third, go to Vancouver. The Sunday meeting is public. It should be supported volubly. In other words, we have been whining long enough. The time has come to act. - *April 13, 1987*

After ten years, the Western Assembly's eastern venture is still in grave doubt

It was exactly ten years ago that about eight hundred people gathered at the Hyatt Regency Hotel in Vancouver in what was billed as "the Western Assembly." They came from the four western provinces, and they all had grievances.

Manitobans resented the fact that a key aerospace defence contract had been conferred on a Montreal company even though the armed forces recommended a Winnipeg one. Saskatchewan had complaints over grain marketing and freight rates. Albertans were still seething over the Liberal National Energy Program, which the Mulroney Tories were quietly maintaining. British Columbians had the same grievance they'd always had: being generally left out of the Canadian confederation.

I was not a dispassionate observer. I gave the keynote speech that opened the assembly. After a full weekend of intense discussion, it adjourned until the fall at Winnipeg where it became the Reform Party of Canada.

Two people emerged at the assembly as possible leaders. One was the late Stan Roberts, a former vice-president of Simon Fraser University and former president of the Canadian Chamber of Commerce. He was backed by the Edmonton philanthropist, Francis Winspear, who had put up $50,000 to help finance the meeting. (Mr. Winspear died this year.) The other was business consultant Preston Manning, son of the former premier of Alberta. Mr. Manning clearly showed the most promise. He spoke articulately, though not passionately. His ideas on policy were well considered and well stated; he knew where he was going and why. He easily gained the leadership and has retained it ever since.

Something else was less evident, but equally important. Nearly all participants in the Vancouver and Winnipeg meetings were (a) essentially western regionalists, and (b) both fiscally and socially conservative. Mr. Manning was neither, and has never tried to hide the fact. He did not aspire to build a western party but a national one, and he said so. And he was not a conservative, but a populist. He said that too, though it seemed abstruse academic theorizing at the time.

Thereafter he took the party in the directions he wanted it to go. It was an amazing accomplishment - gutsy, even brazen. Here was a party created to be one thing and he made it into another, carrying the rank and file with him. The big question remains, however. Can he carry the country as well? Unless the polls are grievously wrong, the answer will be no. Despite a very impressive and convincing line-up of national policies, what began as a western assembly will probably remain a western assembly. Ontario isn't interested.

Why so? I think the explanation may be found in the second Manning departure. Canada doesn't need a populist party, for the sufficient reason that it already has one. It's called the Liberal party.

The term "populist" as "popularly" understood - and that's the only way I can understand it - means this: that the best authority for deciding public policy is popular consensus. Ultimately, the people, the populace, are more likely to know the best course than anyone else. Government should therefore emerge from the people, rather than impose its will upon them. Naturally there will be "expert opinion" on almost any subject. But this expertise must pass the test of popular assessment before being adopted. Clearly our whole concept of democratic government is infused with populist assumptions.

But populism is not conservatism; there is actually a profound difference, indeed an incompatibility. The conservative begins with a different assumption. All sane human beings, he says, are endowed by nature with an ability to perceive what is good, and true, and beautiful. We may disagree in some respects about these things, but in the main we display a remarkable unanimity. We agree that honesty is good and fraud bad, and that we should think of the interests of others as well as our own, that we should tell the truth, that we should keep promises, and so on. Similarly we agree on the rules of reason - that the same man can't be in two places at the same time, that (as the old axiom decrees) equals plus equals equal equals, and that you can't have your cake and eat it too. Finally, and most controversially, we have wide agreement on what is beautiful. Modern art may challenge this but only briefly; in the end a striking sunset or a sombre dawn will move us all in much the same manner.

Now the first priority of government, says the conservative, is to conserve in public policy these universal values. Civilization itself depends upon them. If they are seriously shaken or lose due respect, chaos will inevitably follow, and all history bears this out. The conservative therefore is not entirely guided by popular consensus. He believes, that is, that two plus two equals four. Told that "informed opinion" currently feels it should equal five, or that the latest Angus Reid poll shows that 68.7 per cent of decided Ontario voters are persuaded it equals three, he will not be impressed. Even if the whole country tells him it equals nine and a half, he will stick stubbornly to four. Such is the conservative.

Can populism and conservatism happily co-exist as the root philosophy of the same political party? As long as popular consensus reflects the traditional view, they can. But when it challenges the traditional, as it now does on every hand, painful schism occurs. That is what afflicts the Reform Party.

It has also gravely weakened Mr. Manning's appeal in Ontario. The really talented populists in Canada are, after all, the Liberals. "Find out which way the parade is going and put yourself as the head of it." That advice is attributed to Mackenzie King, who was recently identified by a panel of intellectuals as Canada's greatest prime minister. He was certainly our most adroit populist. How can the same Liberal party which initiated our vasty array of social programs, people wonder, now so serenely preside over their dismemberment? That's simple. Liberalism is populist, and this year the parade happens to be going the cutback route.

Yet in our best moments we don't respect politicians who try to find out what we want in order to offer it to us. We look for leaders who appear to know what's needed and try to persuade us to follow them. Can a westerner accomplish this in Ontario? One did. In 1957 and 1958 a Saskatchewan country lawyer named John Diefenbaker swept Ontario because he had a vision for Canada which people embraced. He didn't ask them what they wanted; he told them what they ought to do, and they believed him. Neither did he acquire a new coiffure because some poll showed it would endear him to young people. He was undisguised and unashamed to be a plain lawyer from Prince Albert, and young people flocked to his cause.

The flaw, in other words, lies in the Manning populism. Most Reformers aren't populist. And if there's anything else at hand and credible, neither are most Canadians. - *May 5, 1997*

Is Manning learning French to win Quebec?
Or could it possibly be to win Ontario?

The vision of Reform Party leader Preston Manning earnestly taking French lessons this summer has about it a certain quality of cuteness. Here he is, at age 55, delicately shaping his lips to pronounce "u" as in "tu," a sound that does not exist in English. There will be other indispensables: how to order a meal in the parliamentary restaurant, how to greet a Quebec MP in the corridor. And those special necessities of parliamentarians: how to adjourn the debate, how to answer the question without answering the question. Yet beyond all the cuteness lies a puzzle: why exactly is he doing this?

So that he can come to understand Quebeckers, he says. Give us a break. A crash course in French will not make him, even peripherally, one whit better able to understand Quebec politics than he is already. And as he will discover, the subtleties of meaning involved in discussion of the most elemental political issue cannot be acquired in a six-week crash course, however immersive. If he can't actually speak French, he hopes to at least be able to understand the spoken language, he says. Well, he won't. Understanding a language is much harder than making yourself understood in it.

(I know something about this, though not much. I taught French to English-speaking students in the St. John's schools for ten years, even composing a four-year course, with massive amounts of English-to-French translation based on Quebec history. I found jobs for anglo youngsters in Quebec, and for Quebec youngsters in the west, to help them gain fluency. In pursuit of jobs I once addressed the Quebec City Rotary Club - in fairly rudimentary French. Being courteous people, they did not laugh out loud. I was very pro-Quebec back then, when Quebec was still Quebec, before it decided to become Sweden-on-the St. Lawrence. I still retain something of the language, but find I can't begin to deal with the current political crisis in French, whether speaking it or listening to it.)

Now, according to media reports, Mr. Manning has already been advised of this unpromising outcome for his efforts, so the question

"Why?" still remains. He says he hopes it will help him gain access to the Quebec vote. Come on! Will Quebeckers be so enthralled with the efforts of a middle-aged politician to acquire their language as to be overcome with gratitude and admiration? Not too likely. Or maybe feel sorry for him, giving him entry to the province on a sympathy vote? Less likely still. Quebeckers doubtless realize better than we do that we are approaching what could easily be the most politically decisive year in Canadian history. The Bouchard government will surely go to the polls next spring. If it is returned, which is altogether probable, the referendum will follow that might very well end Canada as we know it. And what is the leader of the Reform Party doing? He is learning to say "*tu.*"

Since all this must be entirely obvious to Mr. Manning, it is hard to believe that his summertime linguistic labours have anything to do with Quebec. So could he have the west in mind perhaps? Are the people who account for one hundred per cent of his caucus terribly keen that he should learn French? This proposition truly defies belief.

No, we must look farther for Mr. Manning's real purpose - namely, to enhance his image in Ontario. He is pretending to ingratiate himself with the Quebec voter because he hopes this will actually ingratiate him with the Ontario voter. He must reason that Reform failed to take a single Ontario seat because he was viewed as a threat to national unity, a closet Quebec-hater, waiting vulture-like for Quebec to leave the country so the Reform Party can take over what's left of it. This certainly was the way both the Liberals and Tories tried to portray him. But see him now! Actually learning to speak French, he is. Doesn't that effectively disprove all the ugly talk that he's an anti-Gallic bigot? Bigots don't learn to say "*tu.*" Thus the rationale.

One discerns once again the touch of the handlers, those experts around him at Ottawa, the "people who know," the same who masterminded the Ontario campaign and who for reasons incomprehensible remain on the payroll. Register Preston in the language class, they have cleverly plotted, and put out a press release. How nauseating! And really, how transparent!

Unhappily, "the people who know" plainly do not know the central reason for such success as the Reform Party has achieved. The

Reformers have been elected and are respected chiefly because they do not play the usual political games. They are not given to striking poses, smothering issues in meaningless rhetoric, or saying one thing in one part of the country and the opposite in another. They have a record of facing issues squarely and taking specific stands. That's why they ran those controversial television ads on the Quebec domination of Ottawa. If Canada's political system is so ordered that a successful prime minister must always come from the same province, there's something wrong with the system. That's a fact, and they said so. No federal system can work if one of the provinces is designated as special, either. That's another. And any deal with Quebec must be approved by referendum among all remaining Canadians. That's a third. The Reform policy program contains dozens more. Reformers say what they believe, and people vote for them out of conviction that they will act on those beliefs.

This may not seem the politically clever thing to do, but it has high credentials in the annals of democracy. In the early 1930s after Hitler came to power, a lone figure stood up in the British Commons and demanded immediate war with Germany for violating the terms of the Versailles Treaty. He was booed and jeered, denounced in the press, and deplored by sensitive, well-meaning people as a dangerous warmonger. But events of the following six years hideously vindicated him, and in the dark hour when everything he had warned of began to happen, the people turned to him as the only person who all along had dared to tell them the truth. His name, needless to say, was Winston Churchill.

A dark hour for Canada is approaching. What matters now is not how Ontario will vote in the next election, but if the country will survive at all. At a minimum we will have to renegotiate Confederation, perhaps in a Canada that includes Quebec, and perhaps in a Canada that doesn't. Either way, Reform has a very clear program on the structure of the country that must emerge. Its duty is to defend, advocate and advance that program. That its leader should now be playing little games for the benefit of Ontario voters does not reassure us that his mind is firmly on the job. - *September 1, 1997*

Chapter Fifteen

Finally, on a Personal Note...

"I suppose modernity would say I had a troubled childhood - violent, dysfunctional home, drunken father, etcetera. But that is not so. I believe I was well served by both parents."

-Ted Byfield, 1996.

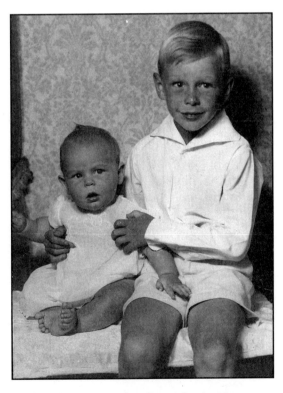

Ted with younger brother John in Toronto in 1937.

Macho males don't produce rednecks;
it's macho females - like this one

It was July 1938, I had just turned 10. I was in a park on the tree-bowered Toronto islands. Hanging from my shoulder was a new canvas bag, labelled *"The Saturday Evening Post."* Several copies of this magazine were in the bag. Another I clutched nervously. I was tearful and dejected.

It had been a bad day. That morning a Post district manager had recruited me as a salesman - a great opportunity. The magazine sold for a nickel; the commission was a cent and a half. I could sell maybe five or seven copies a day to the picnickers in the island parks. Make maybe 30 to 35 cents a week. With hamburgers, soft drinks and chocolate bars all costing a nickel, that was big money. The *Post* had thousands of such boy salesmen.

So I had headed for the park, armed with my first copies and my canvas bag, approached several hundred people, was turned down by them all, and come home in despair to face something even worse: my mother. As I expected, she marched me back to the park, lecturing me on the disgrace of being a "quitter," on how you have to smile to sell, on how you have to "speak up" if you expect to persuade anybody to do anything, and how success would depend not on what the prospect did but on what I did. With me endlessly repeating my sales pitch, we arrived back at the scene of my earlier defeat.

Surveying the park with the practised eye of the professional huckster, she spotted a solitary figure leaning aimlessly against a tree. "Go sell a magazine to that man over there." I approached, fixed my smile in position, and launched loudly into my pitch. To my utter astonishment, he bought the magazine.

"Now go see that one," said mother and, incredibly, he bought too. In the next hour I sold about seven magazines and returned home triumphant, step firm, head high, ruler of the world. Before long I set up a makeshift stand on the island's crowded boardwalk and was selling a hundred or so magazines a week. Which mattered. My father wasn't working and we needed the cash.

I thought of this last week after reading a very silly story on the boyhood of the Republican presidential candidate, Pat Buchanan. The feminist writer attributed his supposedly macho toughness to the male teachers and competitive environment of his all-boy Catholic schools. It was males, she thought, who produced such dreadful rednecks. What nonsense! It was females who produced them. Someone once called them "vampire mothers." I know. I had one.

One of six children of an English house painter, she grew up in small-town Ontario. At 20, she was blonde, beautiful, inadequately educated, unquenchably ambitious and working in Toronto as a clerk. Though courted by many, she fixed her sights on the dubious Vernon Byfield, a news reporter and nephew of the city's longtime mayor, Tommy Church. Their relationship was explosive from the start. He said she talked too much; she said he drank too much; they were both right. After one terrible fight, apparently to spite him, she left town and married an automobile worker in Toledo. Following that, he persuaded her she'd made a serious mistake. So she divorced the automobile worker, returned to Toronto, and married him. Their first child was born a year later, namely me.

Before that, however, father bought a Doberman pinscher the latest trendy breed, which he thought would make a fortune in stud fees. "Either that dog goes, or I go," my mother declared. "Goodbye," was his complacent reply. Laughing, she remained and within a week the dog was more hers than his, and I spent much of my childhood apologizing for it as it methodically killed most of the neighbourhood cats. "They attack him first," mother insisted. She always defended him, however overwhelming the evidence. Anything that was hers was right: children, dog, brothers, sisters, even - to outsiders anyway - her husband.

Insiders knew otherwise. Their quarrels were incessant, articulate, violent and sometimes hilarious. Invariably she would blow up and begin hurling things at him. He never fought back, but took to using a card table as a shield, while assorted dishes, ornaments and other missiles went hurtling by. Her aim was hopeless; she couldn't hit anything, let alone a target concealed by some sixteen square feet of card table who kept poking his head out from behind, making jokes. Finally she would dissolve in laughter and that would be that.

There's a story he once arrived home with a gang of reporters, late and drunk, to find she'd locked all the doors. He put a ladder to a second-floor window. "I will now effect an entrance," he announced majestically. When he reached the window, there was a loud whang as she hit him over the head with a tin frying pan. With great guffaws he and the gang drove away in their Model-T Ford.

In 1936, he swore off booze and they had another son. It didn't work. His drinking resumed, he lost job after job, and she left him. Four subsequent reconciliations all failed and they eventually parted for good. She married two other men, the last a California lawyer whom she pushed into becoming a judge. She would order him about mercilessly, he meekly and happily obeying. It was her dreamed-of perfect marriage and it bored her to tears. When the judge died she went briefly back to my father. It was less rowdy because they were then in their 70s, but again it didn't work. Yet they continued to be fascinated with one another. Orthodox Christian theology has always held that a marriage can "die," thereby making a divorce possible. This marriage, I think, would not have qualified. It never died.

She outlived him by twenty years, spent in Edmonton. They were good years. Her elder son, of course, was still selling magazines, her younger a California radiologist. In her 80s she hosted parties for the magazine staff, promoted the publication wherever she went, danced till midnight and beyond until well into her 90s, and acquired a persistent taste for brandy. This could cause problems. In her last days, though barely able to walk herself, she was caught just in time pushing a fellow nursing home resident in her wheel chair towards the brink of a steep stairway, both of them singing lustily. Near the end her mind faded, yet not entirely. "Do you remember Vernon?" I once asked her. Her face lighted in a broad appreciative smile. "Oh," she replied, "he was a dandy!" As I say, it never died.

Not anyway until she herself died last month at 96. I suppose modernity would say I had a troubled childhood - violent, dysfunction-al home, drunken father, etc. But that is not so. I believe I was well served by both parents. - *March 11, 1996*

If sex 'terrified' Robert Fulford, he didn't belong to our crowd

Last week we were privileged to learn how Canadian literary critic and magazine editor Robert Fulford reacted when he found out about sex. It was, he confides, "terrifying." Nowadays when young people can watch it being done in almost any movie, they escape the "fear-ridden personal discovery" which it used to involve in the bad old days, he said.

Mr. Fulford was writing in *The Globe and Mail* to tell people born after the Sixties what things were like before then. Much as I admire him as a critic, writer and editor, this article was to me deeply offensive. If he had written that he, Robert Fulford, found the whole idea of sex "terrifying," that would be fine. No doubt he did. But when he wrote on behalf of the whole "older" generation, he included me, and all the guys I used to know in those days when we learned about sex, mostly from each other. Frankly, I did not find the idea at all terrifying. Neither did any of us boys in the Grade 7 class at Courcelette Road School back about 1939. Exciting, yes. Absolutely intriguing, yes. Terrifying, no.

It came, I remember, as a sort of rewarding discovery. All along, you had had these strange and exotic feelings. And now, why by heaven, there was actually something you could do about them, something you had already half suspected. It was simply marvellous.

There was, of course, the requisite other half of it - girls. Without girls, it would be nothing. But how could you possibly talk girls into this? They'd have to be crazy to let you do that. But who knows? Someday one of them might.

I had no sisters, so girls were a deep mystery to me. I had a girl cousin, a year older, whom I adored. Yes, I told myself in furtive moments, she was a possible candidate all right. But not a very likely one, which turned out to be disappointingly true.

Some of the other guys had sisters,. But to them, a sister was not a girl - not in this sense. A sister was a sister, meaning usually a pain. The idea of a sister as what we would one day learn to call "a sex object" was, to those of us who had sisters, simply ludicrous. What you needed were girls, and sisters just didn't qualify.

For several years, we of the Courcelette Road School sex discovery set were preoccupied with this subject. We heard and retold countless jokes about it. We pined, we yearned for the chance to actually try it, and as we grew older we recounted to each other our triumphs in this regard, some of them perhaps half true.

But alas, I suspect we had few triumphs, and I myself had none whatever - though God knows it was not for lack of trying, and certainly not for lack of imagining. I added my own contribution to the total corpus of lies. But in fact until I was married sex remained a captivating unknown, about which I could only fantasize.

To me, girls were then, and women have remained to this day, one large mystery. They are so different from men. I don't think I've ever met a man - including those they now call "gay" - with whom I could not instantly feel some sort of rapport. I know immediately, as the saying goes, "where they're coming from," and I assume they know that of me. For we men are boringly the same - great companions on a canoe trip, in a business venture, for a night of song in some bar, or (and this I can only guess) for a struggle to the death on some battlefield. But we are distinctly unmysterious.

I simply cannot say that of women. Be it the one I married and have spent 45 years living with, and without whom now life wouldn't be as much fun; be it the poor, suffering, strident, semi-hysterical feminist I encounter as fellow panellist on some TV show; be it the unclad nymph prancing about in some beer parlour; be it the grande dame, old, decaying, dying and yet still alluring in a nursing home, they are all different and they are all fascinating. In a way you want to love them all.

Mr. Fulford describes the process of discovering this relationship, and the physical expression God has provided for it, as "terrifying." It is an interesting word, and I don't doubt he means it. But I find it very unsatisfactory for such an experience. We were not terrified, not one of us. Captured, but not terrified.

Now there is more to this rambling discussion of sex than there may seem. For when I read of Mr. Fulford's terror, an awful thought occurred to me and it was this.

Most of what I have called "my generation," both men and women, are not as unreserved as Mr. Fulford in our admiration of the present sexual candour. We believe it dangerous and we see it as the direct cause of much of the present abuse and violence that has come to be associated with sex. We believe sex should have remained a mystery, and we think that if you spend twenty or more years assuring people that they must feel unrestrained in their sexual appetites, that the old "taboos" have now been repealed, and that "anything that turns your crank is right for you," you should not be surprised if what turns some cranks are things you do not approve of - such as rape, sodomy, pederasty, zoophilia, sadism and consequent disease.

But much as "our generation" might be unenchanted by the sexual revolution, we must also face the fact it was we who brought it about. The children of the Sixties were our children, and the culture that produced the Sixties was our culture.

Or was it? Who, after all, testified on our behalf during those crucial years? Who were the spokesmen for what could be called "our world?" Who were our artists, our writers, our poets, our ambassadors, as it were, to the age that would follow?

Who but the Robert Fulfords, they whose views were so liberated they were no longer liberal, and whose minds were so open, everything in them (as someone once said) seemed to have fallen out. In eager acquiescence with the spirit of the age, they surrendered every fortress and abandoned every road. And now, with the war all but lost, we find out that they were never of us. They were different. Respectability stupefied them; violence horrified them, and sex terrified them. Such were our supposed champions. No wonder we now fight with our backs to the sea. - *January 25, 1993*

On oratorios and choirmasters and a debt that can't be repaid

In the course of 59 years I've been favoured with more than a few exciting experiences. I've played a part in founding two news-magazines and three boys' schools. I've helped run brigades of big canoes down scores of rapids, paddling most of the way from Portland, Oregon, to Montreal, and all the way from Winnipeg to Hudson Bay. I was fortunate in covering some big news stories and I have published two books and an atlas. I have backpacked through the Howse and Poboktan Passes of the Rockies, and have sailed (somewhat flawfully) a 42-foot sloop from Vancouver to Nova Scotia via the Panama Canal.

All these produced great moments, but none can compare to one other: I've sung in the bass section of a big choir doing Handel's oratorio *The Messiah*. For sheer joy and reward of human accomplishment, that is the peak. It's a kind of raw pleasure, the ultimate delight, the highest thrill, though my own contribution to it was minor indeed.

At Christmas some choir in almost every major city will do Handel's great masterpiece, and for me it always brings back poignant memories of those days. I was in my mid-twenties, had decided for a number of reasons to return to the church, and had made the mistake of praying for direction on how I might contribute. The answer was prompt and unwelcome. Men were needed, announced the clergyman in an appeal that I later discovered was issued seasonally, to sing in the church choir. I groaned within. Surely not this.

Singing was admittedly fun, but it was something provoked in my case solely by another great pleasure called alcohol. Sober and in public I found it just about impossible to sing. Oiled even slightly I found it just about impossible to shut up, and the more public the occasion the better. There had been some regrettable incidents in restaurants where the people did not appreciate unscheduled entertainment.

Singing in a church choir would entail (this seemed inescapable) singing while sober. There was another obstacle too: the need to do it in those ridiculous black and white dresses. It was like being asked to stand naked before the Women's Canadian Club and recite Shakespeare. Very inconsiderate, this God.

Anyway, I wound up doing it - the singing I mean - though not without a fight. I remember pacing up and down in front of the rector's house, trying to get up courage to tell him of my decision. When I finally did, the poor man must have already been in bed. Clad in pants and a pajama top, he peered at the wretched figure on his doorstep. I blurted out something like "I want to sing in the choir." He seemed to grasp immediately what was going on. (A man who held the Military Cross from the Belgium and Holland campaign and still carried in his face and body fragments of the land mine that had blown up his jeep, he was not easily fazed.) He told me he understood, and I should call the choirmaster.

This, needless to say, I neglected to do. Getting to that door was the most I could manage. But now they had my name. The choirmaster called me. When I failed to show up at practice he called me again, and when I failed again he came and got me. They are utterly deceptive people, these choirmasters. Outwardly they may be all sweetness, patience and amiability. This is a mere facade. Put them in front of their charges, and the real animal emerges - demanding, intolerant, stubborn, implacable, humourless, of an appalling diligence and often quite rude.

You have, that is, the marine sergeant personality carefully suited up in an ecclesiastical cloak - a wolf in sheep's clothing, unlike most modern clergy, who are, as somebody has said, sheep in sheep's clothing. But I've never known one that I did not like, nor one that failed to serve his craft with the assiduity that it required. It is this, needless to say, that makes them so cussed when they don't get what they want from their people.

That first choirmaster was a man named Harold Christie, altogether typical of the trade. I recall him as miserable and endlessly dissatisfied when on the job, one of the happiest people I've ever known when off it. (He is now a school principal in Winnipeg, so I had better be careful of what I say.) Each practice, it seemed, was for him a succession of catastrophic disappointments. He would stand before us, hand raised, eyes heavenward, waiting enraptured for us to produce that precise sound, that flawless chord, that delicate balance of tone and pitch which the composer required. It seemed we never once produced it. Down would come the hand on the lectern with a great crash. There would be much shouting, invective, lamentation, denunciation, groaning, acid comment and finally the command to try again. Only this time...But it never worked. Not once.

I think he had one of the best church choirs in the city. He was certainly one of the best choirmasters (and people) I've ever known. And in the four or five years I sang for him I cannot remember his ever once being satisfied with what we or he did. Every performance, every service, fell short for one reason or another of the perfection his soul demanded. The congregation might have loved it; the critics (when there were any) were invariably impressed; we who sang it certainly liked it. But Harold would only rue it. Had we not noticed, not even noticed, that in the fourteenth bar of that anthem the tenors had failed - failed although they had been told a dozen times - etc., etc. Always we failed and always we tried again.

For me, however, the man's whole work in music was one resounding success. Not only did he teach me, me and a lot of other people, to sing while sober. Far beyond that he introduced me to a whole new world, a world I would otherwise have never known, the world of Handel, Bach, Brahms and Mozart, the world of real music. I still find I have to sing while drinking. But even here there were lessons to learn. Was not the best drinking chorus in the whole repertoire of music written by Franz Josef Haydn?

For every human activity - work, love, war and worship - can be set to music, and in that world men like these form the unchallenged oligarchy. For taking me into it, into civilization from barbarism so to speak, I am indebted to one choirmaster. The debt is inestimable and it cannot be repaid. - *December 21, 1987*

I'm addicted to a brilliant cop show
that reveals the exhaustion of the liberal mind

I spotted an old acquaintance last week, peering out from a lavish newspaper picture layout. Mind, I've never actually met this man in person. But I've spent night after night with him at work. He is the actor Michael Moriarty, portrayer of New York assistant district attorney Ben Stone, who for years has prosecuted cases for my edification and amusement on the Arts & Entertainment network program *Law and Order*. I confess to being hopelessly addicted to "cop shows" on television, and for my money *Law and Order* is the best ever produced.

For one thing, it is what I presume to be realistic. Never having lived in New York, nor covered (for very long anyhow) a police beat, and knowing almost nothing about criminal court proceedings, I may not be the most reliable judge of "real." But my late father, who was a police reporter, imparted to me two pieces of information. "The police," he said ("cops" was not a word he used) "never interview a witness alone. They always work in pairs so one can verify the evidence of the other." The other thing he told me was never to lie to the police. "They are in the business of lies," he said. (He meant catching people out in them.) "Besides, the truth is the only thing you can remember with reasonable accuracy, and they know that too."

Criminal lawyers (an unfortunate term, that) have told me that *Law and Order* depicts their work with great fidelity, and a high court judge told me only last month that the show's portrayal of the challenges, pitfalls and occasional errancies of judges is very accurate as well. Finally, the crimes are often crude, messy and depressing, exactly like the ones we read about in the paper.

All of which is not to denigrate other cop shows. I like Miss Marple as well as anybody, but it is altogether fantasy. If any village in England were as smitten with poisonings, revolver shootings, disappearances, suspicious suicides and drownings as St. Mary Mead you'd have to be crazy to live there. Hercule Poirot at least gets called in; he doesn't encounter all this murder and mayhem among his immediate acquaintances. But as with Miss Marple and, for that matter, the American cop Lieutenant Colombo, nobody without money, celebrity or a degree in nuclear physics is ever investigated by Hercule. Only the most highly esteemed and academically qualified are eligible as criminals. The same, of course, is true of of the crimes investigated by the numerous English chief inspectors - Morris, Frost, Wexford, the whole crowd. Everything is so refined.

Well, it isn't on *Law and Order.* You get your real creeps there. Ghastly people. Miss Marple would be appalled, however curious the crime. And it's never very curious anyway. Two slugs in one spinal column in some back alley, or a knifing in a dumpster, or a half-decomposed corpse hauled out of the East River. *Law and Order* does cheat some, of course. The black guy with the purple hair and the muscle shirt and the bashed-in skull tattooed on his rump admits he did the job. But he was actually working for this other guy up town, who turns out to have a connection to that bigwig at the New York Yacht Club. Just as you suspected, the yacht club guy was the real villain, and Ben Stone puts him in jail, after the black killer dies of an overdose and they cut a deal with the middle-man, who turns state witness against Mr. Big. Which leaves just ninety seconds for Ben to philosophize about it all with his black and/or female assistant and the credit lines come up. It's all very satisfying, and it never changes night after night.

There's something else about *Law and Order.* Almost every crime brings in "an issue," some current controversy over morals, the law, lifestyles or ideology, and the show always espouses the liberal viewpoint. This is good reason for conservative-minded people to watch it. You're seeing the enemy, as it were, in action. You can see what he thinks, and how, and often that he doesn't. In short, it reveals the exhaustion of the liberal mind.

Invariably, for instance, the show will expose the traditional family. These people looked so confident, so secure, so caring. But when the two detectives get to the bottom of it all, it turns out the father has a mistress, or is abusing the daughter, or tyrannizing the poor young son, which is what caused him to commit the crime.

The mother, of course, is an alcoholic, and the son secretly gay and terrified the father will find out. Which is why he shot those six people at the Taco Bell. It was actually the father's fault. In fact, almost everything is the father's fault.

Unless, that is, it can be blamed on religion. You can always identify the crazed killer by the cross around his neck. Clergy, who often appear, come in two varieties: the unscrupulous and the asinine. That wonderfully caring evangelical church is in reality a cult whose charismatic leader is milking the poor out of every last cent in order to pay for his house full of concubines on Grand Cayman. And Father Murphy, dear wonderful Father Murphy, isn't it too bad he's such a sap he doesn't even know some of his flock are peddling cocaine out of the parish hall? But Ben Stone will get them every time.

"So why look at this night after night?" my wife asks. Well, for one thing, you notice they have no heroes. Not among the civilians, that is. Everybody the show deals with, whether as criminal or witness, is flawed in some way. Everybody, that is, except one class of people - those who work in what we call the public sector. True, the odd building inspector is corrupt. But all the police are simon pure - dedicated, committed, courageous, selfless. So are all the government lawyers. Any other lawyers are...well, you know what lawyers are like. This same incorruptibility characterizes hospital nurses, laboratory workers and social workers. School teachers are especially caring and sharing. Public school teachers, that is. Private schools, and they often appear, are invariably elitist, discriminatory and money-obsessed.

So there you have it - a program built on values straight out of the Sixties and therefore, of course, doomed. To people my age it is radically modern. Our two youngest children, both Generation-Xers, have never mentioned it, and obviously don't watch it. They doubtless consider it out of date, phony, irrelevant. But it's well done, nevertheless. I wonder if we traditionalists can come up with something for the next generation that is anywhere near as good. - *January 12, 1998*

On death, sex, fat and youth and other points of being 60

I turned 60 this week and somebody suggested I write about it. "Saying what?" I asked. "Saying what it's like," they said. It seems silly. People who aren't approaching 60 don't like to think about getting there, and those who've passed it wish they hadn't. Some audience. However, for what it's worth, here's what being 60 is like to one 60-year-old.

For starters, I can frankly declare that sex is not the problem that it was. I'm no longer prone, that is, to leer at women on the street, mentally undressing them, the sort of things all us bonafide religious fanatics are supposed to resist doing, and sometimes do resist doing, and sometime don't. Well, I don't do it at all anymore, and I told my wife I must be making real progress in the Kingdom of God. She said, "Don't flatter yourself. You're not getting virtuous. You're just getting old." She has a great eye for the probable. Somebody once asked Bob Hope: "Is there sex after 60?" He is supposed to have replied: "You bet. And it's great. Especially the one in the fall." Anyway, that's sex covered. If you don't bring it into a piece like this, people think there's some dreadful thing you're hiding. Well I'm not hiding anything. I'm a respectably retired lecher.

Here's another thing. I've discovered why my mother, who is 88, keeps calling me a "boy." "That boy is working too hard," she'll say to my children, who can't figure out who she's talking about. The point is that you simply never elevate anybody. Last week I referred to a "young clergyman." It dawned on me afterwards that the fellow must be about 40. When I was 40, I never thought of myself as a young anything. It's all defensive, of course. If you allow the young to mature, this creates problems. It might mean conceding they know something. And what does it make you, but irredeemably ancient? So you keep them safely young.

However, there is an up-side to this discovery. The ones who turned 20 in the mid-1960s, and then turned 40 in the mid-1980s (I refer, of course, to those wonderful people, the Flower Children, about whom we have heard so very very much these past 25 years) are now themselves discovering that the bloom, so to speak, is off the rose.

Other flowers are springing up in the garden, things that themselves are now around 20, and who sometimes look a lot more like us than they look like Flower Children. Right from the start, for instance, they get haircuts, they wash and they don't smell too bad. All kinds of promise. Maybe one day, if they can survive the coma of the Flower Children's schools, they might even come to believe in something.

On the down-side, however, is the Fat Problem. It begins at 40, and is not over, I'm sorry to have to report, at 60. (They say it is over by 70 because by then either you have solved it, or it has solved you.) I've never been able to say whether the Fat Problem is the fault of my mother or the fault of my wife. I lived with the former for the first eighteen years of my life and with the latter for the last forty, and remember very little of the year in between because I spent most of it getting drunk.

I suspect that all mothers have two incompatible objectives: One is to feed you as much as possible, and the other is to constantly warn you about your weight. Even now, I notice, if I eat dinner with my mother, she watches my every move. If there are four things on the plate - say, carrots, cabbage, potatoes and meat - and if I start on the cabbage, she'll say: "Eat your potatoes, Teddy." If I go over to the potatoes, she'll say, "I wasn't aware you didn't like carrots, Teddy." Then if I go to the carrots, it's, "Are you going to let that beef go to waste, Teddy? Have you any idea how much it costs?" She chases me like this all around the plate and all through the meal, at the end of which she'll say" "You're simply going to have to watch your weight, Teddy. I remember your father..."

Wives are the same. If I mention on Tuesday that I'm going on a diet, by Wednesday there'll be a great smell in the kitchen. "I just felt," she'll say coyly, "like doing a little baking. It's been so long." So much for the diet. It's instinctive with them, I think. Mothers fatten their sons so they won't be able to find a wife, and wives fatten their husbands so they won't be able to find a girlfriend.

I can honestly say I've never had a girlfriend, but again, it isn't virtue. I never wanted one. It's because of the girlfriend I married. I've never gotten used to her. She's smart, intelligent, always fascinating.

We founded schools together, started magazines, are writing a book. At 50, we took up dancing and I guess we've danced a thousand times. At 55, we took up sailing and have sailed a boat from Vancouver to Nova Scotia via the Panama Canal. Where are you going to find a girlfriend who can do all this? They don't make 'em anymore.

Finally, I've become more conscious of death. It's not so much a fear, as it is a kind of wonderment. People keep dying. In the last six months, there have been two former news cronies, a school pal, a business acquaintance, and a couple of politicians I used to cover. A friend's mother, three years my junior, died last week of a heart attack. Someone else, also younger than I, has been given a maximum ten months with cancer.

You've known about death all along, of course, but when it's all around you, it becomes a much closer reality. I'm wholly conscious of the fact, for instance, that I might go poof! before this gets into print. I knew this at age 50, too. But I knew it the way I knew there were bad things going on in Cambodia. Now, so to speak, it's me who's in Cambodia. That's the difference.

But it isn't frightening. In fact, it's strangely exciting. It's like knowing you're going to be leaving soon on a trip. You don't know how you'll travel, or even where you're going, only that you're certain to be going on it, and that it will be unlike anything you can remember.

Though, come to think of it, not unlike anything that has ever before happened to you. For there must have been a time when we lived comfortably within our mother's womb. It must have seemed very secure, very warm, very permanent. They say we were in fact conscious at that stage, though we have no memory of it. But it seems certain that if anybody had somehow tried to tell us of what lay ahead, we probably wouldn't have believed them.

Maybe the change from this stage to the next is just as drastic, just as programmed and (viewed from here) just as unimaginable. We don't know this, but it's what some of us have been authoritatively told. And I can add one thing. If you believe it, it makes turning 60 a whole lot easier. - *July 18, 1988*